DOROTHY L. SAYERS

a reference guide

A
Reference
Guide
to
Literature

Ronald Gottesman
Editor

DOROTHY L. SAYERS

a reference guide

RUTH TANIS YOUNGBERG

G.K.HALL &CO.

70 LINCOLN STREET, BOSTON, MASS.

Library of Congress Cataloging in Publication Data

Youngberg, Ruth Tanis.
   Dorothy L. Sayers, a reference guide.

   Includes index.
   1. Sayers, Dorothy L. (Dorothy Leigh), 1893-1957—
Bibliography.   I.   Title.
Z8786.55Y68   [PR6037.A95]   016.823'912   81-6992
ISBN 0-8161-8198-5   AACR2

This publication is printed on permanent/durable acid-free paper
MANUFACTURED IN THE UNITED STATES OF AMERICA

Contents

The Author

Ruth Youngberg is a graduate of Wheaton College in Illinois, with a Library Science degree from the University of Illinois Library School. She has retired from her position as a cataloger at the Oregon State University Library. Over the years she has held short-term positions at a number of public and university libraries.

Preface

I present this bibliography with the hope that it will save time for those who wish to learn what the critics have said about Sayers's work. I have attempted to give some analysis of each article and book listed in terms that will make clear whether or not it will be of use in research. Thus, I have tried to use the word "discuss" only to describe what I considered of great enough length to show the development of an author's thoughts. The length of an annotation will have little to do with the merit of a review or book, since the annotations are not critical but informative and the annotation of a short article may be complete enough to eliminate seeing the item itself.

While I had hoped to make this bibliography comprehensive, this turned out to be impossible. As far as possible it includes the citations found in the major American bibliographic tools and in some English ones. Those citations that led only to a listing with imprint have been excluded. Only books and articles in English have been annotated. An asterisk precedes the listing of those items that I was unable to see.

My cut-off date for magazine and newspaper articles was September, 1980. Two books published in 1981 have been included in the bibliography since the publishers kindly sent me review copies in time to include them.

Volume and/or page numbers are missing when these have not been available to me and I have found the material by dates alone. The term "Processed" has been used for all materials duplicated rather than printed by standard printing methods.

Detective literature and reviews are often written pseudonymously. I have used the latest Library of Congress rules of entry for pseudonyms. The author name used for an annotation is that shown on the title page of a book or at the head of an article, without the use of "pseud." In instances of a noun phrase used as a pseudonym (e.g., Laicus Ignotus) I have entered the annotation under the phrase as written, with a cross-reference in the index from the inverted form.

I wish to extend my thanks to all of the following: Dr. Edward Smith, Oregon State University Department of English, for setting me on my course; Rodney K. Waldron, Director of Libraries, Oregon State University, for extending invaluable special privileges; to the following librarians: Patricia Brandt and Agnes Grady, for editorial advice; Helen Horvath and Stanley Swanson, for making certain materials available; and Doris Tilles and her staff, for the many materials secured through Inter-Library Loan; Lieutenant Colonel Ralph Clarke, of The Dorothy L. Sayers Historical and Literary Society, for generous and painstaking assistance; Marjorie Mead, Associate Curator of The Marion E. Wade Collection, for giving time for research, Inter-Library Loans, and for sending much copy; Joe Christopher, always willing to help with details and copy; Leona Sutherland, for assistance in research and typing; and to all who have published bibliographies within the last few years, as they have been of immeasurable worth to me. Finally, I want to thank Dr. Clyde Kilby, Curator of The Marion E. Wade Collection, for his continuing inspiration and encouragement; and Chet, without whose help this bibliography would be no more than an idea.

Introduction

Dorothy L. Sayers, born in Oxford in 1893, began writing early in life. Her education began at home, took her to Godolphin School and on to Oxford's Somerville College where she took a first in French in 1915.

Her first published works were poems. Critical comment on her writing began in 1917 when her book of poems, OP.I, was reviewed in The Times Literary Supplement. From that time until today there has been a steady flow--sometimes lesser, sometimes greater--of critical writing on her work.

Being naturally brilliant and well-educated in the classics, she brought to her writing not only a broad background in literature and languages but also an understanding of the craft of writing. In addition, her work is characterized by intellectual honesty and by a sense of the value of work well done.

She was a popular lecturer. With her love for language and her ability to use it she could hold an audience spellbound or raise a storm of critical comment.

In the 1920s and 1930s, when Sayers was writing mostly detective fiction, using it as her "breadwinner," her works were reviewed primarily in the popular press. By the time her "breadwinner" had ceased to interest her, she had had a taste of writing for the theater. Busman's Honeymoon, written in collaboration with Muriel St. Clare Byrne, and later turned into her final novel, had met with no great success at the box office, but she had learned from it and had fallen in love with the medium.

When she was invited to write a play for the Canterbury Festival she accepted and wrote The Zeal of Thy House, produced in 1937. Her success led to further invitations, and she was on her way to being a religious dramatist of some note. In the reviews for this play and her later ones, particularly The Man Born to Be King, she was commended for her ability to combine spiritual truth with comedy and humor, for her characterization, for her presentation of old truth in new forms, and for her use of language and versification. Adverse criticism complained of her attempt to persuade people to her Church of England beliefs, poor character development, and the use of American slang.

Today some of her plays are being revived for use in Christian drama classes and church groups.

In the 1940s we find Sayers included as an important writer of dectective fiction in books on the subject, while newspaper and magazine article reviews dealt mainly with her religious works. From that time on we see the interest of religious writers added to that of those reviewers who dealt chiefly with her detective fiction.

Kathleen Nott included a long and scholarly discussion of Sayers's religious philosophy in her book, The Emperor's Clothes, published in 1954, creating a stir that continues to this day.

It is interesting to note that in the earlier reviews of Sayers's theological works she was often praised for her brilliance and the manner in which she put forth her ideas even when the critic did not agree with her. In the more recent criticism of these works one finds a growing acceptance of her ideas and praise for her ability to elucidate them. As an example, Edmund Fuller (1979.26) calls The Mind of the Maker her greatest work. Leland Ryken (1979.39) calls it "the classic work on the contribution of Christian doctrine to an understanding of artistic creativity"--a subject much under discussion in the church today.

On 13 December 1980, the British Broadcasting Corporation's Radio Times, carrying an announcement of a radio reading of some of Sayers's works, quotes Vernon Sproxton as saying that she may be remembered for the expression of her "real if somewhat over-intellectualised grasp of 'that love which moves the sun and all the other stars, . . . long after Lord Peter Wimsey and The Man Born to Be King have been forgotten."

It was during World War II that Sayers met Dante through his Divine Comedy. For the remainder of her life a share of her attention was given to a new translation that would help the modern reader to reap the rewards of knowing his work. She became a well-known Dante scholar with a long list of lectures and essays to her credit. Publication of her work included translation and essays as follows: Cantica I, 1949; Introductory Papers on Dante, 1954; Cantica II, 1955; Further Papers on Dante, 1957; and Cantica III, completed after Sayers's death by Barbara Reynolds, 1962.

Compared to the amount of critical attention she received for her other works and her essays on Dante, the number of commentators on her translation is small though drawn from the ranks of scholars. The main thrust of the criticism is in two areas: her versification and her concept of Dante's meanings. There is little agreement among the critics, although Sayers is usually commended for the quality of her notes and her critical introduction.

Early critics of the Dante papers disliked the promotion of her orthodoxy and also what they saw as the influence of Charles Williams and C. S. Lewis. Opposed to them were those people who agreed with Sayers theologically and appreciated her lucid explanation of age-old truths. Others were thankful for her ability to open up the world of Dante to the general reader.

Whatever one's attitude toward Sayers's translation, it is significant that the notes accompanying it are still used in some colleges and universities, sometimes with her translation, sometimes with a different one.

There is a theory that interest in an author wanes during the first twenty years following death. Does this hold true for Sayers? It seems not. While there is a lesser number of critical reviews shown for some of the years from 1959-1968, the importance of the material issued during this period is significant. Her detective fiction was kept in print. Two collections of essays were published, and her story for children, The Days of Christ's Coming, was issued for Christmas 1960, and noted by reviewers. Also in the 1960s we see the beginning of Sayers's inclusion in encyclopedias, in books of general literary criticism, in books on drama--especially religious drama, in books on religion, and we find her as the subject of doctoral theses, and bibliographies. Of significance in the period, too, is the founding of the Wade Collection at Wheaton College, Illinois, which includes manuscripts of all the Sayers novels, manuscripts of many of her speeches and essays, copies of her books in various editions, and other pertinent items.

Beginning in the late 1960s and continuing to the present, there is evidence of a constantly growing interest in all of Sayers's works.

Nineteen seventy-six saw the formation of the Dorothy L. Sayers Historical and Literary Society in what had been Sayers's residence in Witham, Essex. Besides maintaining a collection of Sayers material, the Society holds meetings of general interest, and publishes the papers given at its annual seminar. The Sayers Review, under the editorship of Christie McMenomy was also begun in 1976, in Los Angeles.

The list of books devoted exclusively to Sayers is burgeoning. These include biographies, bibliographies, and critical studies. Two have won awards: A Bibliography of the Works of Dorothy L. Sayers, by Colleen Gilbert (1978.18) won an American Library Association award for academic excellence, and Ralph Hone's Dorothy L. Sayers: A Literary Biography (1979.31) was given the American Mystery Writers' version of the "Edgar" for 1979.

Introduction

There are other evidences of a growing interest in Sayers and her work. Some of her essays, reprinted in <u>Christian Letters to a Post-Christian World</u> in 1969 have been reprinted again in 1978 with the title: <u>The Whimsical Christian</u>. Other essays and parts of some appear in magazines from time to time.

At the time of her death Sayers had not completed her study of Wilkie Collins and his work, begun early in her life. The manuscript has been edited with an introduction by E. R. Gregory and published by the Friends of the University of Toledo Libraries in 1977. During her lifetime Sayers, C. W. Scott-Giles, and others had compiled a "history" of the imaginary Wimsey family. Scott-Giles has brought together all the bits and pieces and had them published in a delightful book, <u>The Wimsey Family</u> (1977.51).

In the field of education Sayers's treatise, "The Lost Tools of Learning" was used as recently as 1973 for background material for a seminar called "Education in a Free Society." The Modern Language Association hosts a Sayers seminar at its annual meetings.

Her two articles "Human, not Quite Human" and "Are Women Human?" are probably quoted more frequently today than at any time in the past as Christian women struggle to learn their proper role at home and in society.

One cannot say that there was ever a decline in the reading of Sayers's fiction. In their enthusiasm, her readers spread word of her books and short stories. Undoubtedly, though, the televising of five of her novels for the British Broadcasting Corporation, later shown on Masterpiece Theatre, is responsible for an increase in the number of her readers. Recent critical consideration of her detective fiction has shown a growing acceptance of Sayers's standing as a first-rate author of novels of manners.

Sister Mary Brian Durkin, in her book called <u>Dorothy L. Sayers</u> (1980.4) has given a tightly written, excellent literary analysis of her novels and short stories. She says of Sayers, "A cool-headed constructionist, she planned each novel meticulously, organized the plot carefully, made the method and the means of murder mystifying but plausible, and worked out all details accurately."

P. D. James, who is becoming noted for her own detective fiction, has written the foreword to James Brabazon's biography (1981.1). In it (1981.3) she summarizes some of the strengths of Sayers's detective fiction. She gives Sayers credit for having created a detective who fits the qualifications Sayers herself has set up for an amateur sleuth. She then commends her for the quality of her writing; her careful attention to detail; her capable handling of the "technical tricks of her trade"; the "freshness, wit and panache" with which she dealt with those tricks; her great sense of humor; and the manner in which her novels reflect their times. She comments that "the

enduring strength of the novels is that they were written to be, and
are, superb entertainment" having "that creative vitality which alone
ensures survival."

Carolyn Heilbrun, in "Sayers, Lord Peter and God" (1968.2)
praises her work highly with comments such as: she wrote "superbly
constructed detective plots, played out in witty comedies of manners";
"the Professor of English could read her books without . . . making
irritable jottings in the margin"; "she seemed to know even more than
the Professors about so many things"; "the conversation of Lord Peter
and his associates is in the best tradition of the comedy of manners."
She ends her article: "Since she has herself compared the mind of
the artist with the mind of God, she would probably not consider
sacrilegious the observation that she has endowed her own creature
with enduring grace."

G. A. Lee, in a paper given before the Dorothy L. Sayers Historical and Literary Society (1977.30) discusses the "consistency of
imagination" that invests the Wimsey novels with a "strong impression
of unity and coherent development." Quoting him: "Artistic success
or failure lies in the extent to which the images do or do not cohere
in the beholder's or reader's mind to produce an impression of whole-
ness." He compliments Sayers on the high degree of consistency she
achieved considering that her Wimsey saga was written over a period
of fifteen years. Surely this is one of the factors in the creation
of Lord Peter that has made of him a personage.

J. G. Cawelti (1976.6) put Sayers's detective fiction at the top
of the form of the classical detective story. Janet Hitchman (1974.8)
says "Wimsey has survived, and will continue to survive, because he
is well written, beautifully constructed, and above all, amusing."
Leroy Panek (1979.35) praised the way in which Sayers revealed in
her novels the changes in her thinking, commenting that "her novels
confront problems and do not give easy answers" and are her "best
pieces of theology."

Jacques Barzun (1971.4) commented on Sayers's staying power and
the excellence of her introductions to Wilkie Collins's The Moonstone
and her editions of Tales of Detection and The Omnibus of Crime. The
latter is still considered one of the best commentaries on detective
fiction ever written.

Not all the criticism has been favorable, especially in the
earlier years. Q. D. Leavis (1937.30) was especially vituperative,
seeing Sayers's fiction as "parasitic, stale, adulterated," her sense
of values shallow and inconsistent, and her writing unworthy of what
literary esteem it received. Edmund Wilson (1945.2, reprinted in
1950.7 and 1956.10) condemned her writing on the strength of skimming
one novel, but admitted that he did not care for detective fiction.

Introduction

Sayers has been accused of snobbishness and of falling in love with Lord Peter; she was derided for creating "a silly ass detective," and for a lack of understanding of the kinds of people she attempted to portray. She was also criticized for using untranslated passages in other languages, particularly French and Latin.

One of the factors in Sayers's continuing popularity is the re-readability of her works. Peter Dickinson (1964.2), saying that re-readability is a curious thing, nevertheless finds Sayers a "great rereadable." He remarks that on the second reading of her novels one is astonished "at the amount of hard work she put in. The jokes are good jokes, for the most part; the backgrounds are carefully thought out and worked in; and the plots are both ingenious and practical."

It is not only the fiction Sayers wrote that is rereadable. Al-most her entire oeuvre is worth rereading. As Jacques Barzun (1942.9) said of her, she was "a woman of immense culture and fine intelli-gence." She faced life's problems and wondered about solutions for them. This comes through in all of her writing, and many of her ideas are pertinent today. We find her ideas on Christian belief, the arts, education, the status of women, materialism and its effects on society, crime and criminal justice, the value of work, and others, running through her fiction and nonfiction alike. Paul Foster (1946.5) commented on the integrity of thought evident throughout her works, a theme we find repeated often in critical literature today.

One of the results of a study such as this is a recognition that nothing is as unpredictable as criticism of an author's writings. There are few areas of agreement about Sayers's works. What one critic sees as wonderful, another considers junk. One thinks the writing itself is excellent, another calls it sloppy. One sees the characterization in her fiction and drama as true to life, the next one finds it totally unreal. Where one finds that the background material gives a novel strength, another sees it as tedious. What is an ingenious plot to one is merely contrived to another. In spite of the variability one cannot complain that Sayers has been treated un-fairly. An overall view of the reviews leaves one with the feeling that here is a person whose works are well worth reading and reread-ing, some for fun, some for enlightenment, and some for both fun and enlightenment.

In spite of all that has been written of her, there remains the feeling that we have still not met the essential Dorothy L. Sayers. We have had glimpses of a lovely person and a great friend hiding be-hind a facade of exuberant, sometimes brash, vitality. One wonders how she was affected by the secret with which she lived--the un-acknowledged fact that her adopted son had really been borne by her. There may well be a few people to whom she showed her real self but thus far no one has revealed that inner being to her readers.

Writings by Dorothy L. Sayers

Only those Sayers works reviewed in the bibliography are listed here. Of these only the first English and/or American edition is listed for each title. Works are listed chronologically within each genre.

NOVELS:

Whose Body? New York: Boni & Liveright, 1923; London: T. Fisher Unwin, 1923.

Clouds of Witness. London: T. Fisher Unwin, 1926; New York: Lincoln McVeagh, Dial Press, 1927 (with title: Clouds of Witnesses).

Unnatural Death. London: Ernest Benn, 1927; New York: Lincoln McVeagh, Dial Press, 1928 (with title: The Dawson Pedigree).

The Unpleasantness at the Bellona Club. London: Ernest Benn, 1928; New York: Payson & Clarke, 1928.

Strong Poison. London: Victor Gollancz, 1930; New York: Brewer & Warren, 1930.

The Five Red Herrings. London: Victor Gollancz, 1931; New York: Brewer, Warren & Putnam, 1931 (with title: Suspicious Characters).

Have His Carcase. London: Victor Gollancz, 1932; New York: Brewer, Warren & Putnam, 1932.

Murder Must Advertise: A Detective Story. London: Victor Gollancz, 1933; New York: Harcourt, Brace, 1933.

Writings by Dorothy L. Sayers

The Nine Tailors: Changes Rung On An Old Theme in Two Short Touches and Two Full Peals. London: Victor Gollancz, 1934; New York: Harcourt, Brace, 1934.

Gaudy Night. London: Victor Gollancz, 1935; New York: Harcourt, Brace, 1936.

Busman's Honeymoon: A Love Story with Detective Interruptions. New York: Harcourt, Brace, 1937; London: Victor Gollancz, 1937.

NOVELS WRITTEN IN COLLABORATION:

The Documents in the Case, by Dorothy L. Sayers and Robert Eustace. London: Ernest Benn, 1930; New York: Brewer & Warren, 1930.

The Floating Admiral, by Certain Members of the Detection Club. London: Hodder & Stoughton, 1931; New York: Doubleday, Doran, 1932.

Ask a Policeman, by Anthony Berkeley, Milward Kennedy, Gladys Mitchell, John Rhode, Dorothy L. Sayers, and Helen Simpson. London: Arthur Baker, 1933; New York: William Morrow, 1933.

Double Death: A Murder Story, by Dorothy L. Sayers, Freeman Wills Crofts, Valentine Williams, F. Tennyson Jesse, Anthony Armstrong, David Hume. Supervised and with a Preface and Prologue by John Chancellor. London: Victor Gollancz, 1939.

SHORT STORY:

The Dragon's Head, retold by L. A. Hill. London: Oxford University Press, 1975.

COLLECTED SHORT STORIES:

Lord Peter Views the Body. London: Victor Gollancz, 1928; New York: Payson & Clarke, 1929.

Hangman's Holiday. London: Victor Gollancz, 1933; New York: Harcourt, Brace, 1933.

In the Teeth of the Evidence and Other Stories. London: Victor Gollancz, 1939; New York: Harcourt, Brace, 1940.

Lord Peter: A Collection of All the Lord Peter Wimsey Stories. Compiled by James Sandoe. New York: Harper & Row, 1972.

Writings by Dorothy L. Sayers

<u>Striding Folly, Including Three Final Lord Peter Wimsey Stories</u>.
London: New English Library, 1973.

COLLECTED NOVELS AND SHORT STORIES BY SAYERS:

<u>Dorothy L. Sayers Omnibus</u>. London: Victor Gollancz, 1933. (Includes
<u>Lord Peter Views the Body</u>, <u>The Five Red Herrings</u>, and <u>Strong
Poison</u>.)

<u>Dorothy L. Sayers Omnibus</u>. New York: Harcourt, 1934. (Includes
<u>Whose Body?</u>, <u>The Unpleasantness at the Bellona Club</u>, and <u>Sus-
picious Characters</u>.)

<u>Strong Poison</u> and <u>Have His Carcase</u>. New York: Harcourt, Brace, 1936.

<u>Clouds of Witness</u> and <u>The Documents in the Case</u>. New York: Harcourt,
Brace, 1938.

<u>The Dawson Pedigree</u> and <u>Lord Peter Views the Body</u>. New York:
Harcourt, Brace, 1938.

<u>Murder Must Advertise</u> and <u>Hangman's Holiday</u>. New York: Harcourt,
Brace, 1938.

<u>Lord Peter Omnibus</u>. London: Victor Gollancz, 1964. (Includes
<u>Clouds of Witness</u>, <u>Unnatural Death</u>, and <u>The Unpleasantness at the
Bellona Club</u>.)

SHORT STORIES EDITED BY SAYERS:

<u>Great Short Stories of Detection, Mystery, and Horror</u>. London:
Victor Gollancz, 1928; New York: Payson & Clarke, 1929 (with
title: <u>The Omnibus of Crime</u>).

<u>Great Short Stories of Detection, Mystery and Horror--Second Series</u>.
London: Victor Gollancz, 1931; New York: Coward McCann, 1932
(with title: <u>The Second Omnibus of Crime</u>).

<u>Great Short Stories of Detection, Mystery and Horror--Third Series</u>.
London: Victor Gollancz, 1934; New York: Coward McCann, 1935
(with title: <u>The Third Omnibus of Crime</u>).

POEMS:

<u>OP.I</u>. Adventures All, no. 9. Oxford: Blackwell, 1916.

<u>Catholic Tales and Christian Songs</u>. Oxford: Blackwell, 1918.

Writings by Dorothy L. Sayers

PLAYS:

Busman's Honeymoon, by Dorothy L. Sayers and M. St. Clare Byrne. London: Victor Gollancz, 1937; New York: Dramatists Play Service, 1939.

The Zeal of Thy House. London: Victor Gollancz, 1937; New York: Harcourt, Brace, 1937.

The Devil to Pay. London: Victor Gollancz, 1939; New York: Harcourt, Brace, 1939.

He That Should Come: A Nativity Play in One Act. London: Victor Gollancz, 1939.

Love All. Produced at the Torch Theatre, 8 April 1940.

The Man Born To Be King: A Play-Cycle on the Life of Our Lord and Saviour, Jesus Christ. London: Victor Gollancz, 1943; New York: Harper, 1949.

The Just Vengeance. London: Victor Gollancz, 1946.

The Emperor Constantine: A Chronicle. London: Victor Gollancz, 1951; New York: Harper, 1951.

COLLECTED PLAYS:

Four Sacred Plays. London: Victor Gollancz, 1948. (Includes: The Zeal of Thy House, The Devil to Pay, He That Should Come, and The Just Vengeance.)

FILMS:

The Silent Passenger. 1935. Film based on an unpublished story.

Busman's Honeymoon. 1940. See also Haunted Honeymoon.

The Haunted Honeymoon. 1940. See also Busman's Honeymoon.

MISCELLANEOUS ESSAYS AND LONGER NON-FICTION

"The Dates in 'The Red-Headed League.'" The Colophon 17, no. 10 (June 1934).

"The King's English." Nash's Pall Mall, May 1935, pp. 16-17, 88-90.

"The Murder of Julia Wallace." In The Anatomy of Murder: Famous Crimes Critically Considered, by Members of the Detection Club. London: John Lane, Bodley Head, 1936; New York: Macmillan, 1937.

"The Greatest Drama Ever Staged." Sunday Times (London) 3 April 1938, p. 20.

"The Triumph of Easter." Sunday Times (London) 17 April 1938, p. 10.

"Wimsey Papers." Spectator, no. 5812 (17 November 1939):672-74; no. 5813 (24 November 1939):736-37; no. 5814 (1 December 1939): 770-71; no. 5815 (8 December 1939):809-10; no. 5816 (15 December 1939):859-60; no. 5817 (22 December 1939):894-95; no. 5818 (29 December 1939):925-26; no. 5819 (5 January 1940):8-9; no. 5820 (12 January 1940):38-39; no. 5821 (19 January 1940): 70-71; no. 5822 (26 January 1940):104-5.

Creed or Chaos? London: Hodder & Stoughton, 1940.

Begin Here: A War-time Essay. London: Victor Gollancz, 1940; New York: Harcourt, Brace, 1941.

"The Human-Not-Quite-Human." Christendom 9 (September 1941):156-62.

The Mind of the Maker. London: Methuen, 1941; New York: Harcourt, Brace, 1941.

Why Work? London: Methuen, 1942.

"Towards a Christian Aesthetic." In Our Culture: Its Christian Roots and Present Crisis. Edward Alleyn Lectures, 1944. London: Society for the Propagation of Christian Knowledge, 1944.

"Creative Mind." In Unpopular Opinions. London: Victor Gollancz, 1946, pp. 43-58.

"'. . . And Telling You a Story'." In Essays Presented to Charles Williams, by Dorothy Sayers et al. London: Oxford University Press, 1947.

The Lost Tools of Learning. London: Methuen, 1948; National Review (Orange, Conn.) 7 (August 1959):237-44.

"My Belief About Heaven and Hell." Sunday Times (London), 6 January 1957, p. 8.

"The Beatrician Vision in Dante and Other Poets." Nottingham Mediaeval Studies 2 (1958):3-23.

Writings by Dorothy L. Sayers

"On Translating the Divina Commedia." Nottingham Mediaeval Studies
   2 (1958):38-66.

"Like Aesop's Bat," by Barbara Reynolds and Dorothy L. Sayers.
   VII: An Anglo-American Literary Review 1 (March 1980):81-93.

COLLECTED ESSAYS:

Strong Meat. London: Hodder & Stoughton, 1939.

Unpopular Opinions. London: Victor Gollancz, 1946; New York:
   Harcourt, Brace, 1947.

Creed or Chaos? and Other Essays. London: Methuen, 1947; New York:
   Harcourt, Brace, 1949.

Introductory Papers on Dante. London: Methuen, 1954; New York:
   Harper, 1955.

Further Papers on Dante. London: Methuen, 1957; New York: Harper
   1957.

The Poetry of Search and the Poetry of Statement and Other Posthumous
   Essays on Literature, Religion and Language. London: Victor
   Gollancz, 1963.

Christian Letters to a Post-Christian World: A Selection of Essays.
   Selected by Roderick Jellema. Grand Rapids, Mich.: William B.
   Eerdmans, 1969.

Are Women Human? Downers Grove, Ill.: Inter-Varsity Press, 1971.

The Whimsical Christian: 18 Essays. New York: Macmillan, 1978.
   (Previously published under the title Christian Letters to a
   Post-Christian World.)

TRANSLATIONS BY SAYERS:

Tristan in Brittany. London: Ernest Benn, 1929; New York: Payson &
   Clarke, 1929.

The Comedy of Dante Alighieri, the Florentine. Cantica I: Hell.
   Harmondsworth, Middlesex: Penguin Books, 1949; New York: Basic
   Books, 1963.

The Comedy of Dante Alighieri, the Florentine. Cantica II: Purgatory. Harmondsworth, Middlesex: Penguin Books, 1955; New York:
   Basic Books, 1963.

The Song of Roland: A New Translation. Harmondsworth, Middlesex: Penguin Books, 1957; Baltimore: Penguin Books, 1957.

The Comedy of Dante Alighieri, the Florentine. Cantica III: Paradise. Translated by Dorothy L. Sayers and Barbara Reynolds. Harmondsworth, Middlesex: Penguin Books, 1962; New York: Basic Books, 1963.

BIOGRAPHY:

Wilkie Collins: A Critical and Biographical Study. Edited by E. R. Gregory. Toledo, Ohio: Friends of the University of Toledo Libraries, 1977.

FOR CHILDREN:

Even the Parrot: Exemplary Conversations for Enlightened Children. London: Methuen, 1944.

The Days of Christ's Coming. London: Hamish Hamilton, 1953; New York: Harper & Row, 1960.

SELECTIONS:

A Matter of Eternity: Selections from the Writings of Dorothy L. Sayers. Chosen by Rosamund Kent Sprague. Grand Rapids, Mich.: William B. Eerdmans, 1973; London: A. R. Mowbray, 1973.

Writings about Dorothy L. Sayers, 1917-1981

1917

1 ANON. Review of OP.I. Times Literary Supplement, 25 January, p. 47.

Comments that there is not a poem in this Sayers collection that should be ignored, and that some have real beauty. Singles out "Hymn in Contemplation of Sudden Death." Considers her failing to be that of preciosity that shows particularly in "Lay" and "The Lost Castle."

1918

1 ANON. Review of Catholic Tales and Christian Songs. Times Literary Supplement, 21 November, pp. 570-71.

Finds in these Sayers pieces a "familiar intimacy with Christ characteristic of the Middle Ages." Comments very briefly on three of the poems.

1919

1 ANON. Review of Catholic Tales and Christian Songs. Catholic World 110 (October):108.

Finds Sayers's attempt to achieve a medieval "divine familiarity" failing to accomplish the divinity while producing only the familiarity, and failing also to show a true "Catholic consciousness." Comments favorably on her introductory poem on the kiss of betrayal.

2 ANON. Review of Catholic Tales and Christian Songs. Nation 109 (27 September):441.

Sayers's book is praised for "reverence and naive boldness," "deep imaginative conceits," and the keen satire in "The Mocking of Christ."

1919

*3   UNTERMEYER, LOUIS. Review of <u>Catholic Tales and Christian</u>
     <u>Songs</u>. <u>New York Evening Post</u>, 1 November, p. 2.
        Cited in <u>Book Review Digest</u>. New York: H. W. Wilson,
     1919, p. 444.

<u>1923</u>

1   ANON. Review of <u>Whose Body?</u> <u>Boston Evening Transcript</u>,
     6 June, p. 4.
        Suggests that this Sayers novel would do for a railway
     journey in spite of its shortcomings--superfluous charac-
     ters and superfluous false scents. Questions the portrayal
     of Lord Peter as a true British younger son and also that
     of Mr. Thipp as a London architect.

2   ANON. Review of <u>Whose Body?</u> <u>Literary Digest International</u>
     <u>Book Review</u> (September):76.
        No other critical comment than that it has an ingenious
     plot and is very entertaining.

3   ANON. Review of <u>Whose Body?</u> <u>Nation</u> 117 (5 September):247.
        Three sentences filled with complimentary phrases:
     "maddest, jolliest crime story," "delightfully mysterious,"
     "attractive gentleman detective," "absorbing story," "well-
     written book."

4   ANON. Review of <u>Whose Body?</u> <u>Times Literary Supplement</u>,
     25 October, p. 709.
        A recap of this Sayers story is accompanied by the re-
     mark that it's good fun even if the characters are un-
     original and the incidents impossible.

5   ANON. Review of <u>Whose Body?</u> <u>New York Times Book Review</u>,
     27 May, p. 27.
        Comments briefly on the characters. Finds Sayers's
     writing very good, the characterization better than in the
     average detective story, and the plot "ingenious and well
     worked out."

6   OSBORN, E. W. "Passing Given Points Along the Fiction Line."
     <u>World</u> (New York), 20 May, p. 6.
        Review of <u>Whose Body?</u> Calls Sayers a "lady of infinite
     mirth." Comments that the cheerfulness of the characters
     takes the edge from the horror. Compares the inquest to
     "an episode in opera comique." Includes lovely pen and ink
     drawing of a young Sayers.

1926

1   ANON. Review of <u>Clouds of Witness</u>. <u>Times Literary Supplement</u>,
      18 February, p. 121.
         A brief review, pointing out that in spite of weaknesses
      --unreal dialogue, too great a dependence on coincidence--
      it really is a fast-moving, suspense-filled story and that
      Lord Peter, silly as he may be, is "quite good company."

1927

1   ANON. Review of <u>Clouds of Witnesses</u>. <u>Boston Evening Tran-
      script</u>, 11 June, book sec., p. 4.
         Discusses Sayers's use of peers as characters, demanding
      trial in the House of Lords--a new element in detective
      stories. Calls it "superior mystery fiction," well written
      and well built, with much better characterization than is
      usually found in detective fiction.

2   ANON. Review of <u>Unnatural Death</u>. <u>Times Literary Supplement</u>,
      29 September, p. 669.
         Examines Lord Peter's role in the solution of what he
      believes to be a case of murder. The crime has to do with
      changes in inheritance laws, which Sayers elucidates well.
      Considers the story "closely and carefully written."

3   CUPPY, WILL. "Detecting Done Here." <u>New York Herald Tribune
      Books</u>, 1 May, p. 11.
         Review of <u>Clouds of Witnesses</u>. Calls this Sayers novel
      "required reading," "richly humorous without balling up the
      clews or destroying the suspense," containing "priceless
      deductions" and "matchless forensics."

1928

1   ANON. Review of <u>Lord Peter Views the Body</u>. <u>Spectator</u> 141
      (8 December):896.
         Brief review commenting that Sayers's selection of
      stories is uneven--some disappointing, some as good as they
      could be. Remarks on her use of good English, her sense of
      humor, and her genius for creating unusual situations.

2   ANON. Review of <u>Lord Peter Views the Body</u>. <u>Times Literary
      Supplement</u>, 6 December, p. 968.
         Gives brief description of themes of these "clever and
      ingenious stories."

1928

3   ANON. Review of The Dawson Pedigree. Boston Evening Tran-
       script, 21 February, sec. 3, p. 3.
           Considers the early pages of the book dull and decep-
       tive. Says that Sayers's style is "facetious" and that she
       attempts to show off. Credits her with an ingenious solu-
       tion and a "keen knowledge of the primary facts of medical
       training."

4   ANON. Review of The Dawson Pedigree. New York Times Book
       Review, 19 February, p. 16.
           Lists the characters and the parts they play. No com-
       ment on the quality of the book.

5   ANON. Review of The Unpleasantness at the Bellona Club.
       Saturday Review of Literature 5 (27 October):301.
           Complains that what should have been a good detective
       story because of its various elements turns out to be a
       poor one. This he blames on Sayers's delay in developing
       the plot, allowing the reader to keep well ahead of the
       story.

6   ANON. Review of The Unpleasantness at the Bellona Club.
       Times Literary Supplement, 16 August, p. 594.
           Feels that this Sayers story will bear the inspection of
       the reader looking for one that sticks to the rules of de-
       tective fiction.

7   B. B. "At the Bellona Club." Boston Evening Transcript,
       15 December, p. 8.
           Review of The Unpleasantness at the Bellona Club. Com-
       mends Sayers for using a true situation to create a detec-
       tive story, and for her use of comic relief. Recommends
       the book for reading elsewhere than in a "lonely mountain
       retreat."

8   CUPPY, WILL. Review of The Dawson Pedigree. New York Herald
       Tribune Books, 5 February, p. 12.
           Suggests that Sayers be put on "the approved list of
       mystery-mongers for good and all." Says she arrives at a
       "grandly grewsome ending" in "graceful" style.

9   H. E. D. Review of The Dawson Pedigree. New York Evening
       Post, 3 March, p. 13.
           Pans this Sayers novel on four counts: murderer's
       identity known, method of killing unbelievably subtle, Lord
       Peter's "line" is "silly-ass," and four of the characters
       are Sapphists.

10   HARTLEY, L. P. Review of The Unpleasantness at the Bellona
        Club. Saturday Review of Politics, Literature, Science,
        and Art, (London) 146 (8 September):305.
            One line of critical comment: "The special qualities of
        Miss Sayers's writing are seen here at their best."

11   MORTIMER, RAYMOND. Review of The Unpleasantness at the
        Bellona Club. Nation and Athenaeum 43 (28 July):564.
            Finds this disappointing in view of Sayers's talent.
        Thinks that "she could write an excellent novel without a
        criminal or detective in it," but considers the book poorly
        written and having jokes that are mostly not funny.

12   PEARSON, EDMUND. "A Good Thriller." Saturday Review of
        Literature 4 (21 April):790.
            Review of The Dawson Pedigree. Praises Sayers for the
        differences between this book and the usual pattern of de-
        tective fiction writing, in her creation of a likeable
        detective, a murderer who is truly a villain, and a new
        type of assistant in Miss Climpson.

13   PURDY, CHARLES McMORRIS. "Murder Will Out!" Bookman 68
        (1 October):233.
            Includes brief notice that Sayers readers will enjoy The
        Unpleasantness at the Bellona Club--an amusing but not in-
        tricate novel.

14   SHANKS, EDWARD. "Fiction." London Mercury 19 (December):
        206-8.
            Includes two-sentence review of Sayers's Lord Peter
        Views the Body. Says that the "worst stories are readable
        and the best excellent."

15   STARRETT, VINCENT. Review of The Dawson Pedigree. New York
        World, 27 May, p. 7M.
            Considers this Sayers novel "well above the average
        claptrap melodrama" with a "literary" flavor both
        Dickensian and modern in characterization and humor.

                                1929

1   ANDERSON, ISAAC. "Miss Sayers Analyzes the Causes of Goose-
        flesh." New York Times Book Review, 11 August, p. 2.
            Commends Sayers's selections for The Omnibus of Crime as
        well as her arrangment of them. Also praises her introduc-
        tion, commenting that it should not be missed by the reader.

1929

2   ANON. Review of <u>Lord Peter Views the Body</u>. <u>Bookman</u> 69 (May):
     xxvi.
        In this two-sentence review the critic comments that
     these Sayers stories are "obviously the work of a practiced
     hand."

3   ANON. Review of <u>Lord Peter Views the Body</u>. <u>Saturday Review</u>
     <u>of Literature</u> 5 (4 May):983.
        Very brief resumé plus one critical sentence: "The sto-
     ries are so slight that Sayers's Lord Peter has plenty of
     room for flippancy."

4   ANON. Review of <u>The Omnibus of Crime</u>. <u>Boston Evening Tran-</u>
     <u>script</u>, 4 September, sec. 3, p. 3.
        Outlines the scope and arrangement of this Sayers col-
     lection. Comments on her extremely well-written introduc-
     tion.

5   ANON. Review of <u>The Omnibus of Crime</u>. <u>Outlook</u> 153 (11 Sep-
     tember):70.
        Would take this Sayers collection as the single one for
     a desert isle without apology to those who consider detec-
     tive fiction an activity of which to be ashamed. Calls
     Sayers's introduction an answer to people who need one, but
     considers the shamefaced attitude one of affectation and
     "the most poisonous form of pseudo-intellectual snobbism."

6   CUPPY, WILL. Review of <u>Lord Peter Views the Body</u>. <u>New York</u>
     <u>Herald Tribune Books</u>, 31 March, p. 11.
        Disagrees with critics who charge Sayers with mere
     flippancy. Avers that she "knows her thrills much better
     than the ponderous boys" in spite of her use of humor.
     Says that these "tales stress the fantastic, grotesque, and
     macabre."

7   _____. "Yours Fiendishly." <u>New York Herald Tribune Books</u>,
     11 August, p. 5.
        Review of <u>The Omnibus of Crime</u>. A lengthy review, dis-
     cussing Sayers's introduction and telling the sorts of
     stories included. Considers the most significant criticism
     his advice to go buy the book--a genuine bargain.

8   HANSEN, HARRY. "As For Detectives." <u>Norfolk Daily Pilot</u>,
     15 August.
        Review of <u>The Omnibus of Crime</u>. With wry humor, sug-
     gests that this Sayers collection was published for the
     sewing circle crowd who do not read newspapers because they
     are too filled with crime. Discusses the idea that

detective stories are changing but still popular and the reason that people read them. Wonders if Yale would offer Sayers an honorary degree.

9   Le CORSE, GEORGE. "Anthology, Scholar Covers Field." Evanston News-Index, 4 September.
      Review of The Omnibus of Crime. Calls this the "social register of thrill writers." Remarks that Sayer's introduction shows a "scholarly plan, a clarity, and a William Jamesian persuasion," and should be read by all students of literature, not just detective fiction addicts. Discusses it briefly.

10   McKAYE, MILTON. "Crime Fiction Goes Respectable in a Standard Anthology. Omnibus Brings Oxford Learning to Mystery Tale. Miss Sayers's 1,000 Pages Most Ably Edited." New York Evening Post, 10 August, p. 6M.
      Review of The Omnibus of Crime. Discusses the contemporary interest in crime and criminals before discussing Sayers's work. Comments on her introduction--the scope, arrangement, and omissions. Considers the detective short story less satisfying than the detective novel although the short story form is excellent for horror. Commends Sayers's choice of horror stories.

11   W. B. R. "Dorothy Sayers Edits Imposing Anthology of Mystery Stories." Dallas News, 8 September.
      Review of The Omnibus of Crime. Criticizes Sayers's limitation of foreign stories to a very few when there are many good French and American ones, especially missing those of De Maupassant. Commends her introduction.

1930

1   ANON. Review of Strong Poison. Bookman 72 (November):xxii. No critical comment.

2   ANON. Review of Strong Poison. Boston Evening Transcript, 13 December, book sec., p. 2.
      Regrets that Lord Peter, Sayers's "literary child and sleuth extraordinary" should descend to mediocrity by determining to marry Harriet. Considers the book uneven in every respect.

1930

3   ANON. Review of <u>Strong Poison</u>. <u>Saturday Review of Politics,</u>
    <u>Literature, Science, and Art</u> (London) 150 (11 October):
    453.
       Remarks that this Sayers novel is "ingenious and amus-
    ing" as her novels usually are, but the reader in this
    instance must know a good deal about toxicology. Impressed
    with Sayers's knowledge of all sorts of things from lock-
    picking to the stealing of wills.

4   ANON. Review of <u>Strong Poison</u>. <u>Spectator</u> 145 (15 November):
    741.
       Finds this Sayers novel disappointing in several ways:
    too much has passed before the story starts, causing the
    story to drag; the murderer is the only one who could have
    done it; and the way in which the crime has been committed
    is unsatisfactory.

5   ANON. Review of <u>Strong Poison</u>. <u>Times Literary Supplement</u>,
    16 October, p. 841.
       Gives an outline of the story, calling it ingenious--the
    only critical comment in the review.

6   ANON. Review of <u>The Documents in the Case</u>. <u>Spectator</u> 145
    (11 October):504.
       Feels that interest is enhanced by the use of letters in
    this Sayers/Eustace collaboration. Comments that the
    characters are "extremely vivid" although not especially
    likable, and that the solution is introduced in an in-
    genious way.

7   ANON. Review of <u>The Documents in the Case</u>. <u>Times Literary</u>
    <u>Supplement</u>, 17 July, 594.
       Remarks that this Sayers/Eustace book not only gives a
    lesson in science but is excellent in another way: the
    letters composing it are as good as genuine ones, espe-
    cially those from the vain, egotistic woman to her lover.

8   ANON. "Tristan in Brittany." <u>Times Literary Supplement</u>,
    30 January, p. 74.
       Review of Sayers's translation of <u>Tristan in Brittany</u>,
    by Thomas. Discusses difficulties to be overcome in trans-
    lating this work, how Sayers handled them, where she suc-
    ceeded, and where failed.

9   ATKINS, STEWARD. "Dorothy Sayers Writes Again." Gastonia
     Gazette, 5 November.
          Review of Strong Poison. Recommends reading this Sayers
     novel at a single sitting in order to keep the chain of
     events unbroken. Calls it a "mind-gripping triumph" and
     a "treat amongst a glut of murder mysteries."

10 COON, RAY. "Lord Peter Solves a Puzzling Murder." State
     (Columbus, Ohio) Journal, 28 December.
          Review of Strong Poison. Finds few women writers of
     detective stories worth reading and not all of the stories
     of the best are good. Admits that the denouement of this
     Sayers book is logical but feels that the book is redeemed
     from dullness only by Miss Climpson and "The Cattery."

11 CUPPY, WILL. Review of Strong Poison. New York Herald
     Tribune Books, 26 October, p. 20.
          Considers this Sayers's best novel to date. Discusses
     the story, the characters, and the development of the plot.
     Says Lord Peter may be a Wodehouse man but he's also lots
     of fun.

12 JOHNSTON, BEN B. "Strong Poison." Macon News, 16 November.
          Says this Sayers novel is not a "credible account of a
     murder case," but an amusing tale of how such a mystery
     might be solved if there were one.

13 P. K. "From Thomas to Mallory." Wheeling Register,
     17 August.
          Review of Sayers's translation of Tristan in Brittany,
     by Thomas. Mentions the three groups of people who would
     especially appreciate this Sayers translation: those who
     enjoy Wagner's Tristan, those who read the poetic versions,
     and the eager scholars who explore the knotty problems in
     the early forms of the romance. Commends Sayers for her
     success in translating it.

14 TOWERS, MARJORIE. Review of The Documents in the Case.
     Nation and Athenaeum 47 (9 August):597.
          Considers this Sayers/Eustace novel satisfying from both
     the intellectual and detective points of view. Appreciates
     most of the character analysis, development of the back-
     ground, "the genius of motive," and the sardonic humor.

1930

15 WEBER, WILLIAM C. "Murder Will Out." Saturday Review of
        Literature 7 (20 December):478.
            Includes a review of Sayers's Strong Poison. Calls it
        "a shining star in the mystery story firmament." Considers
        the characters well portrayed.

*16 WILLIAMS, CHARLES [S]. Review of Strong Poison. News
        Chronicle, 18 September, p. 4.
            Unlocatable. Cited in Charles S. Williams: A Check-
        list, by Lois Glenn. Kent, Ohio: Kent State University
        Press, p. 27.

                                1931

1   ANON. "Murder Mystery in Scottish Setting." Quincy Herald-
        Whig, 25 October.
            Review of Suspicious Characters. Considers this one of
        Sayers's unusually clever books, and says that the element
        of suspense is better done than in most detective stories.

2   ANON. Review of Suspicious Characters. Boston Evening
        Transcript, 16 September, sec. 4, p. 3.
            A long resumé followed by brief critical comments that
        this Sayers book is too long and too involved. Comments
        that it "lacks force, suspense, and thrills."

3   ANON. Review of The Documents in the Case. Bookman 73
        (June):xv.
            Includes a very brief resumé and a sentence of criti-
        cism, calling this collaboration "most effective."

4   ANON. Review of The Documents in the Case. Boston Evening
        Transcript, 10 June, sec. 3, p. 2.
            Implies that this Sayers/Eustace book is too long be-
        cause of the collaboration, neither author wanting to leave
        the other's work out. Characterizes it as "part detective,
        part botanical, part triangle." Suggests that some of the
        letters are relevant to the plot, some not.

5   ANON. Review of The Documents in the Case. Springfield
        (Mass.) Republican, 25 June, p. 8.
            No critical comment.

6   ANON. Review of <u>The Five Red Herrings</u>. <u>Spectator</u> 146
      (9 May):746.
           Remarks that this Sayers novel depends on timetables too
      taxing of the intelligence to be enjoyable. Misses Lord
      Peter and the "other pleasant fantasies wherewith Miss
      Sayers is wont to adorn her novels."

7   ANON. Review of <u>The Five Red Herrings</u>. <u>Times Literary
      Supplement</u>, 9 April, p. 290.
           After giving a recap of this Sayers story the writer
      describes it as "neatly and plausibly contrived" but tedi-
      ous to follow.

8   ANON. Review of Sayers's translation of <u>Tristan in Brittany</u>,
      by Thomas. <u>Living Church</u> (16 January).
           Calls this translation "more than literal--it is exact,"
      and still Sayers was able to follow the meter and rhymed
      couplets of the original.

9   BROOKS, WALTER R. "Behind the Blurbs." <u>Outlook</u> 158 (27 May):
      121.
           Includes review of <u>The Documents in the Case</u>. Gives a
      grade of A, though he misses Wimsey in this Sayers/Eustace
      detective novel.

10   _____. Review of <u>Suspicious Characters</u>. <u>Outlook</u> 159
      (23 September):123.
           Feels let down by Sayers, one of his favorite writers,
      with a book in which the detective conceals a clue until
      the end of the story and in which the train schedules are
      too confusing.

11   CUPPY, WILL. Review of <u>Suspicious Characters</u>. <u>New York
      Herald Tribune Books</u>, 20 September, p. 14.
           An unenthusiastic review of this "over long" Sayers
      novel, called <u>Five Red Herrings</u> in England. Suspects that
      Americans do not know what a red herring is.

12   HARWOOD, H. C. Review of <u>The Five Red Herrings</u>. <u>Saturday
      Review of Politics, Literature, Science, and Art</u> (London)
      151 (7 March):347.
           Comments very briefly that this good Sayers story might
      have been improved by more distinctive characters. Re-
      marks that the murder method is very sophisticated, de-
      manding the full attention of the reader.

1931

13   RAE, BRUCE. Review of <u>Strong Poison</u>. <u>New York Times Book Review</u>, 8 February, p. 25.
        Recommends this Sayers novel for Lord Peter's chatter, not for the "tepid" mystery element.

14   _____. Review of <u>Suspicious Characters</u>. <u>New York Times Book Review</u>, 13 September, p. 21.
        Characterizes Sayers as "one of the most skillful of mystery writers," this book as "first-rate" work, and Lord Peter as at "his amusing best."

15   _____. Review of <u>The Documents in the Case</u>. <u>New York Times Book Review</u>, 19 April, p. 13.
        Gives Sayers good grades for characterization and plot development. Writes a bit about Mr. Eustace, the collaborator.

16   Van VLEEK, SCHUYLER. Review of <u>Suspicious Characters</u>. <u>Chicago Tribune</u>, 19 September, p. 13.
        Contrasts this "well-written . . . thrilling" Sayers novel with those detective stories that have no style. Finds it told with skill and enhanced by humor.

17   WEBER, WILLIAM C. "Murder Will Out." <u>Saturday Review of Literature</u> 7 (18 July):981.
        Includes review of <u>The Documents in the Case</u> by Sayers/ Eustace. Usually objects to the series-of-letters style but credits Sayers with handling both it and the scientific material well.

18   _____. "Recent Mystery Stories." <u>Saturday Review of Literature</u> 8 (26 September):152.
        Includes review of Sayers's <u>Suspicious Characters</u>, predicting that it will "hold the palm for the best all-around mystery novel of the year."

<u>1932</u>

1   ANDERSON, ISAAC. Review of <u>Have His Carcase</u>. <u>New York Times Book Review</u>, 29 May, p. 16.
        Recommends this Sayers story as good entertainment since it includes both Lord Peter and Harriet Vane.

2 _____. Review of The Floating Admiral. New York Times Book
    Review, 21 February, p. 18.
       Expresses amazement that this story, written by fourteen
    people (all members of The Detection Club), each adding a
    chapter to what has gone before, "hangs together and holds
    the reader's interest.' Feels that this shows the "inge-
    nuity of the writers" and their ability to work from clues
    given by someone else.

3 _____. Review of The Second Omnibus of Crime. New York Times
    Book Review, 7 February, p. 12.
       Discusses the subject, brought up in Sayers's introduc-
    tion, of the decline in the number of good mystery short
    stories. Commends her selection.

4 ANON. "Little 'Tecs' Have Little Crooks." New Statesman and
    Nation 3 (7 May):594.
       Criticizes the smallness of most contemporary fiction
    detectives, but excepts Sayers's Lord Peter. Calls him "a
    sort of Hermes of the criminal detection Olympus." Puts
    Have His Carcase along with Sayers's other books for "care-
    ful elaboration," excellent character portrayal, and style.

5 ANON. Review of Have His Carcase. Spectator 148 (18 June):
    874.
       In contrast to some other books reviewed here, feels
    that this one by Sayers is not for cretins. "Written with
    distinction and wit," it is both a psychological study and
    an exercise in detection.

6 ANON. Review of Have His Carcase. Times (London), 12 April,
    p. 20.
       An interesting re-telling of this Sayers story. Calls
    it an intellectual puzzle with a most ingenious finale,
    having "well-drawn" characters.

7 ANON. Review of Have His Carcase. Times Literary Supplement,
    5 May, 333.
       Considers this Sayers novel the better sort of detective
    story--the type that provides a genuine intellectual prob-
    lem; that is, to discover the method of the murder when the
    identity of the murderer is fairly obvious.

8 ANON. Review of The Second Omnibus of Crime. Bookman 75
    (June/July):xiv.
       No critical comment.

1932

9   ANON. Review of The Second Omnibus of Crime. Wisconsin
       Library Bulletin 28 (March):91.
            Brief remarks: "Good value for the money."

10 ANON. "Suspicious Characters." Charleston Evening Mail,
       17 January.
            Views this story by Sayers as an excellent mystery story
       because it keeps one guessing to the end and because it is
       well written from a literary point of view.

11 BROOKS, WALTER R. Review of The Second Omnibus of Crime.
       Outlook 160 (3 February):154.
            Considers Sayers's choice of stories for the section on
       "Detection and Mystery" excellent, but feels she is not as
       "at home" in her choice of stories for the section on
       "Mystery and Horror." Wishes for more recent stories and
       newer talent.

12 CATTON, BRUCE. "Why Detective Story is Losing Its Popularity."
       South Norwalk Sentinel, 1 June.
            Reiterates authors' agents' comment that the detective
       story is losing its popularity, and says, in effect, "No
       wonder." Uses Sayers's Have His Carcase as an example of
       what he considers "atrocious" writing--"humorless and de-
       void of the slightest kinship with reality." This review
       appeared in at least eleven other papers from 1-5 June 1932.

13 CUPPY, WILL. Review of Have His Carcase. New York Herald
       Tribune Books, 29 May, p. 10.
            Says Sayers has become a household word in two hemi-
       spheres. Gives resumé of story, calling it "an elegant
       problem in deduction" rather than a "classical presentment
       of life."

14 _____. Review of The Second Omnibus of Crime. New York
       Herald Tribune Books, 31 January, p. 14.
            Calls this a bargain and a pleasant successor to
       Sayers's earlier collection. Briefly comments on the
       contributors and Sayers's introduction.

15 HARWOOD, H. C. Review of Have His Carcase. Saturday Review
       of Politics, Literature, Science, and Art (London) 153
       (16 April):396.
            Brief but commendatory remarks, saying that Sayers
       relies on some "out-of-this-world" knowledge in writing
       this "clever, amusing and nearly perfect" detective story.

16   McMANIS, RUMANA. Review of Have His Carcase. New York
        Evening Post, 21 May, p. 7.
              Two-line comment, calling it "the best deductive mystery
        of the year--long but Lord Peter keeps it interesting."

17   PARKER, SELMA SABLE. "Have His Carcase." Madison Times,
        24 July.
              Calls this an "absorbing mystery," and in spite of the
        numerous coincidences, so well written that one swallows
        them easily.

18   W. T. S. "Mystery, Alibi, and a Murder." Providence Journal,
        22 May.
              Review of Have His Carcase. Highly recommends this
        Sayers detective story for its "amusing detective," intel-
        ligent writing, "finely woven complications," study of
        human nature, humor, and scientific structure.

19   WEBER, WILLIAM C. "Thrillers." Saturday Review of Literature
        8 (18 June):796.
              Includes review of Have His Carcase. Considers it up to
        Sayers standards, a mystery that "unrolls as it goes
        along," as a result of her close attention to detail.

1933

1   A. B. Review of The Dorothy L. Sayers Omnibus. Saturday Re-
        view of Politics, Literature, Science, and Art (London) 155
        (25 March):290.
              Remarks that, contrary to Sayers's prophecy that the
        higher type of detective story is coming to an end, Lord
        Peter's resources are not failing.

2   ANDERSON, ISAAC. Review of Hangman's Holiday. New York Times
        Book Review, 24 September, p. 25.
              Remarks that the Wimsey short stories give him new
        scope. Discusses Montague Egg more fully, and also com-
        ments on two other short stories.

3   _____. Review of Murder Must Advertise. New York Times Book
        Review, 9 April, p. 12.
              Comments on the amount of material given to the business
        of advertising instead of detection, but considers it good
        reading nevertheless. Remarks on Lord Peter's popularity.

1933

4   ANON. "The Criminal Record." Saturday Review of Literature
    9 (22 April):553.
        No substantial critical comment on Sayers's Murder Must
    Advertise.

5   ANON. "The Criminal Record." Saturday Review of Literature
    10 (23 September):136.
        Favorable comment on Sayers's Hangman's Holiday credit-
    ing Sayers with ingenious ideas plus some O. Henry touches.

6   ANON. "Lord Peter's Impersonation." Cincinnati Times-Star,
    11 April.
        Review of Murder Must Advertise. Discusses briefly
    Sayers's talents both as a detective story writer and as an
    ad writer.

7   ANON. Review of Ask a Policeman. New York Times Book Review,
    18 June, p. 10.
        Believes that, because this was written as an exercise
    in fooling around by its six authors, including Sayers, it
    does not turn out to be a good detective story. Describes
    the manner in which it was put together.

8   ANON. Review of Hangman's Holiday. Times Literary Supplement,
    11 May, p. 328.
        Says Sayers "followers will be glad to have this vol-
    ume." Admires her prolific and whimsical "inventive
    faculty" and her "irrepressible" sense of humor. Dis-
    cusses the merits and problems of the various stories
    included.

9   ANON. Review of Murder Must Advertise. Times Literary Sup-
    plement, 2 March, 149.
        Finds that this represents Sayers at her best: murder
    "ingenious and yet artistic in its simplicity," plenty of
    direct narrative well managed. Yet thinks Lord Peter be-
    gins to be too much a "universal genius" and that she will
    have to get rid of him somehow.

10 ANON. Review of Murder Must Advertise. Wisonsin Library
    Bulletin 29 (May):139.
        Brief remarks: "Complicated, amusing, clever."

11 ARMSTRONG, ANNE. Review of Hangman's Holiday. Saturday
    Review of Politics, Literature, Science, and Art (London)
    155 (13 May):461.
        Says that these are stories to be read through without
    a pause.

12   BECKER, MAY LAMBERTON. "The Reader's Guide." Saturday Review
      of Literature 9 (6 May):581.
            Discusses detective fiction as a genre. Assesses a good
      detective story as one that lasts even when the suspense is
      over. Considers Sayers's Murder Must Advertise one of this
      sort, partly because she thinks it uproariously funny.

13   BRITTAIN, VERA. "Oxford Versus War." In Testament of Youth.
      London: Victor Gollancz, pp. 106, 482, 508, 510.
            Gives a glimpse of Sayers at Oxford from firsthand
      acquaintance.

14   CUPPY, WILL. Review of Hangman's Holiday. New York Herald
      Tribune Books, 24 September, p. 22.
            Briefly discusses the stories, concluding that the "ad-
      vance guard of our short story masters would swoon dead
      away at the simplicity of these tales" but Sayers fans will
      enjoy them anyway and Sayers knows it.

15   _____. Review of Murder Must Advertise. New York Herald
      Tribune Books, 9 April, p. 17.
            Calls this Sayers's gayest baffler.

16   KLEIN, NORMAN. Review of Hangman's Holiday. New York Evening
      Post, 30 September, p. 14.
            Cryptic comments calling Sayers "clever English-woman,"
      welcoming Montague Egg. Gives one-word characterization of
      each of two stories.

17   McMANIS, RUMANA. Review of Murder Must Advertise. New York
      Evening Post, 8 April, p. 7.
            This two-liner says that Lord Peter is "less whimsical
      and more interesting than usual." Recommends it as excel-
      lent both as a detective story and as a picture of a
      British advertising firm.

18   PARTRIDGE, RALPH. "Heavy Spring Calendar." New Statesman and
      Nation 5 (18 March):342, 344.
            Includes review of Murder Must Advertise. Considers
      this book "brightly and intelligently" written except that
      Sayers succumbed to the temptation to introduce an atmo-
      sphere of violence, weakening Lord Peter's actual solution
      of the murder problem.

1933

19 _____. "P. Vance v. J. French Score--Deuce." New Statesman
and Nation 5 (20 May):654.
   Ranks Sayers fourth in the list of detective writers
here reviewed. Says she has "every virtuosity of style,
but is occasionally unsound in her plots." Comments that
her stories "make perfect reading for the tops of buses and
suburban trains.

20 PORTUGAL, EUSTACE. "Death to the Detectives!" Bookman 84
(April):28.
   Interesting summary of Portugal's favorite detectives
and of those he would like to see lined up in Albert Hall
and shot. He would have Lord Peter shot but only after
allowing Bunter to make his last moments comfortable.
Admires Sayers's writing on detective fiction and considers
her compilations well done.

21 POWELL, DILYS. Review of Murder Must Advertise. Spectator
150 (17 February):224.
   Says this "brilliant" Sayers novel is "written with intelligence and education" although with too many compli-
cated details.

22 QUICK, MORTIMER. Review of Murder Must Advertise. Toledo
Times, 4 June.
   Recommends this book to all, especially to those who
have found mystery writers unable to end a book as well as
it began. Comments on Sayers's ability to put "every beam
and bolt" in its place.

1934

1 ANDERSON, ISAAC. Review of The Nine Tailors. New York Times
Book Review, 25 March, p. 11.
   Says this is "Dorothy Sayers at her very best." Discusses the prominence of bell-ringing throughout the story
and Lord Peter's role. Comments on the delightful people
to be met.

2 _____. Review of Omnibus. New York Times Book Review,
30 September, p. 20.
   Lists titles included: Whose Body?, The Unpleasantness
at the Bellona Club, and Suspicious Characters, and calls
this a real bargain for new Sayers readers. No critical
comment.

3   ANON. "Art of Bell-Ringing." Springfield (Mass.) Republican,
      5 April, p. 8.
         Information on bell-ringing as found in notes from
      Harcourt-Brace at the time they published Sayers's The Nine
      Tailors. Mentions three sets of bells in the United States
      on which changes were rung.

4   ANON. "Baker Street Notes." Saturday Review of Literature 10
      (7 July):795.
         Discussing activities of some "Sherlockians," comments
      on Sayers's "astute conjectures" in her paper "The Red-
      Headed League," and also in her presentation of evidence,
      in the forthcoming Baker Street Studies, that Holmes
      studied at Cambridge.

5   ANON. "The Criminal Record." Saturday Review of Literature
      10 (24 March):581.
         No substantial critical comment on Sayers's The Nine
      Tailors.

6   ANON. "The Criminal Record." Saturday Review of Literature
      11 (29 September):144.
         No substantial critical comment on The Dorothy L.
      Sayers Omnibus.

7   ANON. "The Nine Tailors: Dorothy L. Sayers's Mystery of
      Pealing Bells." Springfield (Mass.) Republican, 29 March,
      p. 8.
         Discusses Sayers's appeal over and above the narrative
      interest as lying in the book's overtones--the bell-ringing
      lore, the village atmosphere, the church architecture and
      history, the fen country. Comments on her "humor, wisdom
      and human perception." Sees the closing chapters as rarely
      equaled in descriptive power "in recent fiction," suggest-
      ing Dickens in its depiction of life, both real and sym-
      bolic. Characterizes Sayers as having "a thoroughly
      civilized and delightful mind."

8   ANON. Review of The Dorothy L. Sayers Omnibus. Wisconsin
      Library Bulletin 30 (December):242.
         Comments that the novels are well done but that the
      themes are "morbid."

9   ANON. Review of The Nine Tailors. Boston Evening Transcript,
      21 April, book sec., p. 2.
         Comments that the setting, characters, and circumstances
      make this Sayers novel one of the most "ingenious and

1934

entertaining tales." Calls it a "story of murder, humor,
mystery, and beauty"--a picture of the English countryside
in times of flood.

10   ANON. Review of The Nine Tailors. Pratt Institute Free
      Library. Quarterly Booklist, 5th ser. (Summer):34.
          A single comment--"unusual."

11   ANON. Review of The Nine Tailors. Times Literary Supplement,
      11 January, p. 26.
          Feels that up until now Sayers has fallen short of what
      people have hoped for from her--something more than a de-
      tective novel--and suggests reasons for this. Says that
      in this book she has fulfilled the people's wishes and
      explains in what ways: the characters, including Wimsey,
      are human beings; the technical management is good; and
      the detective interest is kept alive. Suggests that here
      she has bound the creative imagination to the emotions of
      the reader.

12   ANON. Review of The Nine Tailors. Wisconsin Library Bulletin
      30 (May):115.
          Very brief comments on the setting, "good character
      delineation," plot, and "well-handled mystery."

13   ANON. "Woman Edgar Country Parson's Daughter." Daily Express,
      28 February.
          An interview by a Daily Express "Special Representative,"
      gives a glimpse of Sayers in her London flat talking about
      the beginnings of her detective-fiction writing. She had
      just won the Edgar award.

14   CUPPY, WILL. Review of The Dorothy L. Sayers Omnibus. New
      York Herald Tribune Books, 30 September, p. 16.
          No critical comment.

15   _____. Review of The Nine Tailors. New York Herald Tribune
      Books, 25 March, p. 18.
          Opens with "Here's required reading for all and sundry--
      this means you." Considers it way above even Sayers's
      average. Says it contains "some fine English writing, a
      positively grand background, a most ingenious plot, and
      whatever else you like in a Lord Peter Wimsey book." Dis-
      cusses the book briefly.

16   PARTRIDGE, RALPH. "A Bumper Crop." <u>New Statesman and Nation</u>
      7 (20 January):94.
          Includes review of <u>The Nine Tailors</u>. Recognizes that
      Sayers is heading for the straight novel with this one, and
      bemoans the fact that she is so involved with the Fen coun-
      try and its people and with the bell-ringing that she is
      reluctant to go on with the detective plot. He finds this
      a pity, as it is an ingenious plot and could stand a good
      deal of elaboration.

17   QUICK, MORTIMER. "<u>The Nine Tailors</u> Has All the Elements of
      Good Detective Yarn." <u>Toledo Times</u>, 1 April.
          Recommends that this Sayers book be read "for the detec-
      tive, the murder, the plot, the characters, the setting but
      most of all for the bells that go clanging and singing
      through it and the beauty and romance of its telling."
      Comments on the strangeness of the murder, the unusual
      setting, and on the art of bell-ringing.

18   _____. Review of <u>Omnibus</u>, <u>Whose Body?</u>, <u>The Unpleasantness at</u>
      <u>the Bellona Club</u>, and <u>Suspicious Characters</u>. <u>Chicago</u>
      <u>Tribune</u>, 6 October, p. 12.
          Finds that Sayers has made strides in her art in the
      eleven years since <u>Whose Body?</u> was written. Comments on
      the similarity between <u>Whose Body?</u> and <u>The Unpleasantness</u>
      <u>at the Bellona Club</u>. Sees in Lord Peter a mellowing devel-
      opment as he "converts his mannerisms into qualities."

19   ROBERTSON, ARNOT. "More Than a Murder Mystery." <u>Saturday</u>
      <u>Review of Literature</u> 10 (24 March):573.
          Review of <u>The Nine Tailors</u>. A native of East Anglia,
      this reviewer commends Sayers on the vividness with which
      she portrays the people and land. Comments that this is
      his sort of mystery--one in which the corpse will not be
      missed, so his interest is involved, not his sympathy.
      Includes illustration of bell-ringing, showing the bells
      above and the ringers below.

20   SWINNERTON, FRANK. "Dorothy L. Sayers." In <u>The Georgian Lit-</u>
      <u>erary Scene: A Literary Panorama</u>. New York: Farrar &
      Rinehart, pp. 429-32.
          Considers Sayers mysteries a grand mix of "richly spiced
      thoughts and views" drawn from her "mental encyclopaedia."
      Says that, as a result of her study of the craft of de-
      tective fiction as shown in her introduction to <u>The Omnibus</u>
      <u>of Crime</u>, her novels are "increasingly and impressively the
      work of a scholar to whom every formula and every possible
      deviation from formula is already a sentence in single

1934

        syllables." Nevertheless, suspects that she is "leading the detective story into dust" through too much erudition.

21   THOMPSON, WILLIAM S. "<u>The Nine Tailors</u>." <u>Atlanta Journal</u>, 17 June.
        Considers this Sayers at her very best, with an original plot, "excellent characterization, and an appealing style."

22   WALTON, EDITH H. Review of <u>The Nine Tailors</u>. <u>Forum and Century</u> 91 (May):vii.
        Very brief comments on the excellent atmosphere, "novel and intricate" plot, naming it one of the best Lord Peter mysteries.

23   WILLIAMS, CHARLES [S]. Review of <u>The Nine Tailors</u>. <u>News Chronicle</u>, 17 January, p. 4.
        Finds in this book a combination of philosophy and fantasy only hinted at in her earlier novels. The surroundings, the characters, and the plot are informed by laughter, pity, terror, clarity, and mystery, compounded by storm and flood--the whole reflecting "our dark and passionate life itself."

1935

1   ANDERSON, ISAAC. Review of <u>The Third Omnibus of Crime</u>. <u>New York Times Book Review</u>, 24 March, p. 18.
        Quotes Sayers's introduction as most of his comment on the book and concludes that she has chosen well--a good collection to read and keep.

2   ANON. "Crime in College." <u>Times Literary Supplement</u>, 9 November, p. 719.
        Review of <u>Gaudy Night</u>. Gives cryptic comments on the development of this Sayers novel. Finds the interplay of psychology and detection so well portrayed that the book stands out among her novels even as she stands out among writers of detective fiction. Does not consider this primarily a didactic novel on woman and the intellectual life, but rather a novel of character development that moves alongside the development of the detective interest.

3   ANON. "The Criminal Record." <u>Saturday Review of Literature</u> 11 (9 March):538.
        Commenting on <u>The Third Omnibus of Crime</u>, calls it a "superb collection" gathered by a "perfect editor."

4   ANON. "The Exploits of Lord Peter Wimsey." Times (London),
        12 July, p. 9.
            Comments on the reissue of five Sayers novels, each
        prefaced with the short biography of Lord Peter by his
        uncle. Says Sayers's records are almost entirely self-
        consistent and that Holmes's were not.

5   ANON. Review of Gaudy Night. Times (London), 5 November,
        p. 22.
            Judges this Sayers novel on the basis of its psycho-
        logical interest while seeing it as flawless from the
        standpoint of detection. Finds it worthy of praise both
        psychologically and in its "discussion of Woman and the
        Intellectual Life."

6   ANON. Review of The Third Omnibus of Crime. bde, 3 March.
            A poem in honor of this long Sayers collection.

7   ANON. Review of The Third Omnibus of Crime. Booklist 31
        (May):301.
            Brief description of this "fresh, unfamiliar" selection
        of predominantly "British" short stories.

8   BLAKE, NICHOLAS. "Gaudeamus Igitur." Spectator 155
        (15 November):828.
            Review of Gaudy Night. Attempts to analyze Sayers's
        "peculiar merit" in her detective fiction. Decides it lies
        in her "consistent and outstanding readability." Comments
        on the merits of this book, and calls it "a royal perfor-
        mance" even if one sighs to see so much talent used on this
        type of fiction.

9   CUPPY, WILL. Review of The Third Omnibus of Crime. New York
        Herald Tribune Books, 3 March, p. 9.
            Gives the scope of the collection. Quotes from Sayers's
        introduction and comments briefly on the stories.

10   GEROULD, KATHARINE FULLERTON. "Murder for Pastime." Saturday
        Review of Literature 12 (3 August):3-4, 14.
            Compares American and English detective fiction, favor-
        ing the latter and giving thoughtful reasons for doing so.
        Sayers's work is commended in several instances.

11   HUGHSTON, JOSEPHINE. Review of The Third Omnibus of Crime.
        San Jose Mercury-Herald, 7 April.
            Gives a list of some of the prominent authors in this
        Sayers collection of "better-than-average" stories.
        Briefly discusses some of the stories.

1935

12   MARKS, JOHN. "Penny Plain, Twopence Coloured." <u>New Statesman</u>
     <u>and Nation</u> 10 (20 July):95.
          Review of "The Silent Passenger." Classifies this
     movie, a Sayers story, as a "typical talkie--garrulous and
     efficient." It shows the British liking for amateurs in
     Lord Peter's role as unofficial sleuth, tracking down a
     trunk-murderer.

13   PARTRIDGE, RALPH. "<u>Gaudy Night</u>." <u>New Statesman and Nation</u> 10
     (16 November):741.
          Greatly regrets Sayers's downhill slide "into those
     luscious lanes frequented by constant nymphs, autumn
     crocuses, and little boys who never grow up," especially
     since she had begun to show signs of great talent for writ-
     ing straight novels in <u>Murder Must Advertise</u> and <u>The Nine</u>
     <u>Tailors</u>.

14   QUICK, MORTIMER. Review of <u>The Third Omnibus of Crime</u>.
     <u>Chicago Daily Tribune</u>, 16 March, p. 14.
          Calls this "another rich, fat volume" and comments on
     Sayers's wise remarks in the introduction.

15   RUSSELL, LEONARD. <u>Writing for the Press</u>. London: A. & C.
     Black, pp. 25, 120.
          Refers reader to Sayers's essay, "The King's English,"
     included in this book (pp. 88-104) for a lesson in correct,
     attractive writing. Mentions her among other detective-
     story writers in a very brief discussion of the detective
     story.

16   S. S. "Dorothy Sayers Mysteries." <u>Minneapolis Tribune</u>,
     3 September.
          Review of <u>Strong Poison</u> and <u>Have His Carcase</u>. Says that
     Sayers not only writes beautifully but handles a compli-
     cated plot with skill. Preferred these two stories over
     <u>Gaudy Night</u>.

17   SCOTT-JAMES, VIOLET. "Holiday for Highbrows." <u>London</u>
     <u>Mercury</u> 33 (December):228.
          Review of <u>Gaudy Night</u>. Sees Lord Peter very much at
     home at Oxford, but feels that Sayers fails to portray the
     essential character of the women as a group. Preferred
     <u>The Nine Tailors</u> but finds this pleasant reading.

1936

1 ANDERSON, ISAAC. Review of Gaudy Night. New York Times Book
   Review, 23 February, p. 20.
         Follows resumé with comment that the book is too long
   and contains too many quotations. Accuses Sayers of going
   "highbrow" and says the book is not dull but not up to The
   Nine Tailors. The page also carries a good-sized ad for
   Gaudy Night.

2 _____. Review of Strong Poison and Have His Carcase. New
   York Times Book Review, 30 August, p. 20.
         No critical comment except that this combined Sayers
   volume is "a real bargain."

3 ANON. "Blood and Thunder." Review of Reviews 93 (April):21.
         Review of Gaudy Night. A single paragraph with a hear-
   say report that this Sayers novel is one of the best detective stories to appear in a long time. Also second-hand,
   that it is perhaps too long.

4 ANON. "Bloodless Murder." Time 27 (24 February):75.
         Review of Gaudy Night. Agrees with detective-fiction
   readers that Sayers is one of the best. Avers that for
   readers who do not know her works this book will provide
   surprises in the quality of its characterization and setting, its combination of mystery and love story, and its
   lack of a murder. Comments on her knowledge and love of
   Oxford and the way in which she pokes fun of and satirizes
   the academic scene.

5 ANON. "Busman's Honeymoon at the Comedy." Illustrated London
   News 189 (26 December):1200.
         Credits Sayers's first stage appearance of Lord Peter
   with playing fair with her audience as concerns the rules
   of detective fiction. Considers it well up to the standard
   of her fiction.

6 ANON. "Comedy Theatre--Busman's Honeymoon." Times (London),
   17 December, p. 14.
         A descriptive review of the story of this Sayers play
   and its performance that should have whetted the appetite
   of those who like detective plays. Lists the cast.

1936

7   ANON. "Dorothy L. Sayers Oddly Disappoints." <u>Hartford</u>
     <u>Courant</u>, 1 March.
          Review of <u>Gaudy Night</u>. Finds this Sayers detective
     story surprisingly dull. Feels that Sayers would have en-
     hanced her theme of women better in a straight novel.

8   ANON. "Miss Sayers's Mystery of Woman's College."
     <u>Springfield</u> (Mass.) <u>Republican</u>, 8 March.
          Review of <u>Gaudy Night</u>. Comments briefly on the setting
     of this Sayers novel and wonders if this book will not ap-
     peal especially to graduates of women's colleges. Con-
     siders it "refreshing entertainment for the fastidious."

9   ANON. Review of <u>Busman's Honeymoon</u>. <u>New Statesman and Nation</u>
     12 (26 December):1065.
          Comments on Sayers's skillful handling of the plot and
     the performances of the players--saying that Dennis
     Arundell was not great as Lord Peter but that the other
     actors and actresses did well.

10   ANON. Review of <u>Gaudy Night</u>. Pratt Institute Free Library.
     <u>Quarterly Booklist</u>, 5th ser. (Summer):38.
          Two words--"mystery story."

11   ANON. Review of <u>Gaudy Night</u>. <u>San Francisco Chronicle</u>,
     1 March.
          Comments on the pleasant atmosphere and excellent writ-
     ing of this Sayers book "that is really a novel." Objects
     to the ending. Feels that one of the other characters
     would have made a better "poltergeist."

12   ANON. Review of <u>Gaudy Night</u>. <u>Wisconsin Library Bulletin</u> 32
     (April):50.
          Calls it a novel and comments that Sayers handled the
     psychological problem very well. Remarks that the charac-
     terization and setting are good, bringing the town of
     Oxford to life.

13   BUCHANAN, GEORGE. "Country Cottage, Corpse, Cellar." <u>News</u>
     <u>Chronicle</u> (London), 17 December.
          Review of <u>Busman's Honeymoon</u>. A sardonic review of this
     "presumably" good Sayers detective story. Comments on the
     acting. Followed by several protesting "Letters to the
     Editor" for having virtually given away the plot.

14 DENT, ALAN. Review of Busman's Honeymoon. Spectator 157
      (25 December):1122.
            Characterizes this Sayers play as a melodrama. Feels
      that the play, with its improbabilities and "rapid detec-
      tive cross-talk," is rescued only by the acting of the
      cast.

15 G. C. "Escaping Life With Dorothy Sayers." Brooklyn Eagle,
      23 February.
            Review of Gaudy Night. Objects to having detective fic-
      tion singled out as "escape literature" when every book is
      an "escape from life." Considers this Sayers novel far
      above average--a great study in detection with interesting
      characters. Remarks on her literary background.

16 HAMILTON, EDITH. "Gaudeamus Igitur." Saturday Review of
      Literature 13 (22 February):6.
            Review of Gaudy Night. Discusses this book, sometimes
      satirically, from the point of view of its setting, the
      sort of people one finds in it and the kinds of subjects
      they discussed. Gives a paragraph to Lord Peter and one to
      Harriet. Considers the ending entirely appropriate. Feels
      that Sayers accomplished what she set out to do: arouse
      interest through the detection and convincingly discuss
      topics of interest to her.

17 HOLLIDAY, TERENCE. "Some More About Lord Peter Wimsey and
      Miss Harriet Vane." New York Sun, 5 February.
            Reviewer is pleased that Sayers's Wimsey-Vane romance
      has come to a successful conclusion in Gaudy Night. In-
      cludes the Wimsey dossier and comments on Uncle Paul's
      revelations. Mentions the setting, the characters, and the
      action. Wonders why Sayers should squander her talents on
      detective fiction, then answers her question by saying that
      she hasn't, but rather she's raised detective fiction to a
      new level and briefly says why she thinks so.

18 JORDAN-SMITH, PAUL. "Vandal Frightens Women in Shrewsbury
      College: Lord Peter Called by Authorities to Solve Poison-
      Pen Mystery That Baffles Dons." Los Angeles Times,
      23 February.
            Review of Gaudy Night. Says that Sayers has elevated
      the mystery story to something at least near to literature,
      contributing her "gay kind of scholarship and shrewd char-
      acterization" to her writing. Commends her choice of quo-
      tations with which she heads the chapters.

1936

19 McC., W. H. Review of Gaudy Night. America 55 (18 April):43.
Expects this book to engage the interest of intelligent
readers for a long time to come. Says that Sayers's characters have "body and soul" and the setting and atmosphere
are the result of careful study. Mentions its drawbacks:
the implication of sex-starvation among faculty of women's
colleges, the use of American slang, and the seeding of
fraudulent research in the minds of students.

20 McCARTHY, MARY. "Highbrow Shockers." Nation 142 (8 April):
458-59.
Review of Gaudy Night. Using very descriptive language,
gives several reasons for considering this Sayers novel an
abysmal failure as a detective story and a regrettable venture into the novel per se. Comments briefly on the possible "death throes" of the detective story.

21 MATTHEWS, T. S. Review of Gaudy Night. New Republic 86
(11 March):147.
Calls this Sayers novel "an apologia, implicit and ex-
plicit, for the murder story as art," and explains what he
means. Prefers detective stories "straight."

22 NORWOOD, GILBERT. Review of Gaudy Night. Canadian Forum 15
(March):30.
Contends that Sayers writes good novels but is neither
a great novelist, nor a great writer of detective stories,
and definitely not a great crime novelist. Considers
Gaudy Night neither a remarkable novel, nor a good detective story, although it is a good study of life in a
women's college.

23 PHILLIPS, ELIZABETH. "Gaudy Night." Burlingame Advance-Star,
1 August.
Calls this a "delectable concoction of cultivated, intellectual conversation, thrill, mystery and suspense" with
a love interest added. Comments that it gives "depth and
profundity in . . . a sugar-coated pill." Admits that not
all will care for the lengthy discussions. Suggests baring
the head for one able to propose in Latin.

24 QUICK, MORTIMER. Review of Gaudy Night. Chicago Tribune,
29 February, p. 8.
Remarks that Sayers has "achieved true eminence in the
craft of mystery story writing." Wonders if Americans will
react to this book as well as the British have. Says it is
apt to be received either with great interest or great
boredom. Also printed in Toledo Times, 8 March.

25   ____. "Two of Earlier Dorothy Sayers Books in One." Chicago
     Daily Tribune, 12 September, p. 14.
          Review of Strong Poison and Have His Carcase. Says
     Sayers never slips from a high plane in "her plots, exacti-
     tude, and characterization," and "never fails to present a
     good mystery story."

26   R. G. L. "A Detective Story That Threatens to Be a Best
     Seller." Milwaukee Journal, 12 April.
          Review of Gaudy Night. Remarks that Sayers wrote this
     book for herself. Quotes from her introduction to The
     Omnibus of Crime. Says there is a great deal of "verbiage"
     before one gets to the plot, but then the reader will be
     hooked.

27   SHERIDAN, MARY B. "Sayers' Newest." Madison (La.) Journal,
     15 March.
          Review of Gaudy Night. Remarks that Sayers is the top
     representative of detective-fiction writers. Calls this
     book a good one for people who like "'Englishy' conversa-
     tion, an individual style, and intelligent writing." Finds
     it a combination of two separate stories, with more body
     than the usual detective story. Also finds it partly
     "cluttered."

28   WEBER, WILLIAM C. Review of Gaudy Night. New York Herald
     Tribune Books, 23 February, p. 10.
          Commenting that in this book Sayers is announcing her
     intention to switch to a different kind of book, Weber
     calls this "a full-fledged novel with mystery trimmings
     that excels most of her earlier books and is equaled only
     by The Nine Tailors." Discusses the various sorts of
     readers who will enjoy this and why, the characterization,
     and some other qualities of the book.

29   WILLIAMS, STEPHEN. "Lord Peter Wimsey to Take the Stage."
     Evening Standard (London), 5 November.
          Recounts the birth of the idea to write Busman's Honey-
     moon with Miss Byrne. Comments briefly on the play and
     Sayers's determination that every clue should be in plain
     sight of the audience.

1937

1   ANDERSON, ISAAC. Review of <u>Busman's Holiday</u> [sic]. <u>New York
     Times Book Review</u>, 21 February, p. 22.
         Concludes that the best chapters in this Sayers novel
     are those that come before the corpse is found, although
     the book "has everything--mystery, comedy, love interest,
     and drama."

2   ANON. "Canterbury Drama." <u>Times Literary Supplement</u>, 3 July,
     p. 493.
         Review of <u>The Zeal of Thy House</u>. Sees in William's
     recognition of his true sin and deeper spiritual need
     Sayers's awareness that "drama, secular or religious, needs
     a profound theme." Appreciates that Sayers has written a
     play weaving together a deep spiritual truth and a good
     deal of comedy and humor. Praises her rhythmical prose and
     her flexible blank verse, bringing alive this ancient form
     of English dramatic speech. Likes her use of hymns.

3   ANON. "The Canterbury Festival." <u>Church Times</u> 120 (18 June):
     745.
         Review of <u>The Zeal of Thy House</u>. A very complimentary
     review of Sayers's play and its production. Praises her
     detective fiction before discussing elements of the play:
     the humor, the real-life characterizations, the noble lan-
     guage of her blank verse, and the tone of the conversa-
     tions. Concludes with a description of the service that
     followed the presentation of the play.

4   ANON. "The Criminal Record." <u>Saturday Review of Literature</u>
     15 (20 February):18.
         Calls Sayers's <u>Busman's Honeymoon</u> "mush and murder
     mystery."

5   ANON. "Detective Comedy is Given in Mt. Kisco. Mildred
     Natwick Appears as Spinster in a New Play by Dorothy
     Sayers." <u>New York Times</u>, 13 July, p. 22.
         Review of <u>Busman's Honeymoon</u>. No critical comment.

6   ANON. "Detective in Love." <u>Times Literary Supplement</u>,
     12 June, p. 445.
         Review of <u>Busman's Honeymoon</u>. Considers this a highly
     successful story, approaching Sayers's desire to write a
     "straight" novel. Comments on her characterization of
     corpse and murderer--both unsavory. Sees Lord Peter's un-
     happiness at the fate of the criminal as a revelation of

Sayers's thinking. Praises the detection, the village humor, the high plane of the nevertheless human lovemaking, and the wealth of allusion.

7   ANON. "Doodles." Evening Standard (London), 18 September, p. 19.
      Pictures a page of Sayers doodles, with an analysis as follows: "Original, amusing, observant, ingenious, and kindly. An individual who enjoys taking a single idea or character and using ingenuity, wit and humour in the exhaustive presentation of it from a wide variety of angles. Movement rather than subtlety interests her. She has a direct attitude to life, is not complicated or confused, works best by herself."

8   ANON. "Dorothy L. Sayers." Scholastic 31 (11 December):5.
      A brief biography accompanying Sayers's story, "The Stolen Stomach." Quotes her on her recreations. Comments that she "worked out her plots to a logical nicety with wit, grace, and good writing."

9   ANON. "The Grandest 'Hoodunit' of 1937." New York Journal, 2 February.
      Review of Busman's Honeymoon. Characterizes this Sayers novel as a "bang-up murder yarn, flawless in construction." Comments briefly on the characters, plot, dialogue, and solution.

10   ANON. "Lord Peter and Bride." Springfield (Mass.) Republican, 25 February, p. 8.
      Review of Busman's Honeymoon. Finds the novel not up to Sayers's usual standards, lacking the "cohesiveness . . . in which the solution of the crime has been interwoven with an interpretative portrayal of a larger social situation." Sees her attention engaged chiefly with Lord Peter's lovemaking and adjustment to marriage, and with the characters, both those in the neighborhood and Lord Peter's relatives.

11   ANON. "A Peter Wimsey." New York Sun, 20 February.
      Review of Busman's Honeymoon. A very uncomplimentary review of a book considered "unworthy of so smart a woman as Miss Sayers." Wonders why she mushes over Lord Peter and Harriet, "spreading treacle over" their love.

1937

12   ANON. Review of Busman's Honeymoon. Booklist 33 (March):214.
          One-line comment on plot, characterization, and writing.
     Considered of interest mainly to Sayers readers.

13   ANON. Review of Busman's Honeymoon. Boston Evening Tran-
          script, 20 February, sec. 6, p. 4.
          Remarks that Sayers accomplishes the difficult task of
     "mixing a murder mystery and a novel." Gives a resumé of
     the manner in which Sayers's detective-story writing led up
     to this novel with mystery thrown in.

14   ANON. Review of Busman's Honeymoon. London Mercury 36
          (July):312.
          Says Sayers "has sat down to enjoy herself and revel in
     sentiment" now that Lord Peter has won Harriet. Prefers
     Wimsey as sleuth to Wimsey as lover.

15   ANON. Review of Busman's Honeymoon. Pratt Institute Free
          Library. Quarterly Booklist, 5th ser. (Summer):40.
          "A love story with mystery and drama thrown in."

16   ANON. Review of Busman's Honeymoon. Wisconsin Library
          Bulletin 33 (April):87.
          Comments that this Sayers book is more interesting as a
     novel than as a detective story, with excellent characteri-
     zations and entertaining dialogue.

17   ANON. Review of The Zeal of Thy House. Booklist 34
          (15 October):68.
          No critical comment.

18   ANON. Review of The Zeal of Thy House. Time 30 (25 October):
          80.
          No critical comment.

19   ANON. "The Zeal of Thy House." Canterbury Cathedral
          Chronicle (July):19-22.
          Quotes from the review of this Sayers play in The Times
     Literary Supplement of 3 June 1937, then thanks the pro-
     ducer, the Cathedral organist, and the author.

20   B. S. E. "Dorothy Sayers Gives Triple Measure." Living
          Church (3 April).
          Review of Busman's Honeymoon. Very complimentary re-
     view, commenting on Sayers's originality, believability,
     logic, story-telling, and humor. Views the Wimsey-Vane
     marriage as a study worth reading.

21   BEAUJOHN, PAUL. Review of Busman's Honeymoon. New York
      Herald Tribune Books, 28 February, p. 19.
         Reviews this work as a novel rather than as a detective
      story alone. Compares Sayers and Wimsey to Doyle and
      Holmes. Discusses the effect of the Wimsey-Vane relation-
      ship on Sayers's novels.

22   BROWN, IVOR. "Getting Away With Murder." Illustrated London
      News 190 (2 January):27.
         Review of Busman's Honeymoon. Comments that Sayers's
      "Lord Peter" will perhaps appear on the stage often over a
      long period of time. Discusses the contemporary interest
      in crime plays. Includes an illustration.

23   BUCHAN, WILLIAM. "Some Poets." New Statesman and Nation 14
      (11 September):384, 386.
         Review of The Zeal of Thy House. Considers this Sayers
      play "interesting and exciting." Comments on its balance
      and tidiness, the same good sense and wry wit as found in
      her novels.

24   COOKMAN, A. V. "The Theatre." London Mercury 36 (July):277.
         Includes a complimentary review of Sayers's The Zeal of
      Thy House. Comments on the vigor and control with which
      Sayers portrays the worldliness and salvation of William of
      Sens. Praises the acting of Harcourt Williams and Anthony
      Quayle, and Laurence Irving's stage setting.

25   G. K. "Peter Wimsey Has Interrupted Honeymoon." Los Angeles
      Times, 21 February.
         Review of Busman's Honeymoon. Praises Sayers for having
      brought to the mystery story "the finest art." Comments
      that one must judge her work aside from the conventions of
      detective fiction. Calls this "wise, witty, wickedly hu-
      morous, and breathless with mystery."

26   GOODALE, RALPH. Review of Busman's Honeymoon. Christian
      Century 54 (3 March):291.
         Remarks briefly that Sayers "covers the bones of her
      mystery stories with human flesh." Comments that she
      writes entertainingly even though one would not look for
      "social truth in her conservatism."

27   HULING, ELIZABETH. Review of Busman's Honeymoon. New
      Republic 90 (24 March):219-20.
         Comments that Sayers had done more than anyone to make
      the detective story a sister to the arts. Deplores her

attempt to produce a novel. Claims that the literary allu-
sions and use of French are unreal additions to an otherwise "corking mystery" with a great cast.

28   IRVING, LAURENCE. Preface to The Zeal of Thy House. New
York: Harcourt, Brace, pp. v-vii.
     Commends Sayers for "avoiding sham archaism and fusty
language" in bringing this bit of history to life. Veri-
fies the authenticity of the major theme and its characters
except for the relationship between William of Sens and
Lady Ursula. Discusses the development of the theme but
does not assess it as drama. Reprinted: 1939.20 and
1948.6.

29   LAVERY, EMMET. "Rebuilding Canterbury." Commonweal 26
(15 October):582.
     Review of The Zeal of Thy House. Compared to Murder
in the Cathedral it lacks "the resounding clash of
forces . . . but it brings man and God together in a
poignant and memorable conflict." Admires Sayers's
technique.

30   LEAVIS, QUEENIE D. "The Case of Miss Dorothy Sayers."
Scrutiny 6, no. 3 (December):334-40.
     Reviews Gaudy Night and Busman's Honeymoon, with which
Sayers appears to have "stepped out of the ranks of detective writers into that of the bestseller novelists, and
into some esteem as a literary figure." Sees the esteem as
wholly unwarranted. Considers her fiction "parasitic,
stale, and adulterated," her sense of values shallow and
inconsistent, her picture of the university untrue. She
represents a class of "educated popular novelists" writing
bestsellers even as they are aware of what they do the
reading public.

31   LECHLITNER, RUTH. "Detective Turned Poet." New York Herald
Tribune Books, 12 December, p. 29.
     Review of The Zeal of Thy House. Opens with a comment
of surprise to find Sayers turning from detective-fiction
writing to religious drama. Appreciates the "great dignity
and beauty" and the "masterly analysis of a fine, warmly
human character, William of Sens." Discusses her development of the play.

32   McCRACKEN, ELIZABETH. "The 1937 Canterbury Festival Play."
Living Church 97 (4 December):721-22.
     Review of The Zeal of Thy House. Comments on some of
Sayers's "ingenious" touches and on the idea that her works

reveal, through their characters, something of the struggle between good and evil.

33 MOCHRIE, MARGARET. "They Make Crime Pay." <u>Delineator</u> 130 (February):28.
    Brief commendatory notes about Sayers and Wimsey.

34 NOBBE, GEORGE. "Enter Murderers." <u>bde</u>, 28 February.
    In a review of <u>Death Comes on Friday</u> by Lillian Day and Norbert Lederer, says that Sayers's influence is becoming "pernicious." People attempt to copy her fiction and fail because they do not understand character development.

35 NORMAN, SYLVIA. "Murders for All." <u>Spectator</u> 158 (18 June): 1156.
    Includes review of <u>Busman's Honeymoon</u>. Accuses Sayers of having removed from the court of law to the court of love. Obviously she finds the novel less than satisfactory.

36 NORWOOD, GILBERT. "Peter and Harriet." <u>Canadian Forum</u> 17 (April):30.
    Review of <u>Busman's Honeymoon</u>. Considers this a charmingly successful blend of novel and detective story. Discusses enthusiastically Sayers's handling of the various elements of plot, character development, and setting, granting "one artistic flaw"--the attempt to express the emotions of love in spoken language.

37 PARTRIDGE, RALPH. Review of <u>Busman's Honeymoon</u>. <u>New Statesman and Nation</u> 13 (26 June):1050.
    Comments unfavorably on Sayers's use of quotations, the weakness of the detective plot, and the mechanism of the crime.

38 SPECIAL CORRESPONDENT. "The Canterbury Festival." <u>Times</u> (London), 14 June, p. 12.
    Review of <u>The Zeal of Thy House</u>. Lists cast. Designates the play "a sincere and illuminating study of the purification of an artist." Comments that its inventiveness shows the discipline developed in writing detective fiction. Notes the acting, stage-setting and the singing.

39 SWINNERTON, FRANK. "London Sees First Play by Miss Sayers." <u>Chicago Tribune</u>, 16 January.
    Review of <u>Busman's Honeymoon</u>. Suspects that the dialogue is Sayers's although the play was written in collaboration. Says that Sayers's conquering of the stage

1937

adds another victory to her list of accomplishments. Remarks that the discipline of play writing will reduce her "tendency to capriciousness."

40 WOODS, KATHERINE. "To Make the Solutions Fit Some Famous Crimes, Seven Well-Known English Writers of Detective Stories Turn Their Talents to Real Cases." New York Times Book Review, 18 July, pp. 5, 18.
 Review of The Anatomy of Murder. Comments that these seven members of The Detection Club are "sophisticated, scholarly . . . ingenious . . . masters of their subject and their craft." Compares the true stories to those of the imagination. Discusses each case separately, including Sayers's analysis of the murder of Julia Wallace, which Woods considers an excellent analysis.

1938

1 ANDERSON, ISAAC. Review of Clouds of Witnesses and The Documents in the Case. New York Times Book Review, 24 July, p. 12.
 Single paragraph review of this combination of two Sayers novels, recommending it as a good buy. Remarks that in spite of the fact that The Documents in the Case lacks the "light-hearted chatter" of Lord Peter it is not lacking in wit and humor.

2 ANON. "The Criminal Record." Saturday Review of Literature 18 (30 July):20.
 Says that in The Documents in the Case Sayers is at her "mystifying best" although the book tends to be esoteric.

3 ANON. "The Criminal Record." Saturday Review of Literature 18 (27 August):18.
 Little comment on this Sayers double volume: The Dawson Pedigree and Lord Peter Views the Body, other than that the former is a "precious" pre-Harriet Vane story.

4 ANON. "Garrick Theatre--The Zeal of Thy House." Times (London), 11 May, p. 14.
 Calls this a "learned, informative, and, in parts, exceedingly well-observed play, "becoming tedious in the fourth scene, where Sayers is dealing with the spiritual facet of William of Sens's life, causing the play to dry up "in a desert of rhetoric." Mentions the cast.

5   ANON. "The Listener at His Fireside." Times (London),
       27 December, p. 15.
              Includes a review of He That Should Come. Descriptive
       telling of the story as Sayers developed it. Calls it a
       "beautiful, modern Nativity play . . . absolutely realistic
       in treatment."

6   ANON. "Murder Market." Time 31 (28 February):67.
              This discussion of the market for detective fiction in-
       cludes the note that the "erudite" Sayers is one of the
       most popular writers and that her books began to sell well
       as she became better known. Murder Must Advertise sold
       9000 copies to Busman's Honeymoon's 20,000.

7   ANON. Review of Clouds of Witnesses and The Documents in the
       Case. Boston Evening Transcript, 30 July, sec. 3, p. 1.
              Very brief critical comment, considering the first one
       of Sayers's most thrilling Wimsey tales and the second
       highly exciting.

8   ANON. "Westminster Theatre--The Zeal of Thy House." Times
       (London), 30 March, p. 12.
              Discusses the plot, the players, the dialogue, and the
       music. Remarks that "using rhythmical prose and flexible
       blank verse, Sayers reaches and encompasses in moving drama
       a crisis of profound spiritual significance." Lists the
       cast.

9   BROWN, IVOR. Comments on The Zeal of Thy House. Illustrated
       London News 192 (9 April):636.
              Brief comments accompanying an illustration of a scene
       from the play.

10   G. V. Review of The Greatest Drama Ever Staged. Blackfriars
       19 (August):627.
              Book includes The Triumph of Easter and both essays are
       reviewed. Commends Sayers's brilliant exposition of diffi-
       cult doctrines.

11   LAICUS IGNOTUS. "Miss Sayers' 'Nativity'." Church Times 121
       (30 December):723.
              Review of He That Should Come. Remarks that this broad-
       cast play was as unusual as one would expect from Sayers.

12   PHILMORE, R. "Inquest on Detective Stories." Discovery
       (April-September):296-99.
              Reprinted: 1946.7.

1938

13   SIMONDS, KATHARINE. "Bloodhound Into Bridegroom." <u>Saturday
     Review of Literature</u> 18 (3 September):14.
          Discusses several Sayers omnibus volumes: <u>The Documents
     in the Case</u> and <u>Clouds of Witness</u>; <u>Murder Must Advertise</u>
     and <u>Hangman's Holiday</u>; <u>The Dawson Pedigree</u> and <u>Lord Peter
     Views the Body</u>. Follows Sayers's Lord Peter from "in-
     genious, erudite, and elegant sleuth" to the sentimental
     bridegroom. Accuses Sayers of falling more deeply in love
     with him with each novel. Wonders if she will be able to
     turn him back into a true "bloodhound."

14   SPECIAL REPRESENTATIVE. "Religion in the Theatre: Interview
     with Miss Dorothy L. Sayers." <u>Church Times</u> 121 (8 April):
     893.
          Reports on an interview with Sayers at the time that her
     play, <u>The Just Vengeance</u>, had been produced. Reveals her
     ideas concerning Christian drama, detective fiction, and
     the young intellectuals of the day.

<u>1939</u>

*1   AGATE, JAMES. "Faust in the Haymarket." <u>Sunday Times</u>,
     23 July, p. 4.
          Review of <u>The Devil to Pay</u>. Cited in Hone, 1979.31,
     p. 200.

2   ANON. "<u>The Devil to Pay</u>, at His Majesty's." <u>Illustrated
     London News</u> 195 (29 July):216.
          A favorable review of the play--Sayers's "attractively
     simple" version of the Faust legend. Comments on the
     players. Four illustrations on p. 206.

3   ANON. "His Majesty's Theatre--<u>The Devil to Pay</u>." <u>Times</u>
     (London), 21 July, p. 12.
          Commends Sayers's "seriousness of purpose, power of
     lively invention, and clear-cut characterization," which
     makes for a successful play despite her limited command of
     verse. Discusses her development of the play, the charac-
     ters, and the acting. Lists the cast.

4   ANON. "Miss Sayers' Modern Faustus." <u>Times Literary Supple-
     ment</u>, 17 June, p. 353.
          Review of <u>The Devil to Pay</u>. Admires Sayers's courage
     in seeking to reinterpret the Faust legend in modern terms.
     Says she brings it up-to-date by showing the Devil's appeal
     to Faustus through sins more interesting to a person of her
     time than those of the original drama. The denouement fits

what she is trying to do. The poetry of the final scene
fits the grandeur of her theme, otherwise it is "utilitar-
ian." Sustains her purpose with invention and clear-cut
characterization.

5   ANON. Review of In the Teeth of the Evidence. Manchester
     Guardian, 1 December, supp., p. xiv.
          Commends Sayers's ability to "compress into so small a
     space the essence of the detective story," made noteworthy
     by the infrequency with which it is accomplished.

6   ANON. Review of Strong Meat. Times Literary Supplement,
     22 July, p. 443.
          Considers the second article, "The Dogma is the Drama,"
     her best piece of work to date in the field of theology--a
     field which she is successfully challenging after building
     her reputation in the field of detective fiction.

7   ANON. Review of The Devil to Pay. Booklist 36 (1 December):
     130.
          Gives Sayers's long subtitle and comments that this is
     an effective, slightly variant version of the Faust legend.

8   ANON. Review of The Devil to Pay. Christian Century 56
     (4 October):1211.
          Remarks that this Sayers adaptation is a new version of
     the Faust story, simplified but retaining the supernatural
     and fantastic qualities of the original. Comments on the
     effectiveness achieved by her language--modern and humorous
     at times, at times "sonorously religious and apocalyptic."

9   ANON. "The Devil to Pay: Miss Sayers's New Play for London."
     Times (London), 26 June, p. 12.
          Describes the play, announces its presentation at His
     Majesty's Theatre in July, and quotes from Sayers's
     introduction.

10   ANON. Review of The Devil to Pay. New Statesman and Nation
     18 (29 July):177-78.
          Calls down judgment on Sayers for her attempt to "com-
     pete with her betters" and feels that she would have done
     a better original play. Comments on the setting and poor
     production.

1939

11   ANON. "Tales With a 'Twist'." <u>Times Literary Supplement</u>,
      18 November, p. 675.
          Review of <u>In the Teeth of the Evidence</u>. Comments that
      while the Sayers stories in this collection are too short
      the characters in them come alive. Likes those stories
      best that are neither about Montague Egg nor Lord Peter.
      Says the collection will whet the appetites of her readers
      for more.

12   ANON. "Towards Realism. Mystery in Instalments." <u>Times
      Literary Supplement</u>, 4 February, p. 74.
          Review of <u>Double Death</u>. Sayers evolved an excellent
      plot as the first writer in this collaboration for a Sunday
      newspaper. The other contributors failed to follow through
      and the book is only mildly amusing. Edited by John
      Chancellor, the book has been put together with the au-
      thors' notes.

13   ANON. "Two Heads and One." <u>Times</u> (London), 7 February, p. 9.
          Review of <u>Double Death</u>. Considers this an unsuccessful
      collaboration, bringing together individualists whose work
      does not hang together except by John Chancellor's pro-
      logue. Appreciates the glimpse given into the minds of the
      individual authors.

14   BOUTELL, CLARENCE B. "England's Other Crisis." <u>Publishers'
      Weekly</u> 135 (15 April):1427.
          The "other crisis" was the storm over a review of Agatha
      Christie's <u>Hercule Poirot's Christmas</u>, involving several
      "Letters to the Editor." Sayers's letter was considered
      worth inclusion in this article and was preceded by com-
      ments on its quality.

15   BROWN, IVOR. "Miss Sayers on Faustus." <u>Manchester Guardian</u>,
      14 July, p. 9.
          Review of <u>The Devil to Pay</u>. Calls this Sayers version
      of the Faust legend an "ingenious modernisation . . . well
      worked into the mediaeval framework of the myth." Comments
      on her peculiar talent for the task, her verse, and the
      well-balanced finale.

16   BROWNE, E. MARTIN. "<u>The Devil to Pay</u>." <u>Canterbury Cathedral
      Chronicle</u> 33 (July):15-16.
          Commends Sayers for her restatement of an old theme in
      a well-written play, performed in a manner that "leaps to
      grandeur" and ending in an age-old truth. Four full-page
      illustrations added.

17   BUNN, FRANCES. "Faustus Legend in New Guise." <u>Raleigh</u>
      <u>Observer</u>, 8 October.
          Review of <u>The Devil to Pay</u>. Sayers's attempt to re-
      interpret the Faust legend for modern days is met with
      approval by this reviewer who feels that she has achieved
      her goal with great skill.

18   DUKES, ASHLEY. "Summer Season: The English Scene." <u>Theatre</u>
      <u>Arts</u> 23 (October):706-7.
          Includes an uncomplimentary review of <u>The Devil to Pay</u>.
      Finds fault with the execution but primarily with the play
      itself, giving several reasons for doing so.

19   HART-DAVIS, RUPERT. "Murder With Padding." <u>Spectator</u> 163
      (15 December):880.
          Includes review of <u>In the Teeth of the Evidence</u>. Con-
      siders this a collection of unsatisfactory stories, wishing
      Sayers had provided a little more of her usual elaborate
      background material.

20   IRVING, LAURENCE, ed. Preface to <u>The Zeal of Thy House</u>. In
      <u>Famous Plays of 1938-1939</u>. London: Victor Gollancz,
      pp. 13-15.
          Reprint of 1937.28.

21   LECHLITNER, RUTH. "Faust Takes the Stage." <u>New York Herald</u>
      <u>Tribune Books</u>, 12 November, p. 38.
          Review of <u>The Devil to Pay</u>. A complimentary review.
      Discusses Sayers's modern handling of an old legend, while
      retaining its "sixteenth-century compound flavor of witch-
      craft and miracle-making, medieval humanism and theology."
      Comments on the poetry.

22   M. K. "Canterbury Festival Play: <u>The Devil to Pay</u>, Dorothy
      Sayers' Version of Faust." <u>Church Times</u> 122 (16 June):656.
          Complains that Sayers has given the devil all the best
      jokes, and he has taken advantage of the situation and
      stolen the show. Nevertheless, feels that her re-telling
      of the Faust legend is pertinent and a very fine play.

23   PARTRIDGE, RALPH. Review of <u>In the Teeth of the Evidence</u>.
      <u>New Statesman and Nation</u> (23 December):934, 936.
          Two sentences give the scope and comment that Sayers "is
      supremely competent in everything she touches" with regret
      that she quit writing in this genre.

1939

24 REED, EDWARD. "Post-Freudian Faustus." <u>Washington Post</u>,
    29 October.
        Review of <u>The Devil to Pay</u>. Calls Sayers "an accredited
    dramatist." Comments that her subsidiary characters por-
    tray the "variety and charm" found in her detective fiction
    characters. Nevertheless, while she is commended for up-
    dating a fascinating character, she is criticized for not
    making a real contribution to dramatic literature.

25 SEARS, WILLIAM P. Review of <u>The Devil to Pay</u>. <u>Churchman</u>
    153 (15 November):18.
        Recommends this Sayers play as excellent reading on
    account of the "clear-cut characterization," and calls it
    "highly provocative."

26 SPECIAL CORRESPONDENT. "The Canterbury Festival." <u>Times</u>
    (London), 12 June, p. 10.
        Review of <u>The Devil to Pay</u>. Discusses the special tal-
    ents Sayers brings to bear on this play. Attributes some
    of her success to the fact that her Faustus presentation is
    totally different from those of Goethe and Marlowe and suc-
    ceeds by "sheer alertness of invention, always intellec-
    tually coherent and always couched in the spiritual idioms
    of the present." Comments on the acting. Includes
    illustration.

27 STRACHEY, JOHN. "The Golden Age of English Detection."
    <u>Saturday Review of Literature</u> 19 (7 January):12-14.
        Discusses English detective fiction in relation to two
    other classes of English literature--best sellers and in-
    tellectual novels. Follows with a discussion of several
    detective novelists of his day, including Sayers.

1940

1   ANDERSON, ISAAC. Review of <u>In the Teeth of the Evidence and
    Other Stories</u>. <u>New York Times Book Review</u>, 18 February,
    p. 23.
        Mentions the number of stories devoted to Wimsey, to
    Egg, and those devoted to neither. Considers the collec-
    tion remarkable, a good addition to Sayers's reputation.
    Finds the non-Wimsey and non-Egg stories more filled with
    suspense as a result of unfamiliarity.

2   ANON. "The Criminal Record." <u>Saturday Review of Literature</u>
    21 (17 February):18.
        Deprecating remarks about Sayers's <u>In the Teeth of the
    Evidence</u>, calling it "clever . . . but empty."

3   ANON. "For Christian Civilization." Tablet 175 (17 February):
    156.
        Review of Begin Here. After quoting from Sayers's book,
    calls it a "powerful apologia" and discusses its merits and
    defects. Commends the publisher for publishing this pro-
    Catholic Christian treatise.

4   ANON. "Miss Sayers's Stories: In the Teeth of the Evidence."
    Springfield (Mass.) Republican, 31 March, p. 7E.
        In the course of discussing this Sayers book, brings up
    the question of the proper scale for a mystery story--how
    long must it be to achieve its end? Comments on Sayers's
    perception and "vivacity of observation."

5   ANON. "Miss Sayers's War-Time Essay." Church Times 123
    (9 February):100.
        Review of Begin Here. Highly complimentary comments on
    the advice Sayers gives to readers, her interpretation of
    two difficult contemporary writers, her ability to deliver
    the Christian message without sermonizing, and her basic
    philosophical argument.

6   ANON. "New Beginnings: Miss Sayers's Hope." Times Literary
    Supplement, 27 January, p. 48.
        Review of Begin Here. Considers this Sayers's philosophy
    of history. Discusses her main points in which she calls
    for a new look at the future, based on a dynamic Chris-
    tianity and a more complete concept of man than was
    prevalent. Finds a weakness in her starting-point--the
    medieval Christian Empire.

7   ANON. Review of Begin Here. Nature 145 (25 May):815.
        Comments on Sayers's thinking brought to bear on the
    subject of planning for the post-war world.

8   ANON. Review of Busman's Honeymoon. New Statesman and Nation
    20 (14 September):259.
        Considers this American production of Sayers's play
    merely good fun. Remarks that it has been changed too much
    from the original and that the American players, Robert
    Montgomery and Constance Cummings, remain just themselves.

9   ANON. Review of Creed or Chaos? Times Literary Supplement,
    27 July, p. 367.
        States that Sayers has attempted "this lucid and vigor-
    ous defence of Christian dogma" to show the vital connec-
    tion between "the structure of society and the theological
    doctrines of Christianity." Notes her plea that these
    dogmas be restated in modern language.

1940

10   ANON. Review of <u>Haunted Honeymoon</u>. <u>Time</u> 36 (18 November):85.
      Comments on the play's "fluffy repartee." Briefly dis-
      cusses the wartime difficulties encountered in the filming
      of this Sayers drama.

11   ANON. Review of <u>In the Teeth of the Evidence</u>. <u>Atlantic
      Monthly</u> 165 (April).
      Grouped with reviews of other mysteries, reviewer com-
      ments on the disappointment to readers who like large doses
      of Lord Peter, although this Sayers book contains some ex-
      cellent stories.

12   ANON. Review of <u>In the Teeth of the Evidence</u>. <u>Christian
      Century</u> 57 (29 May):706.
      Says briefly that "the name Dorothy Sayers is as good as
      a money-back guarantee of a good story." Finds "ingenuity
      of plot" the characteristic quality of these stories.

13   ANON. Review of <u>In the Teeth of the Evidence</u>. <u>New York
      Herald Tribune</u>, 18 February, p. 12.
      Recommends this collection with the comment that "Sayers
      has something special on the ball in each and every item,
      whether it be an unusual narrative attack, a peculiar mood,
      or what."

14   ANON. Review of <u>In the Teeth of the Evidence</u>. <u>New Yorker</u> 16
      (17 February):72.
      No critical comment.

15   ANON. Review of <u>Love All</u>. <u>New Statesman and Nation</u> 19
      (13 April):493.
      Gives reasons for thinking that this is "a jolly little
      play for the uncritical." Comments that Sayers would not
      completely fail in anything but light comedy is not her
      metier.

16   ANON [?]. Review of <u>Love All</u>. <u>Time and Tide</u> (13 April):392.
      Calls this Sayers play "well-written, excellently-
      handled comedy," with thoughts about women as inspiration
      for men's work. Comments on the production and cast.

17   ANON. Review of "The Wimsey Papers." Rochester, N.Y.
      <u>Democrat and Chronicle</u>, 18 February.
      Comments that this series running in <u>The Spectator</u> is
      "like meeting old friends in a national emergency."

1940

18 ANON. "Torch Theatre--Love All." Times (London), 10 April,
    p. 6.
        Suggests that Sayers loses the angles of her triangle
    "in the comic pattern of the general struggle for artistic
    self-expression" in this somewhat feminist play.

19 BEVAN, EDWYN. "A Book of Good Counsel." Spectator 164
    (9 February):187.
        Review of Begin Here. Discusses Sayers's thinking about
    the past and "the significance of the present moment as a
    sequel to that past" along with considerations for future
    action.

20 BROWN, IVOR. Comments on Busman's Honeymoon at the Empire.
    Illustrated London News 197 (31 August):292.
        Captioned illustration from the production with Robert
    Montgomery.

21 FAUSSET, H. I'A. "War-time Essay." Manchester Guardian,
    2 February, p. 3.
        Review of Begin Here. Characterizes this "spirited
    essay" by Sayers as "little more than a stimulating sketch
    of the situation in which we find ourselves," but still a
    spur to faith, works, and self-knowledge.

22 FOX, R. M. "The Theatre Goes On: In England." Theatre Arts
    24 (November):787.
        Comments accompanying picture of scene from Haunted
    Honeymoon, the movie version of Sayers's Busman's Honey-
    moon. Names the players.

23 KERNODLE, GEORGE R. "England's Religious Drama Movement."
    College English 1 (February):414-26.
        In this article on religious drama Sayers is given fre-
    quent mention as an outstandingly competent playwright.
    Discusses at length The Zeal of Thy House and The Devil to
    Pay, giving especially high ratings to the former.

24 KIRKUS, VIRGINIA. "A Reader's Almanac: Jan., Feb., March."
    Saturday Review of Literature 21 (3 February):13.
        Calls 15 February a "red-letter day" bringing Sayers's
    In the Teeth of the Evidence, "rattling good stories."

1940

25 THOM, JANET. "Lord Peter Passes His Prime." <u>New Republic</u> 102
    (19 February):253.
        Reviewing <u>In the Teeth of the Evidence</u>, finds these
    Sayers stories "all first-class examples of their genre."
    Considers Sayers best in the crime puzzle projected in the
    comedy of manners. Discusses the waning of interest in
    Lord Peter once he had won Harriet in <u>Gaudy Night</u>--a "drama
    of character."

26 VANN, GERALD. Review of <u>Begin Here</u>. <u>Blackfriars</u> 21 (March):
    198.
        Comments on the vigour and depth of Sayers's thinking.
    Gives the main lines of argument and suggests that much
    good would come of a wide reading. Disagrees with her idea
    of self-consciousness as originating in the Fall of man.

27 WADE, MASON. Review of <u>The Devil to Pay</u>. <u>Commonweal</u> 31
    (19 January):290.
        Comments that Sayers's second best is sometimes better
    than another author's best. Nevertheless accuses her of
    attempting to do too much in a short play, and of inviting
    and deserving unfavorable comparisons with Goethe and
    Marlowe.

28 WIGGIN, MARIAN. "Rogues' Gallery." <u>Boston Evening Transcript</u>,
    17 February, sec. 6, p. 2.
        Review of <u>In the Teeth of the Evidence</u>. Very brief com-
    ments on its scope and contents, "all excellent reading."

1941

1   ANON. "Christ in Woman Novelist's 'Radio Oberammergau'."
    <u>News Chronicle</u> (London), 11 December, p. 3.
        Announces the BBC production of Sayers's <u>The Man Born
    To Be King</u>. Comments that this will be the BBC's first
    impersonation of Christ over the air but that the BBC and
    Sayers were prepared to risk it. Includes Sayers's remark
    to the reporter that the plays would be dramatic but
    reverent.

2   ANON. "Christ's 'Voice' in Radio Play." <u>Daily Mirror</u>
    (London), 11 December, p. 8.
        Announces the BBC presentation of Sayers's <u>The Man Born
    To Be King</u>, the first time in this country that Christ will
    be portrayed on the air.

3   ANON. "Dorothy Sayers' Experiment." <u>Evening News</u> (London),
     11 December, p. 2.
     Three paragraphs of biographical information on Sayers
     accompany the note that she had written twelve plays for
     dramatization on the Sunday Children's Hour of the BBC.
     The series is called <u>The Man Born To Be King</u>.

4   ANON. "Dorothy Sayers Looks to the Future." <u>New York Times
     Book Review</u>, 18 May, p. 8.
     Review of <u>Begin Here</u>. Examines Sayers's philosophy of
     history and its effect on her thinking about the times in
     which she lived. Commends her "lucid soundness" and re-
     marks that the "book has something to say to all of us,
     here and now."

5   ANON [?]. "Imaginative Theology: Miss Sayers's Latest
     Thriller." <u>Church Times</u> 124 [?] (19 September):537.
     Review of <u>The Mind of the Maker</u>. Discusses Sayers's
     theology on the basis of this book. Barely mentions the
     difficulties encountered in discussing the Fall. Concludes
     with the comment: "Theology in Miss Sayers's hand is more
     exciting than crime."

6   ANON. "Problems of Divine Creation: the Analogy of the
     Artist." <u>Times Literary Supplement</u>, 9 August, pp. 382, 385.
     Review of <u>The Mind of the Maker</u>. Commends this work as
     "an essay of great penetration and acumen." Discusses
     Sayers's main ideas and their illumination of both creative
     writing and Christian beliefs.

7   ANON. Review of <u>Begin Here</u>. <u>Booklist</u> 37 (1 June):458-59.
     No critical comment.

8   ANON. Review of <u>Begin Here</u>. <u>Bookmark</u> (November):7.
     Single paragraph commending Sayers for her penetrating
     criticism of various conceptions of man and the state, and
     for her message to citizens of Great Britain to think and
     plan ahead for the future of civilization.

9   ANON. Review of <u>Begin Here</u>. <u>Buffalo Union-Echo</u>, 30 May.
     Says this book will come as no surprise to Sayers
     readers who have gone beyond her detective fiction into her
     Canterbury Cathedral plays. Remarks that <u>The Zeal of Thy
     House</u> invites comparison with Eliot's <u>Murder in the
     Cathedral</u>. Views <u>Begin Here</u> as far from original, but its
     significance lies in its foresight.

1941

10   ANON. Review of Begin Here. Christian Century 58 (14 May):
     659.
         Considers Sayers's exhortation to make a better post-war
     world a valid one that might be considered a statement of
     forward-looking war aims.

11   ANON. Review of Begin Here. Detroit News, 1 June.
         Considers this book the work of a craftsman, interesting
     because of Sayers's knowledge of history and philosophy.
     Nevertheless wonders if she has really said anything new.

12   ANON. Review of Begin Here. New Republic 105 (4 August):166.
         A two-sentence summary of Sayers's analysis of man's
     emotional and intellectual development, advocating a doc-
     trine of the "Whole Man."

13   ANON. Review of Begin Here. Toledo Blade, 31 May.
         Calls this a quietly eloquent book by an "English-woman
     of exceptional intellectual poise and penetration." Says
     that the reader should find new hope for the future in this
     Sayers work.

14   ANON. Review of Begin Here. Wisconsin Library Bulletin 37
     (June):114.
         States Sayers's aim and remarks briefly that she deals
     more with personal attitudes than the national and inter-
     national reconstruction she feels should begin immediately.

15   ANON. Review of The Mind of the Maker. Spectator 167
     (22 August):190.
         Derogatory comments to the effect that Sayers here uses
     a "dangerous analogy" made more dangerous by her personal
     approach to it. Objects to the results of her self-
     criticism.

16   BARZUN, JACQUES. "A Lively Sermon." Nation 152 (10 May):
     561-62.
         Review of Begin Here. Characterizing Sayers as "a com-
     petent historian, a philosopher, and an artist," comments
     that she brings to her writing a "calmness born of histori-
     cal perspective, the clarity of a logician, and the con-
     creteness that belongs to art." Discusses the ideas she
     puts forth, remarking that they deserve close study.

17   BROWN, GRETA E. Review of Begin Here. Library Journal 66
     (1 April):304.
         Comments on the clarity and conciseness of Sayers's
     presentation.

18 ELLIOTT, R. A. "Letter to the Editor." <u>Daily Telegraph</u>
(London), 31 December.
    Protests the outcry against Sayers's <u>The Man Born To Be</u>
<u>King</u>, saying that this BBC production was sincere, reverent,
and dignified. Wonders if the spoken word is more offensive
than the word sung as in Bach's <u>St. Matthew Passion</u>.

19 ERTZ, SUSAN. "Trumpet Call." <u>New York Herald Tribune Books</u>,
4 May, p. 11.
    Review of <u>Begin Here</u>. Discusses Sayers's thinking and
her writing as seen in this book. Commends it to all
"deeply concerned men and women in the democracies."

20 FADIMAN, CLIFTON. Review of <u>Begin Here</u>. <u>New Yorker</u> 17
(3 May):85.
    A complimentary review, remarking on Sayers's wisdom and
courage. Calls her a "downright lady" who believes the future is now, a religious woman whose blueprints involve the
human soul and its liberation.

21 GOLDEEN, MIRIAM. "Faith From England." <u>San Francisco</u>
<u>Chronicle</u>, 1 June.
    Review of <u>Begin Here</u>. Comments on Sayers's popularity
in the United States, her competence in literature and
philosophy as a background for this book, and her wit and
vigor in discussing her subject. Gives a very brief resumé
of her ideas.

22 HAYCRAFT, HOWARD. <u>Murder for Pleasure: The Life and Times of</u>
<u>the Detective Story</u>. New York: D. Appleton-Century,
428 pp., passim.
    History and analysis of the development of detective
fiction, primarily in England and America, including many
references to Sayers and her writing. Includes bibliographies, "Who's Who in Detection," and some portraits.
Chapter eleven, "The Rules of the Game," reprinted in
<u>Writing Detective and Mystery Fiction</u>, edited by A. S.
Burack (1945.1). Enlarged edition: 1951.5; Reprinted:
1968.1.

23 JOHNSON, F. ERNEST. "Ladder of Destiny." <u>Survey Midmonthly</u>
77 (December):371-72.
    Review of <u>Begin Here</u>. A long resumé of Sayers's thought
accompanied by a single paragraph of critical comment.
Sees Sayers, the self-styled "amateur," as being wiser than
many specialists in the field. Says her judgments are
sound, "formulated against a background of historical
knowledge and touched with exceptional insight."

1941

24 L. L. R. Review of Begin Here. Churchman 155 (June):35.
    Calls this a "war book worth reading."

25 LEEDY, PAUL D. Review of Begin Here. Christian Advocate,
    26 June.
        Views this as a significant, stimulating study of democ-
    racy in relation to World War II. Gives a brief resumé of
    Sayers's ideas.

26 M. W. B. "Thinking the Thing Through." Christian Science
    Monitor, 18 September, sec. 2, p. [24A].
        Review of Begin Here. Several paragraphs given to
    resumé. No critical comment.

27 R. L. "Creeds and the Artist." Manchester Guardian,
    1 August, p. 3.
        Review of The Mind of the Maker. Mentions the fact that
    this Sayers work is the first of the Bridgeheads series,
    providing a bridge between the mind of God and that of
    creative man. Praises her use of illustration to clarify
    her statements.

28 RYND, REGINALD F. Review of Begin Here: A War-Time Essay.
    Hibbert Journal 39 (January):213-15.
        Summarizes briefly Sayers's main ideas, discussing areas
    in which he agrees and disagrees.

29 VANN, GERALD. Review of The Mind of the Maker. Blackfriars
    22 (October):562-63.
        Considers this Sayers book a failure for its unevenness,
    confused thinking about evil, lack of a clearly defined
    purpose, and a failure to communicate the idea of rever-
    ence which should be inherent in creativity, since human
    creativity is generated in and copies divine creativity.

30 WILLIAMS, CHARLES [S.]. "Renovations of Intelligence." Time
    and Tide 22 (16 August):689-90.
        Review of The Mind of the Maker. Discusses Sayers's
    thesis and concludes that "her realism is sound and her
    rationality accurate" after he had approached the book
    with apprehension. Considers it an aid "to a renovation
    of our true intellectual nature."

1942

1   A. L. [?]. Review of The Mind of the Maker. Studies (Dublin)
    31 (December):544.
       Remarks that Sayers sees a direct relationship between
    God as Maker of the world and man's creativity, using the
    writing of a book as her example. Thinks that while her
    knowledge of orthodox dogma is sound and her insight into a
    writer's mind acute, her coordination of the two gives rise
    to doubt. Since the concept of the Trinity remains a mys-
    tery outside of revelation, her treatment remains a meta-
    phor. Still, sees the book as refreshing, its literary
    criticism enlightening, and many of her ideas in advance of
    their time.

2   ANON. "B.B.C. Life of Christ." Times (London), 9 January,
    p. 2.
       Announces that the Central Religious Advisory Committee
    of the BBC had fully considered the objections to the air-
    ing of Sayers's The Man Born To Be King and decided to con-
    tinue the broadcasts.

3   ANON. "The Bread of Heaven." Weekly Review, 23 April.
       Review of The Man Born To Be King. Episode five. Com-
    plains that the Lord Chamberlain's relaxation of rules con-
    cerning the portrayal of divine persons on the stage was a
    great mistake. Criticizes the lack of a major climax in this
    episode of Sayers's play series and finds fault with the
    amount of noisy shouting. Also objects to the use of un-
    dignified colloquial language.

4   ANON. "Creation." Tablet 179 (10 January):20.
       Review of The Mind of the Maker. Commends Sayers's
    writing on literary creation and the fact that her ideas
    throw new light on theological truths. Nevertheless dis-
    agrees with some important aspects of her theology. Com-
    ments that the book can teach us much and should be studied
    with care and caution.

5   ANON. "Dorothy Sayers on Creation." Springfield (Mass.)
    Republican, 15 February, p. 7E.
       Review of The Mind of the Maker. Considers this book a
    logical sequel to Sayers's Begin Here. Calls it "fascinat-
    ing reading for anyone, but especially for those who com-
    bine a curiosity about creativity with an interest in
    theology." Quotes from the book to give an idea of what
    she is saying, and comments that "she writes with wit and
    distinction."

1942

6 ANON. "English Detection." <u>Times Literary Supplement</u>,
    31 January, p. 49.
        Reports on Sayers's address, given at the Czechoslovak
    Institute, but gives no criticism.

7 ANON. Review of <u>The Mind of the Maker</u>. <u>Booklist</u> 38
    (1 March):225.
        Quotes from <u>Religious Book Club Bulletin</u>, which calls
    Sayers's analogy between God and the creative artist
    "fascinating."

8 ANON. "Sayers, Dorothy Leigh." In <u>Twentieth Century Authors</u>.
    Edited by Stanley J. Kunitz and Howard Haycraft. New York:
    H. W. Wilson, pp. 1237-39.
        Gives some biographical data on Sayers. Comments on
    some of her books and various of her characters. Quotes
    some contemporary critics. Concludes with the remark that
    "she remains one of the four or five most literate and
    accomplished writers of detective fiction." Includes
    bibliography of principal works.

9 BARZUN, JACQUES. "Aesthetic Theology." <u>Nation</u> 154
    (21 February):238.
        Review of <u>The Mind of the Maker</u>. Discusses this book in
    the light of Sayers's overall thought and writing, calling
    her "a woman of immense culture and fine intelligence."
    Finds the book less successful than some of her others and
    gives reasons for thinking so.

10 BEVAN, EDWYN. Review of <u>The Mind of the Maker</u>. <u>Hibbert
    Journal</u> 40 (January):202-3.
        Compares Sayers's notion of God with that of other
    scholars, finding her view incomplete, really an implica-
    tion rather than a proposition to which she is committed.
    Discusses her main theme as worked out in her analogies.
    Questions some of her statements.

11 CONNOLLY, FRANCIS X. Review of <u>The Mind of the Maker</u>.
    <u>America</u> 67 (9 May):133-34.
        Comments briefly that Sayers "roughly" achieves her goal
    in an "erudite, argumentative, and indirect fashion." Con-
    siders her exegesis of the Trinity theologically inaccurate
    but her discussion of the dilemmas of fiction-writing
    stimulating.

12   COURNOS, JOHN. "The Creative Artist." New York Times Book
        Review, 27 September, p. 29.
              Review of The Mind of the Maker. Dwells at length on
        the metaphysical aspects of this Sayers book, then says
        they are the "least attractive part." In one sentence
        Cournos expresses admiration for her literary criticism,
        of which there are "pages and pages."

13   EGAN, JAMES M. Review of The Mind of the Maker. Thomist 4
        (July):538-39.
              Quotes Sayers's intent to "trace the image of the
        Trinity in the mind of the creative artist." Suggests that
        in concentrating on one set of analogies, she loses sight
        of the scriptural basis of the traditional analogies.
        Nevertheless finds the book a "treasury of wise observa-
        tions on the mind of the creative artist."

14   HOLMES, JOHN HAYNES. "New Light." New York Herald Tribune
        Books, 1 March, p. 23.
              Review of The Mind of the Maker. Calls this a fascinat-
        ing work in which Sayers attempts to justify the theologi-
        cal dogma of creation and provides a "brilliant exposition
        of her thesis." Comments on the development of her ideas.

15   KUNITZ, STANLEY J., and HAYCRAFT, HOWARD, eds. Twentieth
        Century Authors. New York: H. W. Wilson, pp. 1237-38.
              Combines biographical data with a running commentary on
        Sayers's works. Includes bibliography of her principal
        works to date. Supplement published in 1955 (1955.15).

16   LANDON, KENNETH P. Review of The Mind of the Maker. Journal
        of Philosophy 39 (May):307-308.
              Considers this an important book for all thinking per-
        sons. Discusses briefly some of Sayers's main ideas.

17   LEWIS, C[LIVE] S[TAPLES]. Review of The Mind of the Maker.
        Theology Magazine [1942?]:248-49.
              Differs with Sayers on one point he considers important.
        To Lewis there is a "far greater difference between the
        'mind of the maker and the Mind of his Maker'" than Sayers
        allows. Otherwise he finds her development of the analogy
        illuminating from both literary and theological points of
        view.

18   MILLER, RANDOLPH CRUMP. Review of The Mind of the Maker.
        Churchman 156 (1 March):17.
              Recommends this book as a help toward an understanding
        of theology and the Trinity in particular. Calls Sayers a
        conservative theologian.

1942

19 PATRICK, JOSEPH. "Man and God as Creators Compared." Chicago
    Sun, 14 February.
        Review of Mind of the Maker. Calls this a book for
    readers who are willing to "roll up your sleeves" and get
    to work, though not as heavy as the title sounds. Dis-
    cusses Sayers's procedure in writing this book and her use
    of analogy.

20 PEPLER, CONRAD. Review of Why Work? Blackfriars 23 (Decem-
    ber):489.
        Recommends this Sayers pamphlet, whose "main theme is
    sound and forcibly set out."

21 QUEEN, ELLERY. The Detective Short Story: A Bibliography.
    New York: Biblo & Tannen, 146 pp., passim.
        See 1969.11.

22 RIGGS, T. LAWRASON. Review of The Mind of the Maker.
    Commonweal 35 (27 March):572.
        Takes exception to Sayers's theology, and gives the
    reason for doing so. Remarks that her discussion of
    creative writing is "keen and suggestive" and could lead
    to "spiritually valuable conclusions."

23 WOOLBERT, R. G. Review of Begin Here. Foreign Affairs 20
    (January):378.
        One-line description with no critical comment.

                              1943

1   A. L. [?] "Why Work?" Irish Monthly 71 (February):92.
        Agrees with Sayers on principle that "A man should
    work . . . to satisfy a need of nature and, therefore, to
    find delight in his work and ultimately to carry out God's
    purpose." Remarks on the fact that she gives no satis-
    factory answers to the problems of making this economically
    feasible. Takes issue with her idea that the Church has
    failed to understand the sacredness of work. Rather, he
    blames the people for not listening to what the Church is
    saying.

2   ANON. "The Bible and Today." Listener 29 (20 May):592.
        Review of The Man Born To Be King. Says Sayers is in
    the company of earlier Morality playwrights and artists in
    depicting the life of Christ on earth in these plays.
    Finds her writing of them true to Biblical scholarship of
    the last fifty years. Avers that her use of modern

language in place of King James English makes Christ un-
comfortably real, but brings a new understanding of the
Gospel.

3   ANON. "The Life of Christ in Drama: Miss Sayers's Radio
    Play." Times Literary Supplement, 19 June, p. 289.
        Considers the presentation of Sayers's The Man Born To
    Be King as a story of real people in a real world a great
    service to the English world. States that the drama de-
    mands a verdict, and herein this series of plays, uneven as
    they are, is a noteworthy achievement. Discusses some of
    her methods toward the achievement of the above end.

4   ANON. "Religious Drama." Times Literary Supplement,
    19 June, p. 295.
        Praises Sayers and the BBC for the courage to face the
    barrage of criticism encountered in bringing The Man Born
    To Be King to the radio audience. Believes that dramatic
    art is born of life itself and is therefore closely allied
    to worship. To portray life it must submit to professional
    standards, and there is no reason to believe that such
    drama need be irreverent.

5   BARTON, JOHN M. T. "Notes on Recent Work: Holy Scripture."
    Clergy Review, n.s. 23 (September):417-19.
        Reviews The Man Born To Be King, saying it is "difficult
    to praise too highly the skill with which the author has
    managed to present many of the great scenes in our Lord's
    life in a vivid, natural, attractive and entirely truthful
    manner." At the same time he notes that many of the char-
    acters and scenes are too obviously fictitious. He is not
    wholly satisfied with Sayers's theology concerning Christ's
    humanity and deity. Stresses the need to read her intro-
    duction in order to do justice to the book.

6   CONLAN, THOMAS M. Review of The Mind of the Maker. Dublin
    Review 212 (January):87-90.
        Comments on Sayers's thesis and her development of it,
    particularly praising her chapter, "Problem Picture." Dis-
    cusses what he considers three "blemishes" in her reason-
    ing, but commends her attempt to relate art and dogma.

7   DENT, ALAN. "Broadcast Drama: Unsecular Matters." Listener
    29 (1 April):400.
        A review of the fifth in the series The Man Born To Be
    King called "The Bread of Heaven" which he heard on radio,
    and of the series as published in Sayers's book. Praises
    both the author and producer as giving the "most remarkable

1943

and striking" contribution to broadcast drama thus far
within his experience. Describes it as sensible and reverent and with an immense spiritual value for the "rational
and unprejudiced." Considers the plays works of art.

8   ELLIOTT, W. H. "The Man Born To Be King." Sunday Graphic
     (London), 30 May, p. 7.
         Calls for an honest reading of Sayers's dramatic retell-
     ing of the Gospel. Deplores the fact that people turn away
     from Christianity without ever discovering the reality of
     it. Feels that this is partly due to their being influenced
     by the unloving behavior of people who call themselves
     Christian but do not understand the way of life that true
     Christianity demands. This might be changed by the kind of
     view of Christ given in this work.

9   ELLIS-FERMOR, UNA. Review of The Man Born To Be King.
     English (London) 4 (Autumn):195-96.
         Commends Sayers on having recognized and worked to over-
     come three main artistic difficulties in producing these
     plays for radio: reconciling theme and form, building an
     integrated series of plays, and working in a new medium.
     Recommends Sayers's introduction to the book to would-be
     producers of radio drama.

10   FOSTER, PAUL URBAN. "The Man Born To Be King." Blackfriars
     24 (November):425-28.
         First comments on Sayers's detective fiction, giving
     succinct statements about the moral standard upheld in each
     of several novels. Follows with a brief discussion of her
     non-fiction writing before discussing The Man Born To Be
     King. Comments on her intellectual approach to the devel-
     opment of the characters, especially that of Christ. Dis-
     cusses her achievement in harmonizing the human and divine
     natures of Christ, and the spiritual depths that show
     through the surface of the play.

11   J. M. Review of The Man Born To Be King. Month 179 (May/
     June):233-34.
         Notes briefly some of the facts about this play series:
     its origin, Sayers's goal, its acceptance by the listening
     audience, and some areas of disagreement.

12   SCOTT-JAMES, R. A. "According to Miss Sayers." Spectator 171
     (9 July):42.
         Review of The Man Born To Be King. Feels that Sayers
     would have produced a better work if she had used the sim-
     ple language of the Authorized Version of the Bible in

presenting Christ in the Gospel story. Nevertheless, comments that when she invented an imaginary situation in which Christ did not appear, she "produced quite good stories." Regrets that Sayers, with her talents, should have failed to achieve full success in this venture.

13   STONIER, G. W. "Miss Sayers's Christian Drama." New Statesman and Nation 26 (10 July):28.
    A two-column commentary on The Man Born To Be King discussing the background situation in England which brought the plays to life and the BBC's role. Considers Sayers's craftsmanship outstanding and the work as a whole "thorough, intelligent, skillful, and courageous." Takes issue with some of her inventions, particularly her depiction of Judas.

14   WELCH, J. W. Foreword to The Man Born To Be King. London: Victor Gollancz, pp. 9-16.
    Tells the history of the writing of these Sayers plays, including the storm of protest aroused before they were even produced.

1944

1   ANON. "A Classic of Detection." Times Literary Supplement, 4 November, p. 535.
    An overview of what Sayers says about detective fiction in her introduction to Collins's The Moonstone. Classes Gaudy Night with The Moonstone as having the characteristics of detective fiction that has more to offer than just the formula detective story. Other than that there is no critical comment on her work.

2   ANON. "A Touch of Instruction." Times Literary Supplement, 25 November, p. 574.
    Discusses among other children's books Sayers's Even the Parrot. Calls it a parody--not to be taken seriously but as fun reading, even as it must have been fun to write.

3   CHANDLER, RAYMOND. "The Simple Art of Murder." Atlantic Monthly 174 (December):53-59.
    Discusses detective fiction as a class. Takes issue with Sayers's remark in her introduction to The Omnibus of the Crime that the detective story is "literature of escape" and not "literature of expression." Suggests that she was tiring of the "arid formula" of her detective fiction because she failed to give her characters the freedom to make

1944

a mystery but used them in unreal ways. Considers her
minor characters true to life. Reprinted: 1947.10 and
1959.3.

4   KRUTCH, JOSEPH WOOD. "Only a Detective Story." <u>Nation</u> 159
     (25 November):647-48, 652.
          Discusses the reading of detective fiction. Includes,
     in one paragraph, the comment that Sayers writes well,
     develops believable characters, and provides the proper
     atmosphere in her best works.

*5   SANDFORD, ERNEST. "Sayers and Sleuths." <u>Central Lit[erary]</u>
     <u>Magazine</u> (November):132-35.
          Cited in <u>Subject Index to Periodical Literature</u>. London:
     Library Association, 1944, p. 320.

6   SANDOE, JAMES. "Contributions Toward a Bibliography of
     Dorothy L. Sayers." <u>Bulletin of Bibliography</u> 18 (May/
     August):76-81.
          Perhaps the first attempt to bring Sayers's works to-
     gether in a bibliography, and therefore limited both by
     time and inaccessibility of her works, which Sandoe admits.
     It includes detective fiction, plays, poetry, one transla-
     tion, articles and letters, and her works translated into
     other languages.

                              <u>1945</u>

1   BURACK, ABRAHAM SAUL, ed. <u>Writing Detective and Mystery Fic-</u>
        <u>tion</u>. Boston: Writer, 427 pp., passim.
          A compilation of writings on the craft of detective fic-
     tion. Includes Sayers's introduction to <u>The Omnibus of</u>
     <u>Crime</u> with the title: "Detective Fiction: Origins and
     Development." Her work is mentioned in chapters by the
     following authors: Todd Downing, Howard Haycraft, Elliot
     Paul, and Lee Wright.

2   WILSON, EDMUND. "Who Cares Who Killed Roger Ackroyd?: A
        Second Report on Detective Fiction." <u>New Yorker</u> 20
     (20 January):59-66.
          Following a series of letters in response to his article
     "Why Do People Read Detective Stories?" in the 14 October
     1944 issue, tells of his attempt to give detective fiction
     another trial. Since Sayers's <u>The Nine Tailors</u> was urged
     upon him, he skimmed it, picking up the thread of the
     story. Criticizes her writing adversely on the strength of
     this incomplete reading. Reprinted: 1950.7 and 1956.10.

1946

3   ZWEMER, SAMUEL. "The Doctrine of the Trinity." <u>Moslem World</u>
     35 (January):1-5.
        Strongly recommends <u>The Mind of the Maker</u> as dealing
     with the Christian mystery of the Trinity, and Sayers's
     approach to the subject "not as dogma but as life, not as
     doctrinal formula but as experience." Should be essential
     reading for every missionary to the Moslems. Considers
     Sayers a skillful reinterpreter of the ancient creeds, with
     a "fine grasp of theological distinctions in their rele-
     vance to everyday life and thought."

1946

1   ANON. Comments on <u>The Just Vengeance</u>. <u>Illustrated London
     News</u> 208 (22 June):671.
        Comments accompanying an illustration of the finale of
     the play, after which Sayers was presented to the Queen.

2   ANON. "From Theology to Sherlock Holmes." <u>Times Literary
     Supplement</u>, 9 November, p. 550.
        Review of <u>Unpopular Opinions</u>. Outlines the essays in
     this book, commenting that the ideas are no longer un-
     popular but in many instances have become platitudes.
     Attributes this to the success of the increased number of
     Christian traditionalist writers of whom she is one. For
     the most part considers Sayers's subjects worthwhile and
     the essays well-written, deserving of a better than average
     reception.

3   ANON. "Theological Drama." <u>Church Times</u> 129 (21 June):365.
        Review of <u>The Just Vengeance</u>. Praises both the drama
     and the poetic form in which it is written, commenting on
     Sayers's "gift of transcribing the dramatic realities of
     faith into the idiom of commonplace existence."

4   FAIRCLOUGH, ALAN. "Dorothy Sayers and Religious Drama in
     England: <u>The Just Vengeance</u>." <u>Christian Drama</u> 1 (Novem-
     ber):3-9.
        Recognizes Sayers's ability as a Christian playwright,
     commending her on several aspects of this play. In accord
     with his stated belief that Christ cannot be portrayed on
     the stage, he discusses the points at which he feels that
     Sayers failed to produce a Christ who is both God and man.
     Compares her attempt to do so with the work of other play-
     wrights who have presented a more believable Christ by
     keeping him off-stage. Also considers the scene of the
     trial of Jesus a weakening factor in the play.

5   FOSTER, PAUL. "Dorothy Sayers." In <u>Writers of Today</u>.
    2 vols. Edited by Denys Val Baker. London: Sidgwick &
    Jackson, 1:111-20.
        Discusses the underlying integrity of Sayers's works,
    ending his criticism of the detective novels with the re-
    mark that they are "tracts in disguise." Goes on to con-
    sider her further works in the light of her need to
    elucidate what she believed to be the truth.

6   McLUHAN, HERBERT M. "Footprints in the Sands of Crime."
    <u>Sewanee Review</u> 54 (1946):617-34.
        Says that detective fiction as an escape valve "is a
    barometer for a deeply resentful and humanly wasteful
    society." Suggests that the Donne quotations Sayers used
    to express Lord Peter's thoughts and feelings betray the
    "emotional illiteracy and confusion" characteristic of a
    technological society. Calls Lord Peter a "degenerate heir
    of Renaissance megalomania."

7   PHILMORE, R. "Inquest on Detective Stories." In <u>The Art of
    the Mystery Story</u>. Edited by Howard Haycraft. New York:
    Simon & Schuster, pp. 423-35.
        A reprint of a two-part article issued in April and
    September of 1938 in <u>Discovery</u>. Part I was co-authored by
    Dr. John Yudkin who gives his opinion of the medical proba-
    bility of five fictional deaths. Of the five submitted to
    him two were Sayers novels: <u>Unnatural Death</u> and <u>Strong
    Poison</u>. Part II examines the motives for murder used by
    fiction writers. Includes two Sayers novels: <u>Have His
    Carcase</u> and <u>Busman's Honeymoon</u>. Reprinted: 1947.10.

8   POLING, JAMES W. "Post Mortems." <u>New York Post</u>, 21 February.
        Review of <u>Gaudy Night</u>. Commends Sayers both for having
    written a mystery without a corpse, and for having produced
    a "full-bodied novel." Finds that the loving picture of
    Oxford and Oxford life contributes much to the book's
    charm.

9   SMALLEY, T. "A Modern Miracle Play." <u>Month</u> 182 (September):
    387-88.
        Review of <u>The Just Vengeance</u>. Primarily a recapitula-
    tion of the play. Commends Sayers for performing a diffi-
    cult task in presenting the old truths in acceptable,
    up-to-date form, commenting on some of the problems.

1   ANON. "Doctrine and Persuasion." <u>Times Literary Supplement</u>,
    31 May, p. 270.
        Review of <u>Creed or Chaos?</u> Finds it easy to understand
    the public demand for the reproduction of these essays by
    Sayers. Commends her willingness to have them issued with-
    out further editorial comment. Disagrees with her on some
    points but finds them basically "pungent and well-reasoned."

2   ANON. Review of <u>The Just Vengeance</u>. <u>Blackfriars</u> 28
    (February):88.
        Likens this to a jigsaw puzzle with a background from
    many writers into which Sayers is fitting her pieces,
    adroitly but with a hint that the intellect sometimes takes
    precedence over the worship of God.

3   ANON. Review of <u>Unpopular Opinions</u>. <u>Booklist</u> 44 (1 November):
    87.
        Includes one line of critical comment, calling these
    essays "distinctively individual commentaries."

4   <u>Chimera</u> 5, no. 4 (Summer):2-79.
        This issue of several articles on detective fiction in-
    cludes frequent brief references to Sayers and/or Wimsey,
    some favorable, some unfavorable. In "A Trinity of 'Tecs'
    from There to Where?" by Ruthven Todd, Sayers is accused of
    sentimental snobbishness and poor writing.

5   CLARK, BARRETT H., ed. <u>A History of Modern Drama</u>. New York:
    Appleton-Century, p. 216.
        A single paragraph for Sayers, to the effect that she
    displayed a surprising dramatic flair for a writer who had
    achieved fame with her detective fiction. Considers
    <u>Busman's Honeymoon</u> a "pleasant melodrama," <u>The Zeal of Thy
    House</u> and <u>The Devil to Pay</u> dramas of "high quality,"
    "sensitiveness of expression, and dramatic sweep."

6   DEVOE, ALAN. "The Garden Gate." <u>Catholic World</u> 165 (May):
    159-62.
        Discusses some of the ways in which men and women are
    drawn to the Christian philosophy when some aspect of
    Biblical truth seems to fit into the field of his/her en-
    deavor. Includes a paragraph on Sayers's finding a rela-
    tionship between God and man as creator, as put forth in
    her book <u>The Mind of the Maker</u>.

1947

7   FERGUSON, DeLANCEY. "From Grave to Gay." New York Herald
    Tribune, 5 October, p. 10.
        Review of Unpopular Opinions. Following the comment
    that at her best "Sayers writes on controversial subjects
    with a trenchancy that recalls early Chesterton and at her
    worst, she scolds," discusses the three groups of essays in
    the light of the remarks she made in the foreword concern-
    ing their unpopularity.

8   GARRISON, W. E. Review of Unpopular Opinions. Christian
    Century 64 (31 December):1616.
        Says briefly that Sayers's mind is one of England's
    "most alert and interesting." Comments that her style
    makes her work interesting even where her ideas are not
    always right.

9   GRAY, JAMES. "Witty Dorothy Sayers, Known for Her Mystery
    Stories, Offers 'Unpopular Opinions' on Variety of Sub-
    jects." Chicago Daily News, 30 September.
        Compares Sayers's title to an answer sometimes given by
    a woman complimented on her dress, "What! This old thing!"
    Says "she knows perfectly well that her intellectual garb
    is original and smart and that it is cut to the best pat-
    tern of the thought of our time." Goes on to discuss the
    book, analyzing the thinking behind Sayers's essays. Also
    in Newark Star Ledger, 30 September.

10 HAYCRAFT, HOWARD, ed. The Art of the Mystery Story: A Col-
    lection of Critical Essays. New York: Simon & Schuster,
    574 pp., passim.
        Essays by various authors about mystery, crime, and
    detective fiction, in which Sayers is frequently mentioned.
    Includes her introduction to The Omnibus of Crime and her
    essay "Gaudy Night." Includes bibliographies. Reprint of
    1946 edition, with index added. Includes Chandler,
    Raymond, (1944.3), and Philmore, R. (1946.7).

11 I. E. Review of Unpopular Opinions. Blackfriars 28
    (August):382-83.
        Finds Sayers's theological opinions of greatest impor-
    tance. Sees in her an ally to the Catholic Church, uncom-
    fortable with "the confused and contradictory answers of
    various Christian bodies."

12 KNIGHT, MARCUS. "An Anglican Prophetess." Spectator 178
    (11 April):410.
        Review of Creed or Chaos? Discusses briefly the salient
    features of this book, questioning the clarity of some of

Sayers's statements and commending her for her "robust and cheerful common sense."

13 L. F. C. "Briskness and Bite in Dorothy Sayers' Opinionated Essays." Milwaukee Journal, 12 October.
    Review of Unpopular Opinions. Comments that this work reflects both Sayers's detective interests and her "distinguished academic background" in its wide range of subjects. Would call her opinions controversial rather than unpopular.

14 SUGRUE, THOMAS. "A Lady-Novelist Speaks Her Mind." New York Times Book Review, 30 November, p. 20.
    Review of Unpopular Opinions. For the most part Sugrue finds this collection "repetitious, undistinguished" and poorly arranged. He disagrees rather forcefully with some of her basic ideas. Concerning Sayers's remark that the English editors suppressed these essays, he says "The answer may be that the English editors decided that the female mind in theology is like the male knee in society, something which should not be exposed."

15 T. K. C. Review of Unpopular Opinions. Dominicana 32 (December):291-92.
    While not agreeing fully with Sayers, commends her for taking time to prepare these essays for the public. Calls them "tasty" and "interesting."

16 WAGENECHT, EDWARD. "Miss Sayers' Essays Show Brilliance." Chicago Tribune, 5 October.
    Review of Unpopular Opinions. Views this book as its own evidence of Sayers's qualifications for its writing. Credits her with the ability to be entertaining even when serious, giving her works their whimsy. Compares her works to that of Virginia Woolf, though he had never paid anyone that compliment before, and to C. S. Lewis, with the comment that she is worthy to stand beside him as a "modern apologist."

1948

1 ANON. Survey Taken by The Pleasures of Publishing of the Columbia University Press. Chicago Tribune, 18 April.
    Article on a survey which places Sayers still at the top of "whodunit" authors, although she had not published a new story in eleven years. Mentions that she had also placed first in 1941.

1948

2   ANON. "Collected Sayers." <u>Tablet</u> 191 (5 May):308.
        Review of <u>Four Sacred Plays</u>. Briefly gives the scope
and a comment that these plays "reveal Miss Sayers' genius
for making religious truth tolerable for a generation that
will accept its by-products but dislikes the substance it
presupposes."

3   ANON. "Reading Plays." <u>Church Times</u> 131 (14 May).
        Includes Sayers's <u>Four Sacred Plays</u> in this review, com-
menting only on <u>The Just Vengeance</u>. Remarks that her verse
is "smooth, yet profound."

4   ANON. "Telling Stories." <u>Times Literary Supplement</u>,
    19 June, p. 345.
        Criticism of <u>Essays Presented to Charles Williams</u> in-
cluding Sayers's chapter, "And Telling You a Story." Calls
her "expert in the business of setting nerves tingling."
Strongly disagrees with her idea that Dante's <u>Divine Comedy</u>
holds "all the master cards in story-telling," though
otherwise agrees with her about the excitement of reading
Dante.

5   D. D. Review of <u>Four Sacred Plays</u>. <u>United Church Observer</u>
    (Toronto), 15 June.
        Considers these plays interesting, beautiful, and highly
inspirational.

6   IRVING, LAURENCE. Preface to <u>The Zeal of Thy House</u>. In <u>Four</u>
    <u>Sacred Plays</u>. London: Victor Gollancz, pp. 9-12.
        Reprint of 1937.28.

7   SANDOE, JAMES. "Crime Can Be Popular." <u>Chicago Sun</u>,
    30 April.
        Comments on the survey in <u>Pleasures of Publishing</u> of the
Columbia University Press (1948.1). Remarks that Sayers's
staying power is astonishing.

8   WARE, HARLAN. Review of <u>The Man Born To Be King</u>. <u>Pasadena</u>
    <u>Star News</u>, 11 December.
        Characterizes these Sayers plays as "a superb contribu-
tion to the literature of Christ," and calls her "the
greatest religious dramatist of our day." Quotes from her
introduction to show how she attempted to accomplish her
goal.

1949

1   ANON. "Everyday Dogma." Time 53 (30 May):56-57.
       Review of Creed or Chaos? Composed mainly of quotations
    from the book but includes the comment that this work is
    "turned out with all the phrase-making flair of a veteran
    bestseller writer." Calls Sayers a "pert, pince-nezed
    . . . crack writer of whodunits."

2   ANON. Review of Creed or Chaos? Booklist 45 (15 March):233.
       Includes one line of critical comment, calling it "con-
    sidered, provocative."

3   ANON. Review of Creed or Chaos? New Yorker 25 (4 June):95.
       A brief resumé with the comment that while "much of what
    Sayers says is thought-provoking, her treatment of socio-
    logical problems is reactionary."

4   ANON. Review of Sayers's translation of the Divine Comedy.
    I: Hell. New Statesman and Nation 38 (10 December):709.
       Criticizes Sayers's translation as obscure and unequal,
    only occasionally attaining the "grandeur of the original."
    Gives three examples to illustrate.

5   ANON. Review of The Man Born To Be King. Booklist 46
    (15 December):139.
       Brief discussion of Sayers's attitude and her recogni-
    tion of likenesses between Roman-Jewish and Anglo-Indian
    relations. Considers it an effective retelling of the
    Gospel story.

6   BIXLER, J. S. Review of Creed or Chaos? Crozer Quarterly 26
    (October):374.
       Suggests that, while this book is very interesting,
    Sayers is more convincing on the subject of work than on
    that of theology. Comments briefly on some of the essays.

7   CASWELL, WILBUR L. Review of The Man Born To Be King.
    Churchman 163 (15 December):16.
       No critical discussion.

8   COMFORT, NICK. "The Greatest of All Dramas." Oklahoma City
    Oklahoman, 25 December.
       Review of The Man Born To Be King. Comments that the
    reading of these plays "leaves one with a deeper longing to
    be true, pure, and good." Nevertheless feels that if
    Sayers had heeded her own advice, they might have been
    better art and less obviously didactic.

1949

9 DOWD, S. J. Review of Creed or Chaos? America 80 (2 April):
      722.
          Sees the book as characterized by the title essay.
      Agrees that the Church has watered down the beliefs Sayers
      discusses in these essays and that the fundamental dogmas
      of the Incarnation and Redemption are vital to the preven-
      tion of disaster in the world. Briefly describes the sec-
      tions into which the book is divided.

10 FREEDLEY, GEORGE. Review of The Man Born To Be King. Library
      Journal 74 (15 October):1605.
          In two sentences remarks on its "monumental" scope, its
      "moving" effect, and its great success in England.

11 GARRISON, W. E. "Art With and Without Dogma." Christian
      Century 66 (30 November):1424.
          Review of The Man Born To Be King. Compares this work
      with Houston Harte's In Our Image, commending both authors
      for their attempts to interpret religious thought into art
      to be enjoyed by readers and non-readers of religious
      works. Remarks on Sayers's craftsmanship and her concep-
      tion of the theology underlying the Gospel narrative.

12   ____. "Beautiful Dynamite." Christian Century 66 (13 April):
      466.
          Review of Creed or Chaos? A philosophical review con-
      tending that Sayers and her colleagues dogmatically uphold
      opinions that lead to chaos rather than to an orderly,
      peaceful society. Comments that she "puts a very attrac-
      tive wrapper around a highly explosive package."

13 HOLMES, JOHN HAYNES. "New Book About Jesus." New York Herald
      Tribune Books, 13 November, p. 38.
          Review of The Man Born To Be King. Commends Sayers's
      achievement of "fine artistry and reverent spirit," her
      purpose, and the handling of the dialogue. Nevertheless
      finds her somewhat pompous and regards the plays and the
      introduction dull when read.

14 HUGHES, RILEY. "'A Religion for Adult Minds'." Saturday
      Review of Literature 32 (16 July):15.
          Review of Creed or Chaos? A complimentary review, giv-
      ing the basic tenets Sayers discusses. Compares some of
      her thinking on various subjects to that of other writers.
      Comments on the unity of these papers, their "subtlety and
      vigor."

1949

15   JOHNSTON, MARGUERITE. "Infinitely Worth Reading." Houston
       Post, 30 October.
           Review of The Man Born To Be King. Considers Sayers
       "one of the truly remarkable living women." Finds her
       scholarship wide-ranging and "precise," showing an ability
       to combine it with the unique talent for translation of the
       "old and ecclesiastical into something eternally new and
       vivid."

16   KUMNICK, H. H. "Re-emphasis on Doctrine." Cresset
       (September):51.
           Review of Creed or Chaos? Praises this Sayers work,
       claiming that "she is a woman of profound Christian convic-
       tion and sound scholarship."

17   McINNIS, J. R. "The Man Born To Be King." America 82
       (5 November):134-35.
           Finds Sayers's distinctive style and sound dramatic
       instinct "ennobled" in this work. Admires her ability to
       limit her imagination for the sake of reverence. Considers
       her introduction proof that she was aware of the signifi-
       cance of dramatizing a divine personality in human terms.
       Mentions a few negative features but comments that there is
       "no positive error."

18   MILLER, PERRY. "The Dream of Humanity." New York Times Book
       Review, 29 May, p. 13.
           Review of Creed or Chaos? Appreciates Sayers's honesty
       and sincerity while questioning the validity of her "im-
       passioned pleading." Wonders if she is guilty of over-
       simplification. Quotes from her work in his discussion of
       her main ideas.

19   REYBURN, WEBB. "Author Defends Dogma in Religious Volume."
       Dallas News, 23 April.
           Review of Creed or Chaos? Comments that the "intellec-
       tual spanking" Sayers administers is well deserved by a
       "wayward society." Feels that her book shows the integrity
       of which she writes.

20   SUGRUE, THOMAS. "Plays About Jesus." New York Times Book
       Review, 23 October, p. 49.
           Review of The Man Born To Be King. Remarks that Sayers
       is inconsistent in her alternation of rigid theology with
       peasant ignorance in the radio drama. Considers many of
       her characters "puppets of medieval scholasticism." Com-
       mends her depiction of Judas. Credits her skill in writing
       and her considerable scholarship, but believes the play un-
       successful in what she attempted to do.

1949

21   SUPPLE, JAMES O. "Special Reading for Lenten Season."
     Chicago Sun Times, 2 March.
          Includes brief review of Creed or Chaos? Compares
     Sayers to C. S. Lewis in bringing "clarity, logic and wit
     to the field of religious writing."

22   TAINTON, EDGAR M. "The Bible in Modern English." San
     Francisco Chronicle, 11 December.
          Review of The Man Born To Be King. A critical discus-
     sion of Sayers's aims and how they are reflected in her
     achievement. Comments on the impossibility of entering an
     alien culture and seeing it clearly. Nevertheless recog-
     nizes that some attempt of this sort must be made in order
     to bring the Bible to life.

23   WAGENECHT, EDWARD. "Play Cycle Masterpiece About Jesus."
     Chicago Tribune, 30 October.
          Review of The Man Born To Be King. Highly recommends
     the purchase of this "masterpiece" from the pen of Sayers,
     a "detective novelist." As drama, considers these plays
     "overwhelming," a wedding of form and substance.

24   WEBSTER, DEBORAH. "Reinterpreter: Dorothy L. Sayers."
     Catholic World 169 (August):330-35.
          With a series of succinct comments Webster discusses
     Sayers as author, her writing, and her Anglo-Catholic
     stance.

1950

1   ANON. "Dante as Story-Teller: The Comedy of Dante Alighieri
     the Florentine. Cantica I: Hell (Inferno)." Translated
     by Dorothy L. Sayers. Times Literary Supplement, 14 April,
     p. 224.
          "Fresh, exploring minds" will be won for The Divine
     Comedy through this Sayers translation. Those who hold it
     in reverence may not like her renderings, but even they may
     find new excitement in the story as she translates it.
     Says her sympathy with "medieval ways of thought and feel-
     ing invests her conversational diction with a good deal of
     charm.

2   FREEMAN, ELMER S. "The Man Born To Be King." Advance (May).
          Comments briefly and primarily on Sayers's portrayal of
     the various characters, but also on the language. Con-
     siders this "religious drama at its best."

3 PUBLIC ORATOR. Durham University, 24 May 1950. Speech in
   honor of Dorothy L. Sayers. Typescript, 2 pp.
       Presents Sayers's claims to the degree of Honorary
   D.Litt. being presented to her, in descriptive language
   using the titles of her books. Adds that her novels have
   "given more pleasure to educated readers than any since
   Conan Doyle's immortal series." Comments on the manner in
   which her novels convey her attitude to society. Remarks
   that her later works are based on a "lively and uncompro-
   mising Christianity."

4 RUSSELL, PETER. "The Penguin Dante." Nine 3, no. 1
   (December):73-74.
       Complains that Sayers brought neither the "genius of a
   minor poet" nor the "care of a serious scholar" to her
   translation of The Divine Comedy. Credits her with hard
   work and a love for the text and for an excellent commentary.

5 SINGLETON, CHARLES S. Review of Sayers's translation of The
   Divine Comedy. I: Hell. Speculum 25 (July):394-95.
       Remarks that since Sayers will have a wide audience
   because of her reputation it is tragic that her translation
   is so poor. Accuses her of padding to translate in terza
   rima, giving one example. Regrets Charles Williams's influence on her thinking. Commends some of her views on
   allegory and symbol, but is not specific.

6 SWAIM, J. CARTER. Review of The Man Born To Be King.
   International Journal of Religious Education (April).
       Quotes from the play series to give a picture of this
   work of Sayers. Recommends the series highly as "perhaps
   one of the finest things done for Christendom this century."

7 WILSON, EDMUND. "Who Cares Who Killed Roger Ackroyd?" In
   Classics and Commercials: A Literary Chronicle of the
   Forties. New York: Farrar, Straus, pp. 258-60.
       Reprint of 1945.2.

1951

1 ANON. "Emperor Constantine Comes Back to Colchester: World
   Premiere of a Mighty Chronicle by Dorothy Sayers." Church
   Times 134 (6 July):453.
       Front-page review mixes critical comments with mention
   of the historical highlights brought out by Sayers.
   Though long, considers it fast-moving, enjoyable, filled

1951

with apt humor. Commends her use of modern language and the play's teaching. Comments on the enthusiastic response of the audience.

2   ANON. "Playhouse Theatre, Colchester--The Emperor Constantine." Times (London), 4 July, p. 8.
Views this as a pageant rather than as a play, calling it long and not otherwise "a big work." Criticizes Sayers for filling out some details too much and rushing through others, making them difficult to understand. Praises the director for providing a "smoothly decorative" production and the players for an "unflaggingly good performance."

3   ANON. "Three-year-old Dreams [. . .] Have Come True [. . .]" Essex County Standard, 6 July.
Discussion of the Colchester Festival includes some lines on Sayers's drama The Emperor Constantine, saying that it is compelling in spite of being "vast and unwieldy in scale." Gives quotations about it from The Times and Daily Mail.

4   BLAIR-FISH, W. W. "Pride and Gratitude for Constantine." Essex County Standard, 6 July.
An accolade by the chairman of the Drama Panel of the Festival Committee for Sayers's play The Emperor Constantine. Congratulates the author, producer, designers, and players. Commends the excellent blending of professionals and amateurs.

5   HAYCRAFT, HOWARD. Murder for Pleasure: The Life and Times of the Detective Story. Enl. ed. New York: Mercury, 448 pp., passim.
Enlargement of 1941.22.

6   I. H. "The Emperor Constantine." Manchester Guardian, 4 July.
Decries Sayers's use of "'light relief' of the most banal and embarrassing sort" in her attempt to make entertainment of this historical play. Says her work only "achieves dramatic distinction" when she "writes simply and seriously out of her own interest."

7   LASSANCE, R. A. Review of Creed or Chaos? Thought 26 (Winter):621-22.
Commends Sayers for her clear thinking and lucid writing. Discusses several of the essays briefly. Criticizes her failure to relate her ideas to an authoritative church.

8   SOPER, DAVID WESLEY. "Dorothy Sayers and the Christian
       Synthesis." <u>Religion in Life</u> 21:117-28.
          Uses Sayers's writings to illustrate his concept of the
       Christian synthesis as a right relationship between philos-
       ophy, religion, and science.

<u>1952</u>

1   ANON. Review of <u>The Emperor Constantine</u>. <u>Booklist</u> 48
       (15 June):335.
          Considers it rewarding only to readers interested in
       early church history.

2   ANON. Review of <u>The Emperor Constantine</u>. <u>Wisconsin Library</u>
       <u>Bulletin</u> 48 (July/August):170.
          Comments that this will appeal to those interested in
       church history.

3   BURNHAM, PHILIP. "Christian Emperor." <u>Commonweal</u> 56
       (4 July):326.
          Review of <u>The Emperor Constantine</u>. Tells the scope of
       the play, quotes from Sayers's preface to describe the
       themes, discusses the requirement of some dullness in the
       beginning to achieve the fullness of the ending, and com-
       mends Sayers for achieving a vehicle that embodies tragedy,
       while teaching lessons of the Christian faith.

4   FLETCHER, JOSEPH. Review of <u>The Emperor Constantine</u>.
       <u>Churchman</u> 166 (1 November):17.
          No critical discussion.

5   GARRISON, W. E. Review of <u>The Emperor Constantine</u>. <u>Christian</u>
       <u>Century</u> 69 (18 June):724.
          Complimentary, calling it "entertainment of a high
       order." Comments that since Sayers wrote it it "would be
       superfluous to say that it is immensely clever." Considers
       it historically accurate and sincerely religious.

6   GREENWOOD, ORMEROD. "<u>The Man Born to be King</u>." <u>Radio Times</u>
       (22 February):1944.
          Wonders if Sayers's play will have an impact equal to
       that of its airing a decade earlier. Feels that, if it
       does, it will be because she had the "courage, discretion,
       and true simplicity" to write a noteworthy drama on a
       great theme. Enlarges briefly on this idea.

1952

7   H. W. F. Review of The Emperor Constantine. Church Manage-
    ment (September).
         Says that Sayers brings church politics to life. Calls
    this a fascinating way to bring history to life for the
    "average illiterate religionist."

8   RYAN, JOHN K. Review of The Emperor Constantine. American
    Ecclesiastical Review 127 (December):479-80.
         Calls it "drama upon the grand scale although not always
    in the grand style." Finds it believable, both in plot and
    characterization, and historically accurate. Considers
    Sayers's handling of theology convincing.

9   WILLIAMS, LILLIAN. "The Emperor Constantine." International
    Journal of Religious Education (September).
         Remarks that Sayers has the ability to make ancient
    characters come alive for today's audience and that Chris-
    tian truths can be interesting.

1953

1   ANON. Review of The Zeal of Thy House. Times (London),
    11 May, p. 3.
         Praises the Epsom College company who staged this Sayers
    play for concentrating on the dramatic possibilities,
    thereby covering its theatrical weakness.

2   HAMILTON, K. M. "Murder and Morality: An Interpretation of
    Detective Fiction." Dalhousie Review 33 (Summer):102-8.
         Discusses the philosophy of detective fiction, espe-
    cially from a moral point of view. Comments that Sayers
    brings too much realism into Busman's Honeymoon, removing
    it from the category of allegory to which detective fiction
    belongs.

3   MILLER, KENNETH D. "Exciting Religious Drama." Saturday
    Review of Literature 36 (21 February):55.
         Review of The Emperor Constantine. Avers that only
    Sayers could make exciting drama out of this historical
    material. Comments on her gift for writing, her spiritual
    depth, and her knowledge of church history.

4   SCOTT, SUTHERLAND. Blood In Their Ink. New York: Stanley
    Paul, pp. 56-57.
         While mentioned elsewhere in the book, two paragraphs
    are devoted exclusively to Sayers's work. Comments on her
    "unusual murder methods" and, more importantly, "her

1954

ability to insert a first-class mystery" into a non-
dramatic background. Considers her worst fault the development of too much sympathy for the criminal.

5   SOPER, DAVID WESLEY. Review of The Emperor Constantine.
       Interpretation 7 (January):120-21.
          Believes that Christians owe Sayers a debt of gratitude
for her "unique presentations of central events in Christian history and central dogmas of the church." Praises
this play for its dramatic power, characterization, and
background.

1954

1   ADAMS, J. DONALD. "Speaking of Books." New York Times Book
       Review, 3 October, p. 2.
          Discussing the future of the detective novel, he quotes
Sayers ("master of the mystery") as saying that "the old
lady is not what she used to be" but that she would persist
--perhaps in a different form. Adams agrees that "she" at
least needs a shot of literary vitamins.

2   ANON. "Aristotle's Poetics." Times Literary Supplement,
       5 February, p. 96.
          Remarks on Sayers's letters in which she comments on
L. J. Potts's translation of Aristotle's Poetics.

3   ANON. "The Living Dante. Dorothy L. Sayers." The Times
       Literary Supplement, 17 December, p. 823.
          Review of Introductory Papers on Dante. These papers,
first delivered to students of Italian, combine with her
translation to make Dante accessible to the non-academic
person. Sayers combines "an earnest attitude to religion
with a great deal of lucidity and common sense." Refresh-
ing touches not often met with in academic research, even
though her taste is not always sure.

4   NOTT, KATHLEEN. "Lord Peter Views the Soul." In The
       Emperor's Clothes. Bloomington: Indiana University Press,
       pp. 253-98.
          Compares Sayers and C. S. Lewis, calling them "funda-
mentalists," with other contemporary writers who compare
and contrast science and theology. Discusses their attempt
to "discredit scientific thinking . . . in order to make
theology paramount again." Her discussion of Sayers takes
off from The Mind of the Maker and Creed or Chaos?

1954

5   REYNOLDS, BARBARA. Preface to <u>Introductory Papers on Dante</u>.
    New York: Harper, pp. vii-ix.
        Introduces Sayers's essays, recommending them to those
    who are willing to expend some mental effort to experience
    the exhilaration provided through her efforts to bring
    Dante's <u>Divine Comedy</u> to today's reader.

1955

1   ANON. "Departure from Crime." <u>Newsweek</u> 46 (22 August):82-83.
        On the appearance of Sayers's translation of Dante's
    <u>Purgatory</u>, gives a recapitulation of her career as an
    author.

2   ANON. Review of <u>Introductory Papers on Dante</u>. <u>Booklist</u> 51
    (15 July):464-65.
        Considers this a help toward an understanding of Dante's
    <u>Divine Comedy</u>.

3   ANON. Review of <u>Introductory Papers on Dante</u>. <u>New York
    Herald Tribune Book Review</u>, 12 June, p. 9.
        No critical comment.

4   BERTRAM, ANTHONY. "Dante Diluted." <u>Tablet</u> 205 (19 February):
    182.
        Review of <u>Introductory Papers on Dante</u>. Commends
    Sayers's exposition of Dante's theology and her courage to
    maintain that his belief in the supernatural is worth hang-
    ing on to. Deplores her folksiness, giving several examples
    of what the reviewer calls "the language of a cozy chat by
    the awfully jolly governess."

5   BRIFFAULT, HERMA. "Dante." <u>New York Times Book Review</u>,
    20 November, p. 58.
        Expresses amazement in this letter to the editor that
    Fitts (1955.10) should be "harsh and unjust" in his criti-
    cism of Sayers's translation, which made <u>The Divine Comedy</u>
    enjoyable to this reader for the first time.

6   CIARDI, JOHN. "Dante for the Missionaries." <u>New Republic</u> 133
    (22 August):18-20.
        Review of <u>Introductory Papers on Dante</u>. Considering
    Sayers's scholarship--"both profoundly well-informed and
    deeply thought"--this could have been a better book. Dis-
    cusses reasons for his conclusions. Accuses her of "criti-
    cal looseness--passionate, knowledgeable, and sometimes

brilliant--but generally unrestrained." Admits to being
hard on her but still recommends the book to those who care
about Dante.

7   _____. Review of Introductory Papers on Dante. Nation 181
       (17 December):540.
            Very brief but scathing remarks about her zeal and her
       poor writing.

8   COURTINES, PIERRE. "Introductory Papers on Dante." America
    93 (3 September):539.
            Comments on the clarity of Sayers's writing, having
       geared herself to readers whose knowledge of Dante was
       limited. Still, considers it challenging and rewarding.

9   FAHY, CONOR. "Italian Studies." Dublin Review 229 (Third
    Quarter):482-84.
            Reviews Introductory Papers on Dante. Praises Sayers's
       attempt to show that the allegory "conceals a moral and
       religious conception of life as intelligible and valid for
       modern readers as for Dante's contemporaries" and her at-
       tempt to explain some of the religious ideas she considers
       fundamental to the Commedia. Criticizes her failure to
       give credit to other Dante scholars who agree that Dante
       wrote to be read by the people, and also for her misprints
       of foreign words, some of which obscure the meaning of a
       given passage.

10 FITTS, DUDLEY. "An Urge to Make Dante Known." New York Times
    Book Review, 6 November, p. 59.
            Review of Sayers's translation of The Divine Comedy of
       Dante Alighieri the Florentine. I: Hell; II: Purgatory.
       Credits Sayers with considerable success in the arduous
       task of bringing this work to the people through a new
       translation. Considers her philosophical emphasis too like
       C. S. Lewis's but appreciates the quantity of information
       she provides. Does not consider her an accomplished poet
       and discusses this through half the article.

11 FOSTER, KENELM. Review of Introductory Papers on Dante.
    Blackfriars 36 (March):87-89.
            Recommends this book of Sayers essays as an introduction
       to certain aspects of The Divine Comedy, especially its
       theological structure. Discusses her thinking about the
       work and her qualification for writing on it. Comments
       briefly on the negative aspects.

1955

12 GILMAN, RICHARD. Review of Introductory Papers on Dante.
Jubilee 3 (June):58.
Calls this a great introduction to the art of Dante.
Says Sayers does not "drown him" in speculations about his
work but brings his work up from the ocean floor to "gleam
and dazzle us with its long-buried splendor." She does not
ignore Dante's theology, nor the political and psychologi-
cal elements, but she keeps them in their places, revealing
a "vision of man in his choices, his commitments, his de-
ceptions, and his glories." Comments on her "rich and com-
plex" mind and her love for Dante.

13 HUGHES, SERGE. "Exploring the Divine Comedy." Commonweal 62
(5 August):452-53.
Review of Introductory Papers on Dante. Commends Sayers
for the quality of her essays and the theological and philosophical understanding she brings to them. Also discusses
the shortcomings.

14 KIESSLING, E. C. "Vigorous Volume of Dante." Milwaukee
Journal, 23 October.
Calls Sayers's translation of The Divine Comedy. II:
Purgatory "readable and vigorous." Gives a sample. Con-
siders her competent to translate Dante following her other
writings.

15 KUNITZ, STANLEY J., ed. Twentieth Century Authors. Supplement I. New York: H. W. Wilson, p. 874.
Continues the information and commentary on Sayers in
the basic volume (1942.15) adding to the bibliography works
published since 1940.

16 MILANO, PAOLO. "A Lasting Experience." New York Times Book
Review, 29 May, p. 7.
Review of Introductory Papers on Dante. Wonders if
Sayers's best story will turn out to be the story of her
varied life. Looks forward to the completion of her Dante
translation. Quotes from her works to show her concept of
Hell. Credits her thorough and wide knowledge of Dante
although she uses it to further her missionary efforts--
"literary, moral, and religious." Summarizes briefly the
scope of this work. Questions whether or not her view of
The Divine Comedy is an accurate one.

17 PRICE, JAMES HARRY. Review of Introductory Papers on Dante.
Catholic World 181 (September):477.
Considers these Sayers papers a "first-rate contribution
to the literature on Dante," quoting from her introduction

to show her purpose in translating The Divine Comedy.
Gives an example of her further development of a theme
found in Dante's work.

18   SEMPER, I. J. "Dante Studies." Month, n.s. 13 (March):
       185-86.
          Review of Introductory Papers on Dante. Commends Sayers
for concentrating on the literal and allegorical meaning of
The Divine Comedy, and for addressing these papers to the
general reader. Disapproves of her acceptance of Charles
Williams's "erratic theories" in her interpretation.

19   SINGLETON, CHARLES S. "Dark Wood of Allegory." Kenyon Review
       17 (Autumn):656-61.
          Review of Introductory Papers on Dante. Follows a very
brief discussion of some of the papers with a look at
Sayers's interpretation of the poems. Commends her knowledge of how to study poetry, her understanding of the
medieval mind, and her ability to look at the poem as a
whole, not just its parts. Then criticizes her for seeking
the truth in the allegory and not in the story, separating
two elements that should be inseparable.

20   SMITH, S. STEPHENSON. Review of Introductory Papers on Dante.
       Library Journal 80 (15 June):1499-1500.
          Commends Sayers on moving Dante into the twentieth cen-
tury. Gives these essays high praise and discusses his
reasons for doing so.

21   SORIA, REGINA. "The Second Part of Dante's Great Poem Trans-
       lated." Baltimore Sun, 23 November.
          Thinks that Sayers has dealt successfully, for the most
part, with the translation of this part of The Divine
Comedy. Mentions some disagreement. Commends the completeness of her explanatory material and the critical
value of her introduction.

22   SVENDESEN, KESTER. "Sayers' Best To Be Issued." Oklahoma
       City Oklahoman, 19 February.
          Review of Whose Body? and of Clouds of Witness. Wel-
comes Harper's decision to reprint the Wimsey novels as a
relief from the "featureless sequence of blunderbust who-
dunits." Comments briefly on the characteristics that make
Sayers's stories good.

1956

1   ANON. "The Criminal Record." Saturday Review of Literature
      39 (3 March):47.

1956

>   Calls Lord Peter the "world's ranking private eye" in
> this notice of the reissue of Clouds of Witness.

2   BAIRD, J. W. "Dorothy L. Sayers on Dante." Expository Times
>   67 (January):109-10.
>   Review of Introductory Papers on Dante finds evidence of
> Sayers's sense of humor in a book that is not intended for
> the scholar and yet demands close study. Emphasizes her
> awareness that Dante wrote for the common man and says that
> her gusto should persuade people to read him. Her lengthy
> discussion on the meaning of Heaven, Hell, and Purgatory is
> worth more than most treatises on eschatology.

3   BOUCHER, ANTHONY. "Criminals at Large." New York Times Book
>   Review, 30 December, p. 15.
>   Review of Unnatural Death. Considers this a histori-
> cally important book in the detective-fiction genre, and a
> good story as well--giving the reader a chance to follow
> Sayers's thinking from a known situation to the motive be-
> hind it.

4   _____. "Criminals at Large." New York Times Book Review,
>   22 January, p. 20.
>   Review of Whose Body? Considers Sayers as important a
> mystery novelist as she is controversial. Says she both
> created and destroyed the modern detective story. Charac-
> terizes Whose Body? (just reprinted) as "short, relatively
> simple in puzzle and characterization, and highly satis-
> factory."

5   E. R. H. Review of Introductory Papers on Dante. Anglican
>   Theological Review (January).
>   Opens with the comment "Blessed is the introduction that
> really introduces, encouraging one to read the work." Dis-
> cusses the essays.

6   JAMES, MONTAGUE RHODES. Letters to a Friend. Edited by
>   Gwendolen McBryde. London: Edward Arnold, pp. 15, 199,
>   217.
>   Contains three brief references. According to McBryde,
> James's favorite Sayers novel was The Nine Tailors. One of
> his letters to her records his reading of this "excellent
> thriller." In a later letter he praises Sayers's detective
> novels in spite of her use of the "intolerable" Dian de
> Momerie in Murder Must Advertise.

7   MYSTERY WRITERS OF AMERICA. The Mystery Writer's Handbook.
>   Edited by Herbert Brean. New York: Harper, 288 pp.,
>   passim.
>   "A handbook on the writing of detective, suspense,
> mystery and crime stories." Includes Michael Gilbert's

"Technicalise," on pp. 57-65, in which Sayers's The Nine
Tailors and Unnatural Death are used briefly to illustrate
points the author is making. Other brief mentions of
Sayers and Wimsey.

8   RAYMOND, JOHN. "White Tile or Red Plush?" New Statesman and
Nation 51 (30 June):756-58.
    Reminisces on his school day enjoyment of Sayers's
Wimsey novels. Takes Mrs. Q. D. Leavis (1937.30) to task
for her harsh criticism in Scrutiny, December 1937. Comments that Gaudy Night and Scrutiny prefigured the literary
discontents of the 1950s and that one must seemingly choose
between "sad, bad hocus-pocus" of the "literary Left" and
the trivially absurd writing of authors like Nancy Mitford.

9   SCHOEK, R. J. Review of Introductory Papers on Dante.
Thought 31 (Autumn):462-64.
    Compares Sayers's work very briefly to that of Charles
S. Singleton in Commedia: Elements of Structure, then
tells its scope. Discusses the quality of her translation
and the intelligence, scholarship, and Christian understanding she brings to bear on it.

10 WILSON, EDMUND. "Who Cares Who Killed Roger Ackroyd?" In A
Literary Chronicle: 1920-1950. New York: Doubleday
Anchor, pp. 339-41.
    Reprint of 1945.2.

1957

1   ABBOTT, BROMLEY. "A 'Fortune with Strings' Awaits the Wimsey
Heirs." Sunday Despatch, 22 December, p. 2.
    Concerning D. L. S.'s will which had not been located at
this date. Mentions various people who knew or did not
know of one, with conjectures as to its contents.

2   ANON. ". . . And Therefore the Daily Express Begins
Tomorrow . . . Murder Must Advertise." Daily Express
(London), 19 December.
    Quotes several famous mystery and detective fiction
writers on Sayers and her novels, particularly Murder Must
Advertise. Title completes that of 1957.33.

1957

3   ANON. "Dante for an Anglo-Saxon Public." <u>Times Literary</u>
      <u>Supplement</u>, 13 December, p. 759.
         Review of <u>Further Papers on Dante</u>. Quotes what he con-
      siders Sayers's attempts to lure people to the reading of
      Dante's <u>Divine Comedy</u>. Comments on the freshness she
      brings to the study of Dante, gives some illustrative
      quotations. Considers the papers remarkable but the chap-
      ter on Charles Williams the least convincing.

4   ANON. "Death of Miss Dorothy Sayers." <u>Manchester Guardian</u>
      <u>Weekly</u> 77 (26 December):7.
         Biographical information joined to a commentary on the
      success of Sayers's career. Briefly compares her work with
      that of Conan Doyle and such crime writers as Symons,
      Chandler, and Simenon.

5   ANON. "Died: Dorothy Leigh Sayers Fleming." <u>Time</u> 70
      (30 December):64.
         Characterizes Sayers as "erudite, cherub-faced who-
      duniteer, translator, playwright, rapier-witted Anglican
      writer on theology."

6   ANON. "Died: Dorothy L. Sayers." <u>Newsweek</u> 50 (30 December):
      44.
         One-line notice of Sayers as "witty British mystery
      writer."

7   ANON. "Dorothy Sayers, Author, Dies at 64: Writer of Detec-
      tive Stories and Theological Works Did Translations of
      Dante." <u>New York Times</u>, 19 December, p. 29.
         Cites cause and circumstances of her death. Comments on
      the scope and quality of her writing. Remarks that she
      will probably best be remembered for her detective fiction
      but that she had changed fields in her writing, perhaps as
      a result of the maturing of her Christian faith. Gives a
      brief biography.

8   ANON. "Dorothy Sayers Dies." <u>News of the World</u>, 22 December.
         Details of Sayers's death, brief comments on her detec-
      tive fiction and membership in the Detective Club.

9   ANON. "Dorothy Sayers is Found Dead." <u>Evening Standard</u>
      (London), 18 December.
         Brief factual account of circumstances surrounding
      Sayers's death. Includes several lines about her writing.

10   ANON. "Literary Studies." <u>Virginia Quarterly Review</u>
     (Autumn).
          Review of <u>Further Papers on Dante</u>. Feels that Sayers
     stands head and shoulders above all contemporary writers on
     Dante, breaking through the roadblock of "literary appre-
     ciation." Especially commends her essay "On Dante and
     Milton."

11   ANON. "Miss Sayers, 64, Mystery Story Writer, is Dead."
     <u>Chicago Tribune</u>, 19 [?] December.
          Very brief biographical notes accompany this obituary.
     Incorrectly states that Sayers had become a convert to
     Roman Catholicism.

12   ANON. "Mystery Story." <u>Time</u> 69 (21 January):36.
          Review of "My Belief About Heaven and Hell." Describes
     Sayers's concept of life after death as "a cogent, striking
     version of one Christian view." Gives the main ideas she
     presented.

13   ANON. "Miss Dorothy L. Sayers: Christian Apologist and
     Novelist." <u>Times</u> (London), 19 December, p. 12.
          Obituary. Says that "sudden death would have had no
     terrors for Sayers since she combined an adventurous
     curiosity" with a strong religious faith. Discusses her
     work, commenting that the diversity of her success was
     founded on an inner unity of character.

14   ANON. Obituary. <u>Illustrated London News</u> 231 (28 December):
     1137.
          Comments on Sayers's accomplishments as a detective-
     fiction writer, her deep religious faith, and the bril-
     liance of her theological writings.

15   ANON. "<u>The Song of Roland</u>. A New Translation by Dorothy
     Sayers." <u>Times Literary Supplement</u>, 25 October, p. 646.
          Finds Sayers's introduction lucid, but the translation
     "completely missing the grace and simplicity of the origi-
     nal." Characterizes it as pompous and archaic on the one
     hand and comic on the other.

16   ANON. "Writer of <u>The Man Born To Be King</u>, Author Found Dead
     by Servant." <u>Braintree and Witham Times</u>, 19 December et
     seq. Witham, Essex: Dorothy L. Sayers Historical and
     Literary Society. Archives, 10.2. Processed, 1 p.
          Some biographical data, a brief appreciation, announce-
     ment of a memorial service, and mention of the will.

1957

17 BERGIN, THOMAS G. "Paths to a Poet's Stately House." <u>New
York Times Book Review</u>, 22 September, p. 29.
Review of <u>Further Papers on Dante</u>. Considers this
"exciting" collection of essays to be for intelligent
readers, not for specialists and says that they should be
judged on that basis. Uses the analogy of a house of many
mansions to show that Sayers's approach to Dante is one of
many. Her essays show the influence of C. S. Lewis and
Charles Williams. Her own preconceptions of medieval atti-
tudes and dogma lead her to an Anglo-Catholic mansion "full
of glamour and glitter" which is not open to all.

18 BERTRAM, ANTHONY. "Looking at Dante." <u>Tablet</u> 210 (13 July):
38-39.
Review of <u>Further Papers on Dante</u>. Repeats his objec-
tion given in his earlier review of <u>Introductory Papers on
Dante</u> (1955.4) that her flippant style is a hindrance to
the appreciation of what she has to say. Regrets that
Sayers, with all her talents and with "the power to draw a
great many readers to Dante," should falsify the effect he
intended to produce.

19 BOUCHER, ANTHONY. "Criminals at Large." <u>New York Times Book
Review</u>, 17 February, p. 25.
Review of <u>The Unpleasantness at the Bellona Club</u>. Brief
comments to the effect that this Sayers novel makes agree-
able reading although it falls below her earlier <u>Unnatural
Death</u> as "Wimseyana."

20 CAREY, GRAHAM. "The Unity of Artistic Experience." <u>Catholic
Arts Quarterly</u> 21 (Christmas):28-31.
Review of <u>The Mind of the Maker</u>. Compares Sayers's
book with Etienne Gilson's <u>Painting and Reality</u>, based on
the random thinking of many artists while hers is written
from her own experience. Values her book for its authen-
ticity--the result of experience plus her considerable
scholarship in the field of letters.

21 CLARKE, MOLLY. "Dante, Divinity, and Death." <u>Braintree and
Witham Times</u>, 13 November, p. 6.
A biographical study that reveals a good deal about
Sayers in a succinct way.

22 FOSTER, KENELM. "Dorothy Sayers on Dante." <u>Blackfriars</u> 38
(October):426-30.
Review of <u>Further Papers on Dante</u>. Characterizes this
work, along with Sayers's earlier <u>Introductory Papers on
Dante</u>, as consisting of "close study of Dante's thought

and art mixed with much cheerful conversation about him, often shrewd, suggestive and even brilliant, but also sometimes intemperate and often tiresomely assertive." Elaborates on this.

23 GIELGUD, VAL. British Radio Drama: 1922-1956, A Survey.
London: G. Harrap, pp. 93, 101, 103, 165, 170-73.
Comments that Sayers did not snub radio drama--the "poor relation of the literary family." Remarks on his pleasure that she selected him to produce The Man Born To Be King. In his chapter on difficult occasions in radio drama, discusses the storm brought on by the airing of The Man Born To Be King.

24 _____. "Literature's Loss." Sunday Times, 22 December.
In this Sayers obituary Gielgud tells of his final visit with her, calling her "a curious and lovable combination of the academic, the professional, and the almost childishly naive." Comments on her attitude toward her works and on her friendliness.

25 _____. "Why I Killed Peter Wimsey--By Dorothy Sayers."
Sunday Dispatch (London), 22 December.
Report of an interview with Sayers which took place for the purpose of learning why she had quit writing Wimsey novels and turned to theology in The Man Born To Be King and to the translation of The Song of Roland.

26 HAGUE, RENE. "Dauntless the Slug-horn." Tablet 210
(19 October):334-35.
Review of Sayers's translation of The Song of Roland. Criticizes, in Sayers's introduction, her discussion of the term "romantic" as applied to this poem, then discusses what she considers problems with Sayers's translation.

27 HOLMES, THEODORE. Review of Sayers's translation of The
Divine Comedy. Comparative Literature 9 (Summer):275-83.
Compares translations of G. L. Bickersteth, T. G. Bergin, John Ciardi, and Sayers. Of Sayers and Ciardi complains that they sacrificed meaning to more formal poetic devices, and in some instances, used their own interpretation of a passage rather than an accurate translation. Nevertheless, remarks that Sayers and Ciardi have given us the best in verse to date.

1957

28 J. C. "A Door to Dante." <u>Saturday Review of Literature</u> 40
    (9 November):44.
        Review of <u>Further Papers on Dante</u>. Expresses gratitude
    for Sayers's insights on Dante but objects to her Anglican
    proselytizing and wishes to be left alone concerning his/
    her [?] soul.

29 J. H. A. "Lord Peter Wimsey Probes Death at the Bellona
    Club." <u>New Bedford Standard</u>, 17 September.
        Review of <u>The Unpleasantness at the Bellona Club</u>.
    Enumerates Sayers's talents brought to the writing of de-
    tective fiction: talent of a first-rate novelist, "per-
    ception of a psychologist," and the "culture of an educated
    woman." As a result, her stories have style and taste, and
    are "tautly" written with unequaled characterization. Re-
    marks that Lord Peter brings a breath of fresh air to a
    field being taken over by "turgid, sex-stuffed epics of
    sadism, perversion, and inanity."

30 MORALL, JOHN B. Review of <u>Further Papers on Dante</u>. <u>Studies</u>
    (Dublin) 46 (Winter):493-94.
        Says that essays are "contributions to original critical
    appreciation of Dante" and therein lie both the book's
    strengths and weaknesses. Comments that Sayers ignores
    previous scholarly studies, "weakening her assertions in
    the realm of the history of philosophy." Some of the es-
    says are particularly criticized for lack of sound scholar-
    ship in the interest of promoting her own brand of "High
    Anglican medievalism" and her distaste for "modern science."
    Scolds her for speculating on the effect of sexual expe-
    riences on the poetry of Dante and Milton.

31 SHIRAS, MARY. "The Spontaneous Response." <u>Commonweal</u> 66
    (23 August):524-25.
        Review of <u>Further Papers on Dante</u>. Comments that Sayers
    brings to the <u>Divine Comedy</u> literary judgments rather than
    scholarly speculations--a benefit to the general reader.
    Discusses some of the essays.

32 SMITH, S. STEPHENSON. Review of <u>Further Papers on Dante</u>.
    <u>Library Journal</u> 82 (1 September):2030.
        Calls this "interpretive criticism at its finest."
    Comments on Sayers's broad knowledge of Dante and her
    ability to relate what she knows.

33 SPAIN, NANCY. "Dorothy L. Sayers, Creator of 20th Century Top
    Detective, Found Dead in Mysterious Circumstances. . . ."
    Daily Express (London), 19 December.
        Eulogizes Sayers in a running commentary on her life and
    work. Some "facts" are not in agreement with other biog-
    raphers', some are additional. See 1957.2 for rest of
    title.

34 SQUIRREL NUTKIN. "Inside of the Week." Church Times 140
    (27 December):5.
        Comments on what Sayers would have thought of "her"
    obituary notices precede two vignettes: Author attended
    performance of The Emperor Constantine at Colchester, de-
    scribes her appearance there and remarks that she had suc-
    ceeded in "making drama out of dogma." Second vignette
    mentions some of her characteristic actions, concluding
    with "But underneath the severity she was kind and human,
    and it was a revelation to hear the ripple and flow as she
    quoted Dante with great fluency."

35 WHISTON, LIONEL A. Review of The Mind of the Maker. Journal
    of Bible and Religion 25 (October):378-79.
        Gives five reasons for believing this book to be impor-
    tant to college teachers of religion. Feels that by this
    time Sayers's reputation in the field of religion and drama
    is stronger than in fiction.

1958

1 ANON. "Dante Up to Date." Times (London), 8 November, p. 7.
       Reviews Sayers's article, "On Translating The Divina
   Commedia," in Nottingham Mediaeval Studies 2 (1958):38-66.
   Briefly discusses her thinking. Concludes with the idea
   that, no matter which translation is chosen, Dante can
   never be brought up to date because he spoke of the
   "religious, political, and aesthetic trends of his time"
   and judged his contemporaries in all those fields.

2 ANON. "Dorothy L. Sayers." English (London) 12 (Spring):10.
       Notes the death of Sayers, a former vice-president of
   the English Association, commenting on her position as
   "one of the century's leading women of letters."

1958

3　ANON. "Dorothy L. Sayers." Friends of Canterbury Cathedral.
　　Annual Report (April):31-32.
　　　　Announces with regret the death of Sayers who had been a
　　Friend in both senses of the word. Remarks that they had
　　looked forward to her lecture on The Song of Roland to be
　　given in June. Quotes comments from The Times of 10 Decem-
　　ber 1957 and Margaret Babington's letter to The Times on
　　9 January 1958 (1958.8).

4　ANON. "Dorothy Leigh Sayers." Publishers' Weekly 173
　　(3 February):52.
　　　　Obituary. Mentions Sayers's death and lists her works
　　published in the United States.

5　ANON. "In Memoriam." Daily Telegraph and Morning Post,
　　16 January.
　　　　An announcement of the service for Sayers, the partici-
　　pants, and some of the audience.

6　ANON. "Translation." Times Literary Supplement, 5 December,
　　p. 705.
　　　　Reviews Sayers's articles in Nottingham Medieval Studies
　　2 (1958): "The Beatrician Vision in Dante and Other Poets"
　　and "On Translating the Divina Commedia." Says she deserves
　　many thanks for bringing Dante to the "literate" not just
　　the "educated." A brief comment on the first essay is fol-
　　lowed by a discussion of her philosophy of translation.
　　Comments on the worth of this essay on a subject about which
　　so little had been written. See 1958.9.

*7　ANON. [?] [Sayers's translation of The Divine Comedy].
　　Sunday Times, 8 November, p. 7.
　　　　Cited in Times Index (November-December):182.

8　BABINGTON, MARGARET. "Miss Dorothy Sayers." Times (London),
　　9 January, p. 14.
　　　　In this letter to the editor, Sayers is praised for her
　　humility, shown in her comments about writing the Canterbury
　　play, The Zeal of Thy House. Calls her "a delightful
　　friend."

9　BICKERSTETH, GEOFFREY L. "Translation." Times Literary
　　Supplement, 12 December, p. 721.
　　　　Letter to the editor following the article of 5 December
　　(1958.6) suggests that Sayers should have spent more time
　　studying Italian Dantists instead of seeing Dante through
　　the eyes of Charles Williams. Comments on several of what
　　he considers her mistakes.

10   HAWKINS, DAVE. "Whimsical Lord Peter is Revived." <u>Shreveport</u>
      <u>Times</u>, 3 August.
          Review of <u>Strong Poison</u>. Views Sayers's novel as a fair
      example of a British detective story and comments briefly
      on recent changes in detective fiction. Prefers the British
      detective, dull as he may be, to the modern hard-boiled
      type. Remarks that glimpses of London people and places
      are of sociological interest in this novel of manners.

11   McDONNELL, LAWRENCE V. Review of <u>Further Papers on Dante</u>.
      <u>Catholic World</u> 186 (February):398-99.
          Comments briefly on Sayers's purposes in presenting
      these papers and on a few of the papers.

12   McLAUGHLIN, PATRICK. "Dorothy L. Sayers, 1893-1957."
      <u>Christian Drama</u> (Spring):11-13.
          Sees in Sayers's death a loss to "the nation of a great
      entertainer, a distinguished scholar, and a superb crafts-
      man of letters" and a loss to "the Church of a devoted
      servant, a powerful apologist, and a soul of remarkable
      sanctity." Comments on the integrity of her work resulting
      from the discipline learned through her varied writing ex-
      periences and through the suffering and disillusionments of
      her life. Remarks on her zealous service to the church.

13   PHILLIPS, IVY. "Obituary: Dorothy Leigh Sayers, 1909-1911."
      <u>Godolphin School Magazine</u>, pp. 46-47.
          An account of Sayers's Godolphin School days and the
      characteristics recognized there that shaped her later
      life. Includes the Sayers translation of Leconte de
      Lisle's "La Mort du Soleil" done while she was at
      Godolphin.

14   SPEAIGHT, ROBERT, ed. <u>Letters from Hilaire Belloc</u>. London:
      Hollis & Carter, pp. 292-93.
          His letter to Major-General Guy Dawnay, 4 July 1940,
      comments on Sayers's <u>Creed or Chaos?</u> commending the quality
      of the writing while accusing her of a fatal lack of defi-
      nition and of avoiding the main issue.

15   THORPE, LEWIS. "Editorial." <u>Nottingham Mediaeval Studies</u>
      2:1-2.
          Comments on the inclusion of two Sayers lectures in this
      issue and discusses the quality of her work in medieval
      literature.

1958

16   WALLACE, DOREEN. "Miss Dorothy Sayers." <u>Times</u> (London),
      1 January, p. 13.
          Notes of a Somerville friend of Sayers, commenting on
      her impressive intelligence, fun-loving nature, and an
      awareness of her among literary young people.

17   WHITEHEAD, F. Review of Sayers's translation of <u>The Song of
      Roland</u>. <u>French Studies</u> 12:364.
          Remarks that the translation "fails because it tries to
      push beyond the bounds of the possible" from the standpoint
      of poetry. Discusses briefly both the poetry and the mean-
      ing Sayers finds in it.

1959

1   ANON. "The Criminal Record." <u>Saturday Review of Literature</u>
     42 (8 August):32.
         No substantial critical comment on Sayers's <u>Murder Must
     Advertise</u>.

2   BOUCHER, ANTHONY. "Criminals at Large." <u>New York Times Book
     Review</u>, 12 July, p. 21.
         Review of <u>Have His Carcase</u> and <u>Murder Must Advertise</u>.
     Comments on the unevenness of Sayers's detective stories.
     Considers the first a lesson in "padding" of a very poor
     detective story. By contrast, <u>Murder Must Advertise</u> is
     well-plotted, tightly written, and still timely in its
     assessment of the advertising business.

3   GILBERT, MICHAEL, ed. <u>Crime in Good Company: Essays on
     Criminals and Crime-Writing</u>. Boston: Writer, 251 pp.,
     passim.
         Not a "how-to" book but a collection of philosophizing
     about crime-writing. Sayers is mentioned briefly in essays
     by Michael Underwood, Cyril Hare, Raymond Chandler (1944.3),
     Michael Gilbert, Jacques Barzun, and L. A. G. Strong. Vita
     of Josephine Bell mentions that Sayers and she were at
     Godolphin at the same time.

4   MEYERSTEIN, E. H. W. "Letter to John Freeman, May, 1925." In
     <u>Some Letters of E. H. W. Meyerstein</u>. Edited by Rowland
     Watson. London: Neville Spearman, pp. 73-74.
         Describes a meeting with Sayers in a restaurant and her
     subsequent visit to his home, including a bit about her
     appearance and manner.

1 ANON. "The Realm of Christmas." <u>San Francisco Chronicle</u>,
   13 November, p. 17.
       Review of <u>The Days of Christ's Coming</u>. Describes this
   Sayers volume as a "pint-sized" volume, handsomely printed,
   richly illustrated, telling the Christmas story.

2 ANON. "Religion Without Tears: Keeping Faith With the Good
   Book." <u>Times Literary Supplement</u>, 25 November, p. 17.
       Includes two-sentence highly commendatory review of
   Sayers's <u>The Days of Christ's Coming</u>.

3 BOUCHER, ANTHONY. "Criminals at Large." <u>New York Times Book
   Review</u>, 27 March, p. 28.
       Review of <u>Gaudy Night</u> and <u>Busman's Honeymoon</u>. Even as
   he calls them "classics" he deplores their wordiness. Says
   Sayers's attempt to fuse "suspense" and "straight" fiction
   fails. Considers both books interesting, but not the ones
   to establish her place in the history of detective fiction.

4 BRITTAIN, VERA. <u>The Women at Oxford: A Fragment of History</u>.
   London: G. G. Harrap, pp. 122-23, 156, 213, appendixes.
       Reminisces about Sayers as a fellow student at Oxford
   and about the day she received her M.A. Also tells of her
   death. Includes her in a list of students, their colleges,
   subjects, degrees, graduation dates, and occupations, and
   in a list of guest speakers at Somerville.

5 BUELL, ELLEN LEWIS. "For Younger Readers." <u>New York Times
   Book Review</u>, 4 December, p. 66.
       Review of <u>The Days of Christ's Coming</u>. In comparison to
   other books for Christmas, finds this "unremarkable" and
   the illustrations by Fritz Wegner "well-drawn and richly
   colored" but "trite."

6 GOODWIN, POLLY. "Surefire Ways to Please a Child's Mind and
   Eye." <u>Chicago Tribune</u>, 4 December, p. 33.
       Includes a two-sentence review of Sayers's <u>The Days of
   Christ's Coming</u>, calling it simple and reverent with "ex-
   quisite illustrations."

7 HEINS, ETHEL L. Review of <u>The Days of Christ's Coming</u>.
   <u>Library Journal</u> 85 (15 November):4218-19.
       Briefly comments on its elegance and reverence.

1960

8   JACKSON, CHARLOTTE. "Books for Children: A Christmas List."
Atlantic 206 (December):130.
     Includes one-line review of Sayers's The Days of
Christ's Coming. Says it is "handsomely printed and richly
illustrated."

9   LELAND, DOROTHY E. Review of The Days of Christ's Coming.
Library Journal 85 (15 November):4219.
     Briefly comments that Sayers's retelling is not in the
proper spirit of Christmas.

10   LIBBY, MARGARET SHERWOOD. "Books for Boys and Girls." New
York Herald Tribune, 11 December, p. 39.
     Review of The Days of Christ's Coming. One-line review
characterizes this Sayers book as "reverent," illustrated
in "blazing color."

11   SPEAIGHT, ROBERT. "Loss and Recovery." In Christian Theatre.
New York: Hawthorn Books, pp. 129-130.
     Comments briefly on Sayers's The Zeal of Thy House and
The Man Born To Be King. Characterizes the latter series
as "brilliant in their characterization, firm in their de-
sign and incisive in their dialogue."

<u>1961</u>

1   ANON. "The Criminal Record." Saturday Review of Literature
44 (27 May):31.
     Calls Sayers's introduction to The Omnibus of Crime a
"fine historical survey of the field."

2   CHIPMAN, WARWICK, tr. "Translator's Note." In The Inferno
from The Divine Comedy. London: Oxford University Press,
pp. viii-ix.
     Says he did not know of the "brilliant" Sayers transla-
tion until he was well into his own. Regrets that she was
unable to finish. No further comment.

3   FAIRMAN, MARION BAKER. "The Neo-Medieval Plays of Dorothy L.
Sayers." Ph.D. dissertation, University of Pittsburgh,
processed, 200 pp.
     Sees Sayers's religious plays as an attempt to "communi-
cate Christian principles to the modern mind." Discusses
the philosophical ideas and the three primary Christian
doctrines underlying her work. Analyzes several aspects of
the plays: form, content, setting, characterization, and
the use of verse, comparing them with the medieval plays
after which they are patterned.

4 SYMONS, JULIAN, and CRISPIN, EDMUND. "Is the Detective Story
     Dead?" <u>Times Literary Supplement</u>, 23 June, p. iv.
        "A recorded dialogue between" these two men. Agree that
     1920-1940 was <u>the</u> era of the detective story. Discussion
     centers on the reason for this, mentioning Sayers's idea
     "that the possibilities of elaboration are not limitless"
     and the crime story would become a novel of manners. The
     other reason given is that behind the puzzle story is a
     dream of reason, no longer viable after the beginning of
     World War II. Defining the classical detective story as
     purely a puzzle, they wonder what will replace it.

5 WEALES, GERALD C. "Charles Williams and Dorothy Sayers." In
     <u>Religion in Modern English Drama</u>. Philadelphia: Univer-
     sity of Pennsylvania Press, pp. 164-77.
        While Sayers is mentioned elsewhere in this book, her
     plays are discussed in depth in this chapter.

<u>1962</u>

1 ANON. "Journey to the Stars. <u>The Comedy of Dante Alighieri,
     the Florentine. Cantica III: Il Paradiso</u>." <u>Times Liter-
     ary Supplement</u>, 27 July, p. 544.
        Review of Sayers's and Barbara Reynolds's translation of
     <u>Il Paradiso</u>. Expresses regret that Sayers did not live to
     complete her work on Dante, but finds that Reynolds justi-
     fies Sayers's faith that she would be the best qualified
     to complete it. Commends the translation suggesting that
     it might be accompanied by a selection of Sayers's essays
     in the same format.

2 CHASE, MARY ELLEN. "Five Literary Portraits." <u>Massachusetts
     Review</u> 3 (Spring):514-15.
        Paints an ugly picture of Sayers's appearance and her
     defensive attitude toward her writing. Still, remarks that
     this most unattractive woman could hold a student audience
     spellbound when she spoke.

3 REYNOLDS, BARBARA, tr. Foreword to <u>The Comedy of Dante
     Alighieri, the Florentine. Cantica III: Paradise</u>.
     Harmondsworth, Middlesex, England: Penguin Books,
     pp. 9-11.
        Tells of her eleven-year friendship with Sayers, their
     discussions and correspondence concerning the translation,
     and Sayers's wish that Reynolds should complete the work
     if she did not. Comments on Sayers's insistence upon the

1962

relevance of The Divine Comedy to modern life and the growth in the number of English-speaking readers since 1949.

4   RICKMAN, H. P. "From Detection to Theology: The Work of Dorothy Sayers." Hibbert Journal 60 (July):290-96.
       Discusses the connection between Sayers's detective fiction and her theology as it developed in her writing. Uses Gaudy Night, The Mind of the Maker, and The Zeal of Thy House to show her concern for integrity as she attempted to assess life and work from the Christian point of view. Credits her use of Lord Peter, not as an ideal man, but as the embodiment of some of her ideals--scholarly thoroughness, common sense, a determination to be lucid, and a sense of humor.

5   SORIA, REGINA. "A New Translation of Dante Completed." Baltimore Sun, 29 June.
       This translation of Dante's The Divine Comedy was begun by Sayers and completed by Barbara Reynolds, Italian scholar. In comparing the two, comments that Sayers's witty and timely remarks will be missed but Reynolds is more careful in her examination of the connections between this work and today's concept of the universe. Discusses the translation briefly.

6   SYMONS, JULIAN. The Detective Story in Britain. London: Longmans, Green, 48 pp., passim.
       Appraises Sayers as both writer and critic of detective fiction. Discusses progression in her novels from strict adherence to rules to revolt against them. Recognizes her dissatisfaction with her inability to achieve what she was trying to do. A selected bibliography includes her fiction. An added bibliography includes her critical introductions to short story collections.

1963

1   ANON. "Spiritual Expressions." Times Literary Supplement, 13 September, p. 690.
       Review of The Poetry of Search and the Poetry of Statement. "A timely reminder of Sayers's remarkable achievements." In discussing the essays, compares her to G. K. Chesterton--having "the same fundamentally religious approach to life, the sympathetic view of the Middle Ages, and the high spirits and verbal dexterity with which they

joust against their opponents, especially the pagan intelligentsia." Quotes a passage to show the latter.

2   DONOGHUE, DENIS. "Sense of Superiority." New Statesman and Nation 66 (1 November):621-22.
      Review of The Poetry of Search and the Poetry of Statement. A scathing condemnation of Sayers's "air of native superiority" and some reasons for saying so. Remarks briefly that the best things in the book are the autobiographical fragments.

3   GREEN, MARTIN. "The Detection of a Snob: Martin Green on Lord Peter Wimsey." Listener 69 (14 March):461, 464.
      Calls Sayers "one of the world's masters of the pornography of class-distinction." Says her detective fiction is built around "crude wish-fulfillment appealing to gross and sophisticated appetites." Finds this a result of post-World War I upward aspirations away from the dullness of ordinary life. Followed by "Letter to the Editor," 69 (21 March):505.

4   JOHNSTON, R. C. "Hoese 'Boot' in the Chanson de Roland, Line 641." Modern Language Review 58 (July):391-92.
      Criticizes Sayers's translation of the word "hoese" in the Song of Roland as meaning "poke" instead of "boot," giving reasons for the criticism.

5   LEGMAN, GERSHON. "The Bitch Heroine." In Love and Death: A Study in Censorship. New York: Hacker Art Books, pp. 72-73.
      Grudgingly admits that Sayers is a capable writer, but follows the remark with a brief caustic appraisal of Sayers, Wimsey, and Vane.

6   LEWIS, C[LIVE] S[TAPLES]. "Wain's Oxford." Encounter 20 (January):81-82.
      Commenting on John Wain's Sprightly Running, Lewis says that Sayers was a friend, not an "ally" of the Inklings, and tells how he and she became friends and of his liking for her.

7   RICHARDSON, JOANNA. Review of The Poetry of Search and the Poetry of Statement. Listener (12 September):393.
      Considers this posthumous collection of essays a tribute to both the depth and range of Sayers's scholarship. Says that it also reveals the breadth of her reading and her independent spirit.

1963

8   ROBINSON, J[OHN] A. T.   "God and the Bishop of Woolwich."
        Horizon 5, no. 7 (September):4-7.
        Selections from 1963.9.

9   ROBINSON, JOHN A. T.   Honest to God.   Philadelphia:
        Westminster Press, p. 15.
        Comments that the picture of God "out there" as under-
    lying such presentations of the Gospel as are given by
    Sayers and others is anthropomorphic.   While he recognizes
    that they do not take it literally says they are not em-
    barrassed by it either.   Quoted in 1963.8.

                                1964

1   De SUA, WILLIAM J.   "Craftsmen and Critics: Dante's
        Twentieth-Century Translators."   In Dante Into English.
        North Carolina University Studies in Comparative Litera-
        ture, no. 32.   Chapel Hill: University of North Carolina
        Press, pp. 87-121.
        Discusses briefly Sayers's place in the field of Dante
    translators.   Places her with post-war translators attempt-
    ing to mix Romantic and critical methods of translation.
    Comments that she aimed toward highlighting certain aspects
    of The Divine Comedy with a tendency toward the use of col-
    loquial language.

2   DICKINSON, PETER.   "The Great Rereadable."   Punch 246
        (10 June):871.
        Review of The Lord Peter Omnibus.   To Dickinson, claim-
    ing to read an average of twenty modern thrillers a month,
    Sayers's novels are eminently rereadable.   Attributes this
    partly to the remoteness of "Wimseyland" that renders them
    "ideal for escapists" and partly to the actual amount of
    work that went into her writing of them.   Enumerates sev-
    eral contributing characteristics.

3   WARD, A. C.   Twentieth Century Literature: 1901-1960.   New
        York: Barnes & Noble, p. 78.
        Concise analysis of Sayers's fiction.   Considers Wimsey
    novels better as novels than as detective fiction.   Recog-
    nizes her religious sensitivity, seeing murder as "spiri-
    tual outrage."   Sees her ingenuity shown in The Nine
    Tailors, her ability as a novelist in Gaudy Night, and her
    humor and common sense in Murder Must Advertise.   Other
    brief comments.

1965

1 BURLESON, JAMES BERNARD. "A Study of the Novels of Dorothy L. Sayers." Ph.D. dissertation, University of Texas, processed, 233 pp.
Discusses Sayers's detective fiction chronologically, showing the "progress of her work toward the legitimate novel." Treats the fiction from the standpoint of plot, theme, style, and characterization, and, in some instances humor and weaknesses. Comments on her detective fiction as a training ground for her future work.

2 CURTAYNE, ALICE. "Dante." Studies (Summer-Autumn):217-26.
Opens with a brief section on Dante, followed by a short section on the Italian scholar, Rocco Montano. Reviews Sayers's feelings for The Divine Comedy and her desire to make it available to everyone. Follows this with a discussion of her translation--its merits and its faults.

3 FULTON, ROBIN. "Two Versions of Ulysses' Last Voyage." Studies in Scottish Literature 2 (April):251-57.
Compares Sayers's translation of the second half of Canto 26 of the Inferno (Penguin edition) with that of Tom Scott in his Ship and Ither Poems, published by Oxford University Press in 1963.

4 GIELGUD, VAL. Years in a Mirror. London: Bodley Head, pp. 61, 93-94, 115, 196-97.
High praise for Sayers as a friend and for her behavior as an author with a play, The Man Born To Be King, in production. Includes brief mention of a rebroadcast of the above play and of her gift to him of a cat.

5 MASCALL, ERIC LIONEL. The Secularization of Christianity: An Analysis and A Critique. New York: Holt, Rinehart & Winston, 299 pp., passim.
Praises Sayers's concern for clarity in expressing old truths in contemporary language. Remarks that the principles laid down in her introduction to The Man Born To Be King are evidenced in both her dramatization of the Gospel narrative and in her popular writings on religion. Includes comments on her determination to protect the authenticity of the truths she was expressing in modern language, her "brilliant" discussions on Dante, her apologetics, and her handling of difficult Biblical passages in The Man Born To Be King.

1965

6   REYNOLDS, BARBARA. "The English Awareness of Dante."
     <u>Nottingham Mediaeval Studies</u> 9:4-14.
          In discussing the writers and translators who make Dante
     live in English, Reynolds relates Sayers's experiences as
     told in her book <u>The Poetry of Search and the Poetry of</u>
     <u>Statement</u>. Also comments on the qualities of her transla-
     tion--her "respect for historical and textual accuracy" and
     her clarity. Says Sayers, along with Pound, Eliot, and
     Williams, are leaders toward a reawakening to Dante's
     poetry and its meaning for life today.

                              <u>1966</u>

1   ANON. Review of <u>The Nine Tailors</u>. <u>Bestsellers</u> 26 (December):
     354.
          Two lines describe this Sayers "classic" as "literate,
     intricate, and quite satisfying."

2   ANON. "Sayers, Dorothy." In <u>A Library of Literary Criticism:</u>
     <u>Modern British Literature</u>. 2 vols. Compiled and edited by
     Ruth Z. Temple and Martin Tucher. New York: Frederick
     Ungar, 3:85-88.
          A collection of quotations from critical literature
     some of which are cited elsewhere in this bibliography.
     See 1947.5, 1949.14, 1954.4, 1956.8, 1963.1.

3   ANON. "Sayers, Dorothy L. <u>The Poetry of Search and the</u>
     <u>Poetry of Statement</u>." <u>Choice</u> 3 (May):204.
          Briefly discusses these Sayers essays in groups, finding
     them written with competence. Feels that the group dealing
     with Dante carries more weight than the others.

4   LEWIS, W. H., ed. <u>Letters of C. S. Lewis</u>. New York:
     Harcourt, Brace & World, pp. 208-209, 287, 299.
          Includes two letters to Sayers, in one of which Lewis
     calls her "one of the great English letter writers." In
     the other he comments on their different ideas concerning
     honesty in work. In a letter to Charles Moorman he re-
     marks that Sayers "neither exerted nor underwent any lit-
     erary influence" among the group of authors called the
     Inklings, and in still another he recommends the reading
     of her book <u>The Man Born To Be King</u>.

5   MOORMAN, CHARLES. "The Suburbs of the City: T. S. Eliot,
    Dorothy L. Sayers." In The Precincts of Felicity: The
    Augustinian City of the Oxford Christians. Gainesville:
    University of Florida Press, pp. 101-36.
        Sees Eliot and Sayers as being on the periphery of the
    Oxford Christians but still within their sphere of influ-
    ence. Discusses the concept of the City in the integrity
    of Sayers's work as well as within the work itself. Illus-
    trates from Gaudy Night, The Zeal of Thy House, The Devil
    to Pay, and The Mind of the Maker. Comments on Sayers's
    debt to Charles Williams.

1967

1   ANON. Review of Murder Must Advertise. Publishers' Weekly
    192 (7 August):57.
        Briefly announces the paperback issue, calling this one
    of Sayers's "best and liveliest novels."

2   ANON. "Sayers, Dorothy L." In The New Century Handbook of
    English Literature. Edited by Clarence L. Barnhart. Rev.
    ed. New York: Appleton-Century, p. 966.
        Brief critical note followed by a partial bibliography.

3   CORBISHLEY, T. "Sayers, Dorothy Leigh." In New Catholic
    Encyclopedia. New York: McGraw-Hill, p. 1110.
        Primarily a brief commentary on Sayers's works from the
    Christian standpoint.

4   CUNNINGHAM, GILBERT F. "Dorothy Leigh Sayers." In The Divine
    Comedy in English: A Critical Bibliography, 1901-1966.
    New York: Barnes & Noble, pp. 211-20, 278-79.
        Comments on the competent way in which Dr. Barbara
    Reynolds completed in Sayers's style what Sayers had left
    of Paradise untranslated at the time of her death. In
    the postscript, pp. 278-79, remarks that the Sayers-Reynolds
    translation of Paradise is superior in every way to the
    Sayers translations of Inferno and Purgatory. In discuss-
    ing Sayers's work, says "Inequality is a marked character-
    istic of Dr. Sayers's writing" and goes on to illustrate.

5   SMARIDGE, NORAH. "Dorothy L. Sayers." In Famous British
    Women Novelists. New York: Dodd, pp. 100-108.
        A biographical commentary on Sayers's life and works.

1967

6 SPANOS, WILLIAM V. The Christian Tradition in Modern British
   Verse Drama: The Poetics of Sacramental Time. New
   Brunswick, N.J.: Rutgers University Press, 416 pp.,
   passim.
       Sayers's work is often mentioned in this critical study
   of Christian verse drama, comparing her work to that of her
   contemporaries. Discusses The Zeal of Thy House and how
   her presentation of the action on human and supernatural
   planes in the "aesthetic of sacramental time" allows her
   "to achieve a multivocal image of an action." Comments on
   her limitations.

7 THURMER, JOHN. "The Theology of Dorothy L. Sayers." Church
   Quarterly Review 168 (October/December):452-62.
       Uses ideas from the following of Sayers's works as his
   basis for comment on her views of creation, free will and
   miracle, the Incarnation, evil, the Holy Spirit, aesthetics,
   and work: The Zeal of Thy House, The Man Born To Be King,
   The Mind of the Maker, "Toward a Christian Aesthetic," and
   Why Work? Mentions several scholars who have held views
   similar to hers.

1968

1 HAYCRAFT, HOWARD. Murder for Pleasure: The Life and Times of
   the Detective Story. Enl. ed. New York: Biblo & Tannen,
   448 pp., passim.
       Reprint of 1951.5.

2 HEILBRUN, CAROLYN. "Reappraisals: Sayers, Lord Peter and
   God." American Scholar 37 (Spring):324-34.
       Looks backward at Sayers's work, especially the Wimsey
   stories, discussing them with "intelligence and wit."
   Commenting on the longevity of Lord Peter, remarks that
   Sayers "has endowed her own creature with enduring grace."
   Reprinted: Lord Peter: A Collection of All the Lord Peter
   Wimsey Stories. (New York: Harper & Row, 1972),
   pp. 454-69.

3 MURCH, ALMA ELIZABETH. "The Golden Age." In The Development
   of the Detective Novel. New York: Greenwood Press,
   pp. 221-23.
       Calling Sayers "scholarly and meticulous," sees her as
   an influence on detective fiction through her "sparkling
   imagination and her love of literature," as well as through
   her introduction to The Omnibus of Crime. Traces the influence of other writers on her novels.

4 ORWELL, GEORGE. Review of Gaudy Night. In Collected Essays,
   Journalism, and Letters of George Orwell. Vol. 1, An Age
   Like This: 1920-1940. New York: Harcourt, Brace & World,
   pp. 160-61.
      Admits to Sayers's being a better writer than others
   under consideration, but goes on to make very uncompli-
   mentary remarks about her and her work. Reprinted from
   New English Weekly, 23 January 1936.

5 ROSTEN, MURRAY. "The Man Born To Be King." In Biblical Drama
   in England: From the Middle Ages to the Present Day.
   Evanston, Ill.: Northwestern University Press, pp. 296-98.
      Believes that Sayers achieved what she set out to do--to
   reaffirm faith in the mystery of the Gospel through her use
   of realism.

6 SHIBUK, CHARLES. "Checklist: Dorothy L. Sayers, 1893-1957,
   Detective Stories Only." Mystery Lover's Newsletter 2,
   no. 2 (December):10-11.
      Lists Sayers's novels and the short stories in her two
   collections: Hangman's Holiday and In the Teeth of the
   Evidence. Continued in 1969.17.

                              1969

1 ANON. Review of Christian Letters to a Post-Christian World.
   Christian Century 86 (25 June):877.
      Comments briefly that while the essays are not up to the
   standard of Sayers's detective fiction they do merit reading.

2 ANON. Review of Christian Letters to a Post-Christian World.
   Choice 6 (October):1030.
      Brief complimentary remarks begin the review of this
   book edited by Roderick Jellema. States that most of the
   essays may be found in other volumes and mentions them.
   Gives two of her themes: the conflict between science and
   theology and the idea that Western civilization has lost
   its imagination.

3 ANON. "Sayers, Dorothy Leigh (1893-1957)." In Chambers Biographical Dictionary. London: W. & R. Chambers, p. 1136.
      Brief complimentary commentary on Sayers's works.

1969

4   ANON. "A Short Sayers Bibliography." Unicorn 1, no. 4
      (Fall/Winter):17.
           The first section of a larger bibliography, here listing
      Sayers's detective fiction. Continued in 1970.11.

5   BOARDMAN, JOHN. "The Whimsy of Dorothy Sayers: Lord Peter
      Views the World." Unicorn 1, no. 4 (Fall/Winter):15-16.
           Says that "next to the Holmes stories, the best evoca-
      tion of a whole society in detective fiction occurs in
      Dorothy Sayers' adventures of Lord Peter Wimsey." Comments
      that she favors a "right little, tight little, hierarchical
      society." Elaborates. Followed by letters in the follow-
      ing issues: 2, no. 1 (Fall 1970):4-5; 2, no. 2 (Spring
      1972):4, 31; 3, no. 1 (Summer 1974):4.

6   GAMBEE, RUTH R. Review of Christian Letters to a Post-
      Christian World. Library Journal 94 (August):2795.
           Comments on Sayers's versatility and her relationship to
      Lewis, Eliot, and Tolkien. Characterizes the essays as
      "stimulating, witty, and literate" and "of more than pass-
      ing value." Remarks on the scope of material covered.

7   HAGEN, ORDEAN. Who Done It? A Guide to Detective, Mystery,
      and Suspense Fiction. New York: Bowker, 834 pp., passim.
           A guide to various aspects of detective, mystery, and
      suspense fiction. Includes bibliographies of the works of
      various authors and several subject bibliographies, of
      which "Writings on the Mystery Novel" is perhaps the most
      complete. Sayers's work is listed in some places, omitted
      in others where it might have been included.

8   JELLEMA, RODERICK, ed. Introduction to Christian Letters to
      a Post-Christian World: A Selection of Essays. Grand
      Rapids, Mich.: William B. Eerdmans, pp. vii-xiii.
           Discusses the reasons for collecting these Sayers essays
      from various sources. Calls them letters because of their
      "feel." Says of them, they "are letters written in England
      from somewhere half-way between the Middles Ages and the
      sun . . . in just such a here-and-elsewhere that we should
      expect to find Dorothy L. Sayers."

9   KILBY, CLYDE S. "A Detective Writer's Sense of Paradox:
      Dorothy Sayers' Essays Lift Christians from Doldrums."
      Eternity 20 (November):74-75.
           Recommends Sayers's Christian Letters to a Post-
      Christian World, agreeing with its "dominant theme of God
      as creator, maker and artist, and of man as most like God
      when he also becomes creator." Recommends it also to

those who disagree with Sayers's thesis but enjoy "wit, humor, and a sense of paradox." Discusses some of her principal ideas.

10 PFATTEICHER, PHILIP H. Review of <u>Christian Letters to a Post-Christian World</u>. <u>Lutheran Quarterly</u> 21 (November):499-500.
    Considers Sayers's work worth knowing and that this book may be an introduction to her in spite of the poor editing and some of Sayers's out-of-date sentiments.

11 QUEEN, ELLERY. <u>The Detective Short Story: A Bibliography</u>. New York: Biblo & Tannen, 152 pp., passim.
    Contains bibliography of authors and their short-story collections, bibliography of detective-short-story anthologies, index of detectives and criminals, and an index of anthology editors. Reprint of 1942 edition.

12 _____. "Dorothy L. Sayers's <u>Lord Peter Views the Body</u>." In <u>Queen's Quorum</u>. New York: Biblo & Tannen, p. 82.
    Attributes to Sayers's writing a higher degree of literary tone than is usually found in detective stories. Rates it HQS according to his scale: Historical importance - H, Literary quality - Q, Value as a collector's item - R (rare) or S (scarce).

13 _____. <u>In the Queen's Parlor, and Other Leaves from the Editors' Notebook</u>. New York: Biblo & Tannen, 204 pp., passim.
    In this book on detective-fiction collecting, some of Sayers's works appear in lists of "bests." She is quoted twice, giving her comment on <u>The Murders in the Rue Morgue</u>, and her inscription to her parents in the presentation copy of <u>Whose Body?</u>

14 _____. <u>Queen's Quorum: A History of the Detective-Crime Short Story as Revealed in the 106 Most Important Books Published in this Field Since 1845</u>. New York: Biblo & Tannen, 146 pp., passim.
    In this history of detective-short-story collections Sayers is quoted several times but only her <u>Lord Peter Views the Body</u> is included for its importance.

15 RUMSCHEIDT, MARTIN. "Book Notes." <u>Canadian Journal of Theology</u> 15 (July/October):285-86.
    This review of <u>Christian Letters to a Post-Christian World</u> speaks of Sayers's "intoxicating sense of amazement of which the New Testament is so full and our ecclesiastical world today so empty." Karl Barth's admiration for

1969

her is a natural result of the clarity of her reflections
on the organized church's irrelevancy to modern man's intellectual needs.

16 SONNEVELDT, NANCY. Review of Christian Letters to a Post-
      Christian World. Reformed Review 23 (Fall):24-25.
          After a review of Sayers's varied literary talents, dis-
      cusses the scope and arrangement of this "well-edited and
      admirably organized" book of essays. Attempts to acquaint
      the reader with Sayers's many worlds and her ideas about
      western culture, contemporary man, and the church as they
      relate to the problems of the sixties.

17 WHITE, WILLIAM. "Dorothy L. Sayers: A Brief Addendum."
      Mystery Reader's Newsletter 3, no. 1 (October):12.
          Continuation of 1968.6, listing Sayers's editions of
      collected short stories and some of her essays, with com-
      ments. Continued in 1970.10.

                           1970

1 CASEY, GENEVIEVE. Review of Christian Letters to a Post-
      Christian World. Sign 50 (November):52.
          Begins with a comment that while English women are not
      typically chic or beautiful, each generation has produced
      "women who are the brightest, the wittiest, the most in-
      cisive, the most civilized" and Sayers is a "case in
      point." Comments on her versatility. Gives a bit of
      biographical information. Discusses more fully the selec-
      tions in this book and remarks that they reveal Sayers as
      a "highly civilized Christian with deep roots in Western
      culture."

2 CHRISTOPHER, JOE R[ANDELL]. "Sayers, Dorothy Leich [sic].
      The Man Born to Be King." Choice 7 (November):1245.
          Comments on the difference between the American and
      British editions, the American giving Sayers's long intro-
      duction. Outlines the general theme.

3 GALLOWAY, A. D. Review of Christian Letters to a Post-
      Christian World. Scottish Journal of Theology 23 (May):
      238.
          Recommends this Sayers collection for anyone needing
      awakening from spiritual torpor. Discusses her special
      talents and skills for "elucidation of the characteristic
      forms of religious discourse."

1970

4   HOWARD, THOMAS. "Old Truths and Modern Myths." New York
    Times Book Review, 15 March, pp. 40-41.
        Review of Christian Letters to a Post-Christian World.
    Calls Sayers the "Carry Nation of secularism" on account of
    her scorn for the way secular theologians attempt to make
    Christianity palatable when they are dealing with the most
    exciting events ever to have occurred. Briefly describes
    several of her essays to make his point.

5   JEFFARES, A. NORMAN. "Some Academic Novels." Wascana Review
    5, no. 1:5-27.
        In a discussion of novels with university or college
    settings, Jeffares says of Sayers's Gaudy Night that it
    gave a sinister picture of an Oxford women's college.

6   PARKS, G. B., and TEMPLE, R. Z., eds. The Literatures of the
    World in English Translation: A Bibliography. Vol. 3,
    The Romance Literature. New York: Frederick Ungar, pt. 1,
    p. 58.
        Lists Sayers's translation of Dante's Divine Comedy,
    completed by Barbara Reynolds. Comments that her transla-
    tion is a good colloquial one and retains Dante's humor
    better than most.

7   ROBSON, W. W. "From Auden to Orwell." In Modern English Lit-
    erature. New York: Oxford University Press, pp. 139,
    146-47.
        Compares the writing of Graham Greene's thrillers to
    that of Sayers, Christie, and Carr. Avers that the latter
    have brought detective fiction to perfection. Complains
    that Sayers's work deteriorated when she fell in love with
    Lord Peter. Considers Gaudy Night and Busman's Honeymoon
    the "worst readable novels in the English language." In-
    cludes her with the "Anglo-Oxford" writers (also called
    the "Inklings") as the weakest of the group. Says her
    religious dramas and her translations are "over-familiar
    in style."

8   RYDBECK, MARGARETA EURONIUS. "Though It Be Madness, There is
    Method In't." Ph.D. dissertation, Lund Universitet,
    Sweden, processed, 46 pp. in 23.
        Outlines the historical use of literary allusions. Dis-
    cusses Sayers's use of them both as quotations and in the
    running text of Busman's Honeymoon. Remarks on the criti-
    cal comment raised. Points out errors Sayers made.

1970

9   SPEAIGHT, ROBERT. "Missions and Transmissions." In The
    Property Basket: Recollections of a Divided Life. London:
    Collins & Harvill Press, pp. 221-22.
        Includes brief descriptions of his experience in his
    performance of Sayers's The Man Born To Be King. Mentions
    Sayers's strengths and weaknesses.

10 WHITTEN, MARY ANN. "Dorothy L. Sayers: A Second Brief
    Addendum." Mystery Reader's Newsletter 3, no. 3 (February):
    2.
        Continues 1969.17, listing Sayers's novels written in
    collaboration with other writers of detective fiction and
    some items gleaned from Sandoe's bibliography (1944.7).

11 WOOD, BARBARA. "A Sayers Bibliography, Part 2." Unicorn 2,
    no. 1 (Fall):25.
        Continues 1969.4, with annotations, listing detective
    miscellany, writings on religion and social problems, and
    religious drama. Continued in 1972.6.

                            1971

1   ANON. Review of Clouds of Witnesses. Bestsellers 31
    (15 July):256.
        Mentions that Sayers's novels are often reprinted, but
    deserve to be called to the attention of new readers.

2   ANON. Review of The Unpleasantness at the Bellona Club.
    Bestsellers 30 (15 February):531.
        Mentions that it's good to have Sayers back in the
    third Avon printing.

3   ANON. "Sayers, Dorothy L(eigh) (1893-1957)." In The Penguin
    Companion to Literature. Vol. 3, English Literature.
    Edited by David Daiches. New York: McGraw-Hill, 3:462.
        Comments more on her works than on her life: her detec-
    tive fiction "scrupulously well written," her desire to
    propagate Christian drama, and her Dante essays and
    translation.

4   BARZUN, JACQUES, and TAYLOR, WENDELL HERTIG. A Catalogue of
    Crime. New York: Harper & Row, 862 pp., passim.
        Reviews Sayers's novels, collaborations, some short
    stories, short-story collections, short-story collections
    edited, and the play Busman's Honeymoon. Comments on her
    staying power and the excellence of her introductions to

The Omnibus of Crime, Tales of Detection, and Collins's The Moonstone, and on her essays on detective fiction.

5 BUTCHER, MARYVONNE. "Sayers, Dorothy." Encyclopedia of World Literature in the 20th Century. 4 vols. New York: Ungar, 3:238-39.
   A short literary biography of Sayers with some brief critical comments on each of the categories of her writing. Includes bibliography.

6 CORAY, HENRY W. Review of Christian Letters to a Post-Christian World. Westminster Theological Journal 33 (May):233-34.
   While "she displays a surprising knowledge of historical as well as current theology" and its relationship to life itself, Sayers's thinking shows confusion in doctrine and the historicity of the Old Testament. Credits her with a warm desire to bring her mind under Christ's sceptre. Includes examples of her writing to establish his reasoning.

7 CRITELLI, IDA J. Review of Are Women Human? Marriage 53 (September):62-64.
   Discusses Sayers's two essays included in this book: "Are Women Human?" and "The Human-Not-Quite-Human." Calls them "witty, enlightening, and sane," remarks especially on their timeliness in view of their having been given as lectures in 1938.

8 La COUR, TAGE, and MOGENSEN, HARALD. The Murder Book. London: George Allen & Unwin, pp. 97, 112, 116.
   A pictorial study of the crime story with an interestingly different point of view from that of American or English writers. Two pages devoted to Sayers--mostly biographical--in which it is mentioned that The Nine Tailors and Murder Must Advertise are still read with enthusiasm. A brief discussion of murder as a crime gives part of her theory of its popularity.

9 LINSENMEYER, JOHN. "Holmes and Wimsey: A Study in Similarities." Baker Street Journal 21:207-14.
   Discusses the similarities of these two in background, career, methods, and taste.

1971

10 SHIDELER, MARY McDERMOTT. Introduction to <u>Are Women Human?</u>
     Downers Grove, Ill.: Inter-Varsity Press, pp. 7-16.
        Speaks of Sayers's position on woman as a part of man-
     kind and her idea that "only the category of personhood is
     adequate for meeting the needs of women, or of society as a
     whole." Also discusses her idea that persons need to work.
     Illustrates from her writings, and comments on the coherence
     of her works.

11 SOLOWAY, SARA LEE. "Dorothy Sayers: Novelist." Ph.D. dis-
     sertation, University of Kentucky, 363 pp.
        Attempts to show that Sayers's novels have considerable
     literary merit for which she is rarely given credit. Dis-
     cusses at length Sayers's theory that the detective novel
     should have a place in the mainstream of literature, and
     could serve as a vehicle for the development of universal
     themes. In order to achieve this, the technical aspects of
     detective fiction must be combined with the development of
     themes and characters as in the novel of manners. Gives
     the plot and analyzes each of the detective novels in
     relation to her theory. Shows how her works offer a
     "criticism of life" and can truly be called "novels of
     manners."

12 STEWART, J. I. M. "Sayers, Dorothy Leigh, 1893-1957." In
     <u>Dictionary of National Biography, 1951-1960</u>. London:
     Oxford University Press, pp. 864-65.
        Aside from a few biographical facts, this is an analysis
     of Sayers's writings.

13 WATSON, COLIN. <u>Snobbery With Violence: Crime Stories and
     Their Audience</u>. London: Eyre & Spottiswoode, 256 pp.,
     passim.
        Says that detective fiction mirrors the thought and be-
     liefs of ordinary men and women. Feels that the tremen-
     dous fear of pauperdom in Victorian England brought with it
     an obsession with the idea of wealth, reflected in the
     literature of the times. Writers' attitudes become evi-
     dent and Sayers, one of the "most accomplished," was among
     the most snobbish. Explores the devices she used that
     showed her social and racial prejudices.

1972

1   ANON. Review of Lord Peter. Library Journal 97 (1 March):
      904.
          Nostalgic comments on Lord Peter as a childhood hero,
      and the impression received then of a debonair man of the
      world. Considers Sayers still one of the "super-stars" of
      mystery fiction.

2   ANON. Review of Murder Must Advertise. Bestsellers 31
      (1 February):496.
          Remarks that Sayers "loomed large in her lifetime" and
      here is a chance to renew or make her acquaintance. No
      other comment.

3   COMB, CLEMENT. "Novels Born in Quiet Fenland." Eastern Daily
      Press, 1 May.
          In this reply to Green's article of 17 April (1972.8),
      writes of Sayers from her days at Christchurch, and wonders
      at her topographical error. Gives some eyewitness accounts
      of where she spent her time writing out-of-doors.

4   DONG, DONNA. "Dorothy Sayers: An Artist for All Seasons."
      Right On (April):6-7.
          Using lengthy quotations from Sayers's work to illus-
      trate her ideas, the author discusses the variety and depth
      to be found in Sayers's writings. Compliments her talent
      for being graphic and dramatic.

5   DUNLAP, BARBARA [J.], and ROCKOW, KAREN. Review of Lord
      Peter. Unicorn 2 (Spring):20, 30.
          Consider this a disappointing collection of Sayers sto-
      ries because it is largely repetitive. Appreciate what
      new material there is. Wish for a better introduction,
      fuller bibliographic detail on the stories, a more imagina-
      tive dust jacket, and a greater unity of type faces. Re-
      mark that the stories are "a delight."

6   DUNLAP, BARBARA [J.]. "A Sayers Bibliography, Part 3."
      Unicorn 2, no. 2 (Spring):27, 31.
          Continues 1970.11, listing, with annotations, poetry,
      literary criticism, books edited by Sayers, her transla-
      tions, and selected secondary works of criticism. Con-
      tinued in 1973.8.

1972

7   EVERSON, WILLIAM K. The Detective in Film. Secaucus, N.J.:
    Citadel Press, pp. 192-93.
        Briefly discusses Lord Peter's role in two Sayers films:
    The Silent Passenger and Busman's Honeymoon (Haunted Honey-
    moon in the United States). Of the first he says it prob-
    ably failed as a result of poor casting. Considered the
    second an "enjoyable light thriller."

8   GREEN, CHARLES. "Action on the Map: East Anglian Topography
    and the 'Whodunit'." Eastern Daily Press, 17 April, p. 6.
        Comments on the value of reading with atlas at hand. In
    The Nine Tailors "the Fenland picture remains essentially
    true," but wonders why Sayers gave an obviously unmapped
    East Anglian background to Busman's Honeymoon. Remarks
    favorably on other characteristics of Strong Poison, Gaudy
    Night, and Busman's Honeymoon. Followed by "Letters to the
    Editor" on 20 April, 27 April, 28 April, 1 May, 2 May, and
    5 May.

9   HITCHMAN, JANET. "Lord Peter." Listener 87 (11 May):623.
        Beginning with a description of Lord Peter from the
    Sayers novels, Hitchman compares Bunter to Jeeves and Lord
    Peter to Bertie Wooster. Considers Sayers a middle-class
    romantic, a typical product of World War I Somerville,
    whose characters, both upper and lower classes, are stereo-
    types. Criticizes the detective novels and gives some bio-
    graphical material. (Taken from Hitchman's remarks on
    "Radio 3" at the time of the serialization of Clouds of
    Witness.) Followed by "Letters to the Editor" in the
    1 June and 15 June issues.

10 KEATING, H. R. F. "Crime." Times (London), 5 October, p. 10.
        Includes announcement of reissue of Sayers's In the
    Teeth of the Evidence. Single sentence calling it a
    "must."

11 LARMOTH, JEANINE, and TURGEON, CHARLOTTE. Murder on the Menu.
    New York: Scribner's, 283 pp., passim.
        A tongue-in-cheek discussion of the settings, atmosphere,
    philosophy, people, and foods found in detective fiction.
    Recipes, mostly British, are in sections at end of some
    chapters. Except for a chapter specifically on Lord Peter,
    the criticism is general and must be studied to understand
    how it deals with particular authors. Recipes are indexed.

12 NEWGATE CALLENDAR. "Criminals at Large." <u>New York Times Book Review</u>, 16 January, p. 42.

Review of <u>Lord Peter</u>. Says that Sayers will long be cherished, especially for her creation of Lord Peter Wimsey, in spite of her many other talents and interests, which he lists. Describes Wimsey and his England in glowing terms and compliments her on bringing them both to life. Says "her Lord Peter short stories are uneven but the Wimsey charm comes through."

13 REYNOLDS, STANLEY. "Clouds of Witness: BBC 1." <u>Times</u> (London), 6 April, p. 10.

Says that this dramatization of Sayers's novel will be watched as much for the reconstruction of the era as for its story. Enlarges on that idea.

14 ROUTLEY, ERIK. <u>The Puritan Pleasures of the Detective Story: A Personal Monograph</u>. London: Victor Gollancz, pp. 137-45, and passim.

Considers Sayers's attempts to combine the detective-story characteristics with those of the novel--noting where she succeeds and where she fails. Also discusses her short-story writing. Touches on the social assumptions on which she based her thinking. Mentions the fact that she was best known in the 1940s for her theological works and her drama: <u>The Man Born to Be King</u>. Thinks that the only religion to be found in her detective fiction is found in her fine portrayal of clergymen.

15 SAYERS, GERALD F. Review of <u>Clouds of Witness</u>. <u>Radio Times</u> (8 June).

Sayers's cousin states his pleasure with the TV performance, remarking that she would have approved of Ian Carmichael's portrayal.

16 SCOTT, WALTER. "Journey to the Fens." <u>Eastern Daily Press</u>, 20 April.

Replies to Charles Green's article of 17 April (1972.8), agreeing with him. Believes that Sayers's error was due to her haste to get <u>Busman's Honeymoon</u> from play to book form and to her being tired of Wimsey and therefore careless. In a further letter on 2nd May he thanks correspondents for their information about the route from Marsh to Downham via Denver, then wishes that some local person would write a biography of this "lucid, ingenious, and (in the Victorian sense) improving writer of our time."

1972

17 SYMONS, JULIAN. <u>Mortal Consequences: A History--From the</u>
    <u>Detective Story to the Crime Novel</u>. New York: Harper &
    Row, 269 pp., passim.
        Comments on the wide divergence of opinion on Sayers's
    novels. Admires her intelligence and craftsmanship in
    plotting the early novels but calls her writing padded,
    "pompous and boring." Feels that the characters are
    stereotyped and poorly portrayed, especially Lord Peter.
    Gives favorable criticism of several short stories, and
    mentions her criticism of crime fiction. British title:
    <u>Bloody Murder: From the Detective Story to the Crime</u>
    <u>Novel</u>.

18 WHITE, JEAN M. "For Vacation Reading." <u>Washington Post Book</u>
    <u>World</u> 6 (16 July):14.
        Mentions <u>Lord Peter</u>, a collection of stories from the
    "incomparable Dorothy L. Sayers."

<u>1973</u>

1   ALPERT, HOLLIS. "Will You Take Breadfast in Bed, My Lord?"
    <u>Saturday Review/World</u>, 9 October, p. 38.
        Review of the television version of <u>Clouds of Witness</u>.
    Comments that this series will further enhance Masterpiece
    Theatre's reputation. Remarks on the precision of details
    used by Sayers to show the period, on the touches of humor,
    and on the quality of the writing.

2   ANON. "The Cream of the Crop." <u>Anglican Digest</u> 15, no. 2
    (Second Quarter):27-29.
        Tells how Sayers's <u>A Matter of Eternity</u> originated and
    was edited by Rosamund Kent Sprague. Gives some biographi-
    cal information on both Sprague and Sayers. Quotes from
    Jellema's introduction to his edition of Sayers's <u>Christian</u>
    <u>Letters to a Post-Christian World</u> but offers no other
    critical commentary.

3   ANON. Review of <u>A Matter of Eternity</u>. <u>Choice</u> 10 (November):
    1406.
        Remarks briefly on the arrangement of these excerpts and
    that the editor, R. K. Sprague, considers it to be a devo-
    tional book. Comments on the broad scope of Sayers's
    writings.

4   ANON. Review of <u>A Matter of Eternity</u>. <u>Library Journal</u> 98
    (July):2072.
        No critical comment.

5   BASNEY, LIONEL. "God and Peter Wimsey." Christianity Today
     17 (14 September):27-28.
          Traces the change that takes place in Lord Peter and
     Harriet Vane in the Sayers novels, comparing these changes
     to the conversion of Dante. While Wimsey does not become a
     Christian, he becomes a more complete human being. Harriet
     learns to put aside her proud independence in order to ac-
     cept love. Although the lessons they learn are earthly,
     they reflect divine love.

6   BURLEIGH, ANN HUSTED, ed. Education In a Free Society.
     Indianapolis: Liberty Fund, pp. 17, 172.
          Sayers's paper "The Lost Tools of Learning" (pp. 145-67)
     was used as background material for the seminar at which
     the papers in this book were read and was included for that
     reason. Comments that it received unanimous acclaim. In-
     cludes brief biography.

7   CHRISTOPHER, JOE R[ANDELL]. "A Half-Member of the Inklings:
     Her Essays." Mythprint 7 (April):13.
          Review of Christian Letters to a Post-Christian World.
     Discusses this collection of Sayers's essays from the view-
     point of a Mythopoeic fan who would, from that standpoint,
     not be interested in all the essays. Points out which es-
     says would be of most interest to such a person and why.

8   CHRISTOPHER, JOE RANDELL. "A Sayers Bibliography, Parts 4, 5,
     and 6 (incomplete)." Unicorn 2, no. 5 (Christmas):28-30;
     3, no. 2 (Post-Fall 1974):51-52; 3, no. 3 (Summer 1976):
     87-89, 91.
          Continues 1972.6, listing and annotating the following
     primary materials: unpublished letters and letters to The
     Times; plus secondary materials complete to the letters Le.
     The remainder of the bibliography is awaiting publication.

9   E. S. "Dorothy L. Sayers--Unrecognized Genius." Braintree
     and Witham Times, 28 September.
          Considers the fact that Sayers had been Witham's most
     famous citizen and yet remained unrecognized. Gives bio-
     graphical information including a number of interesting
     facts--much of it from interviews with Sayers's former
     secretary.

10   HARDWICK, MICHAEL. A Literary Atlas & Gazeteer of the British
     Isles. Detroit: Gale Research, pp. 56, 57.
          Negligible for Sayers students, since it includes but
     two locations--both inaccurate: birth in Christchurch and
     living in Somersham, Huntingdonshire.

1973

11 LARSON, ROY. "Sayers' Writing Evokes Sophisticated '50s
      Nostalgia." Chicago Sun Times, 21 April, p. 16.
          Review of A Matter of Eternity. As the fifties welcomed
      Auden and Sayers, Larson wonders if the day will come again
      "when non-fundamentalist Christians will be able to witness
      to their faith with such confidence in themselves and their
      religion?" Discusses modern theology briefly. Remarks on
      Sayers's writings, mistakenly calls her a Roman Catholic.

12 LEJEUNE, ANTHONY. "Variations on a Theme." Tablet 227
      (2 June):516.
          Includes mention that a new edition of In the Teeth of
      the Evidence contains two Peter Wimsey stories not pre-
      viously found in books and one not previously published.
      Comments that "all right-minded lovers of detective fic-
      tion" must admire her.

13 NEWMAN, LOIS. Review of Clouds of Witness (Masterpiece Thea-
      tre production). Fantasiae 1, no. 8 (November):6.
          Happily reports that the BBC had "turned out a first-
      rate production." Comments on the sets, costumes, music,
      its close adherence to the book, and the acting.

14 O'CONNOR, JOHN J. "TV: Delightfully Whimsical Detective with
      Title." New York Times, 17 October, p. 94:3.
          Review of Clouds of Witness (Masterpiece Theatre produc-
      tion). Praises Ian Carmichael's portrayal of Sayers's Lord
      Peter and the evocation of the period through the settings
      used. Reviews in a complimentary way the plot, character-
      ization, some of the dialogue, and ends with some biograph-
      ical details of Sayers's life.

15 POWLEDGE, TABITHA M. "Lord Peter Wimsey Needs His Harriet."
      New York Times, 2 December, sec. 2, p. 19:1.
          Contends that the television versions of Sayers's novels
      pervert the themes with which Sayers attempted to deal in
      all of her fiction--particularly her feminist ideas. Dis-
      cusses Lord Peter and Harriet as persons. Considers Ian
      Carmichael's personification of Peter merely tolerable and
      not at all true to the man Sayers invented.

16 RAY, LAURA KRUGMAN. "The Mysteries of Gaudy Night: Feminism,
      Faith, and the Depths of Character." In The Mystery and
      Detection Annual. Beverly Hills, Calif.: D. Adams,
      pp. 272-85.
          Analyzes Sayers's development of Gaudy Night in terms of
      Sayers's own writing about the detective novel. Uses her
      essay "Gaudy Night" to tell what kind of novel this was

meant to be, then shows how Sayers developed it to accomplish her purpose. Discusses her method of changing Lord Peter from the original in Whose Body? to a fully rounded character in Gaudy Night. Deals at length with Sayers's handling of "the plight of the educated woman in reconciling her public and private roles" (or handling the subject of feminism). Concludes with a discussion of changes in Sayers's thinking revealed in The Mind of the Maker, published six years after Gaudy Night.

17   SCHEPER, GEORGE L. "A Lesser Known C. S. Lewis." National Catholic Reporter 10 (21 December):12-13.
Review of A Matter of Eternity. While hoping that more people will become acquainted with Sayers's non-fiction, does not feel that a book of excerpts does justice to the depths of her thinking or to her competence in writing. Adds Sayers to C. S. Lewis and Charles Williams as authors who state "simple truths wittily," especially valuable to people who have not grown up on G. K. Chesterton and Sister Corita.

18   SPRAGUE, ROSAMOND KENT, ed. Introduction to A Matter of Eternity: Selections from the Writings of Dorothy L. Sayers. Grand Rapids, Mich.: William B. Eerdmans, pp. 11-14.
Introduces Sayers as a writer and some of the Christian ideas on which her writings were based. Tells how Sayers once illustrated a lecture on change-ringing by assigning bell notes to groups of people and having them "ring" a change.

19   THOMSON, HENRY DOUGLAS. Masters of Mystery: A Study of the Detective Story. London: Folcroft Library Editions, 288 pp., passim.
In discussing the history of the detective story, quotes from Sayers's introduction to Great Short Stories of Detection, Mystery and Horror (American title: The Omnibus of Crime) to enforce his points of view. Also uses Sayers as author and Lord Peter as detective to illustrate his ideas. In addition, there are two pages of discussion of some of her stories.

20   WIMSATT, MARGARET. Review of A Matter of Eternity. America 128 (12 May):447.
Characterizes Sayers's writing according to the genre in which she was working. Gives some of her strengths and comments on the sentimentality in her detective fiction. Commends the editor of this collection, R. K. Sprague, on her selections.

1973

21 WILLIS, THOMAS. "Behind this 'Cloud' is a bit of Wimsey."
    Chicago Tribune Tempo, 10 October, sec. 2, p. 6.
        A delighted viewer gives his impression of the TV per-
    formance of Clouds of Witness.

                            1974

1 ACOCELLA, JOAN ROSE. "The Cult of Language: A Study of Two
    Modern Translations of Dante." Modern Language Quarterly
    35 (June):140-56.
        A lengthy comparison of The Divine Comedy translations
    of Sayers and John Ciardi. Considers them revisionist,
    shifting emphasis from the finished work to the tools used
    in producing it, thus leading to serious textual distor-
    tions. Gives examples. Concludes that they must still be
    given credit for viewing Dante in the light of their times.

2 ANON. Review of Lord Peter: A Collection of All the Lord
    Peter Wimsey Stories. Booklist 70 (1 February):573.
        Brief comment calling Lord Peter an "elegant, super de-
    tective," and stories a "delight."

3 BASNEY, LIONEL. "Dorothy Sayers and the Detective Novel."
    Paper read before the Houghton English Colloquium,
    February, processed, 25 pp.
        Examines detective fiction from the point of view of the
    literary critic, differentiating between detective fiction
    and other novels. Comments that a critical vocabulary has
    not been built to accommodate the criticism of detective
    fiction but that does not eliminate the need for such crit-
    icism. Considers Sayers's novels worthy of critical con-
    cern. Discusses the literary values of The Nine Tailors,
    concluding that the development of its plot is "deep enough
    and comprehensive enough for any 'serious' naturalistic
    novel," and that it brings us face to face with the Chris-
    tian perception that "human life is a lost and elusive
    paradise."

4 FEASTER, JOHN. Review of Strong Poison. Cresset 38 (Novem-
    ber):21.
        Expresses a wish that Sayers had been as prolific as
    Erle Stanley Gardner, and suggests giving her novels as
    stocking gifts. Especially comments on the pleasant back-
    ground for this novel--England in the twenties--and the
    cheerful personalities depicted.

5   GRELLA, GEORGE. "Dorothy Sayers and Peter Wimsey." The Uni-
    versity of Rochester Library Bulletin 28, no. 1 (Summer):
    33-42.
        Inspired by the appearance of Lord Peter and by tele-
    vision's adaptation of Sayers's novels, "stylishly done,"
    Grella here praises Sayers highly even while admitting that
    he does not particularly like Peter Wimsey. Accuses Sayers
    of falling in love with Lord Peter beginning with Strong
    Poison. Goes on to analyze the weaknesses of the Sayers/
    Lord Peter fiction--the despised middle class, anti-
    Semitism, a lack of timeliness, hostility to the new and
    unusual. Ends with a sarcastic appraisal of what a
    "gentleman amateur" would really be like and a disparage-
    ment of the American Anglophile.

6   HARRISON, BARBARA GRIZZUTI. "Dorothy Sayers and the Tidy Art
    of Detective Fiction." Ms 3, no. 5 (November):66-69,
    84-86, 89.
        Sees in Sayers's Gaudy Night a revelation of her
    feminism-cum-individualism, along with her talent as "the
    most austerely intelligent, the wittiest, liveliest prac-
    titioner of the tidy art of detective fiction." Discusses
    the feminism at some length.

7   HERMAN, LINDA, and STIEL, BETH. Corpus Delicti of Mystery
    Fiction: A Guide to the Body of the Case. Metuchen, N.J.:
    Scarecrow Press, 180 pp., passim.
        A manual for would-be collectors and/or readers of de-
    tective fiction. Discusses its value, history, develop-
    ment, and available reference works. Brief biographical
    sketch and list of works given for fifty representative
    authors. A summary of Sayers's themes precedes a list of
    her novels.

8   HITCHMAN, JANET. "Introduction: Lord Peter Wimsey and His
    Creator." In Striding Folly, Including Three Final Lord
    Peter Wimsey Stories. London: New English Library,
    pp. 9-31.
        Discusses Sayers's personality, her characterization of
    Wimsey whom she likens to King Arthur, the reflection of
    society in her detective novels, their content aside from
    the detective angle, and their humor. Avers that "Wimsey
    has survived, and will continue to survive, because he is
    well written, beautifully constructed, and above all,
    amusing."

1974

9 KRUITHOF, BASTIAN. Review of A Matter of Eternity. Calvin
   Theological Journal 9 (April):81-82.
       Classes Sayers with C. S. Lewis, Charles Williams, and
   G. K. Chesterton as a "brilliant and stimulating" writer.
   Remarks that this book demonstrates her view that Chris-
   tianity gives a rational explanation of the universe. In-
   cludes examples. Comments at length on The Lost Tools of
   Learning. Concludes that her works deserve wider reading.

10 O'CONN[O]R, JOHN J. "Lord Peter Wimsey is Back in Mystery."
    New York Times, 7 October, p. 71:4.
        Comments that there are enough "delightful moments" in
    the TV dramatization of Murder Must Advertise to make it
    worth watching. Nevertheless says it has several weak-
    nesses, which he discusses.

11 ORTON, PETER. "Campaign of the Century." Campaign (3 May):
    34-37.
        An illustrated story of the beginnings and successes of
    the Mustard Club, an advertising scheme of the firm of
    S. H. Benson for J. Colman. Attributes the idea to Oswald
    Green of the advertising agency. Sayers was a copywriter
    at Benson's at the time. Says Colman's thinks she was a
    contributor but has no confirmed evidence for this.

12 PETERS, MARGOT, and KROUSE, AGATE NESAULE. "Women and Crime:
    Sexism in Allingham, Sayers, and Christie." Southwest
    Review 59 (Spring):144-52.
        Compare the sexist attitudes of Allingham, Sayers, and
    Christie, finding Christie "offends the least, but still
    offends." Use examples from the novels to substantiate
    their conclusions. Credit Sayers with one "redeeming
    quality--her accurate recording of the problems of single,
    intelligent, independent women."

13 ROCKOW, KAREN. "Blowing the Whistle on Dorothy Sayers and
    Lord Peter." Unicorn 3, no. 2 (Post-Fall):37-38, 45.
        Discusses some grievances against Sayers and her Lord
    Peter, appearing at times to be tongue-in-cheek, at other
    times genuine.

14 WHELPTON, ERIC. The Making of a European. London: Johnson,
    pp. 126, 128, 138.
        Discusses his view of the relationship between Sayers
    and himself and of Sayers as a person. Comments on the
    way in which she gathered some of the source materials for
    her detective fiction.

15   WHITAKER, CHRISTE ANNE. "An Introductory Paper on Dorothy
      Sayers." In Mythcon III Proceedings. Whittier, Calif.:
      Mythopoeic Society, pp. 40-44.
         Discusses the integrity of Sayers's work in the light of
      her thinking on creativity. Illustrates from Sayers's
      writings.

                              1975

1   ADAMS, PHOEBE-LOU. Review of Such a Strange Lady, by Janet
      Hitchman. Atlantic Monthly 236 (December):118.
         Remarks that, in spite of limited access to information
      and her own lack of deep interest, Hitchman has managed a
      surface account of Sayers's "rather dismal" life.

2   ANNAN, GABRIELE. "Born To Be Middle." Listener 93
      (30 January):157-58.
         Following a summary of Such a Strange Lady comments on
      Sayers's life and writing. Says she was brilliant, liked
      the company of men, but lacked understanding of non-
      academic and lower class women, "hag-ridden by the spectre
      of spinsterhood." Her detective novels show her limited
      knowledge of any but the "middle middle" classes. She was
      "the captive of her generation of 2,000,000 surplus women--
      and that was the pathos of her life."

3   ANON. "Critics Crowner." Bookseller (8 March):1700.
         A resumé of what a number of critics said about Such a
      Strange Lady, by Janet Hitchman, including quotations.

4   ANON. Review of Further Papers on Dante. Reprint Bulletin
      Book Reviews 20, no. 2 (Summer):32.
         Remarks that while the essays in the earlier work,
      Introductory Papers on Dante, dealt mainly with theological
      and ethical aspects of the Divine Comedy, these deal with
      the literary and poetic aspects. Speaks of Sayers's
      Christian theological point of view and her argument that
      Dante's spiritual creed should not be separated from his
      "poetic achievement."

5   ANON. Review of Such a Strange Lady, by Janet Hitchman.
      Christian Century 92 (3 December):1116.
         Brief comments to the effect that Hitchman found little
      to love in Sayers and presents her as a "most unpleasant
      person."

1975

6   ANON. Review of <u>Such a Strange Lady</u>, by Janet Hitchman.
    <u>Kirkus Reviews</u> 43 (1 September):1035.
        Tells something of what Hitchman says about the book.
    Gives some of its details. Characterizes Sayers in her own
    terms from her introduction to <u>The Omnibus of Crime</u>: "A
    very odd piece of work indeed, a mystery." Concludes that
    further writing about Sayers may not make as pleasant
    reading.

*7 ANON.[?] Review of <u>Such a Strange Lady</u>, by Janet Hitchman.
    <u>Observer</u>, 2 March, p. 25.
        Cited in <u>Book Review Index</u>. Detroit: Gale Research,
    1975, p. 232.

8   ANON. Review of <u>Such a Strange Lady</u>, by Janet Hitchman.
    <u>Publishers Weekly</u> 208 (22 September):125.
        No critical comment.

*9 ANON.[?] "Sayers's Model for Lord Peter Wimsey." <u>Sunday
    Times</u>, 23 March, p. 32.
        Cited in <u>Times Index</u>. London: Times, (January–March),
    p. 295.

10 BACKHOUSE, JANET. Review of <u>Such a Strange Lady</u>, by Janet
    Hitchman. <u>Times Literary Supplement</u>, 14 March, p. 279.
        Criticizes special points in the Hitchman biography for
    lack of research and poor chronology.

11 BARNES, MELVYN. "Queens of Crime." In <u>The Best Detective
    Fiction: A Guide from Godwin to the Present</u>. Hamden,
    Conn.: Linnet Books, pp. 48–50.
        Reviews some of Sayers's work among that of other
    detective-fiction writers whose works represent "the high-
    est standards." Considers <u>The Documents in the Case</u> her
    most unusual, <u>Hangman's Holiday</u> skillful short stories, <u>The
    Nine Tailors</u> well-balanced as to detective puzzle and back-
    ground, and <u>Gaudy Night</u> a well-portrayed university novel.

12 BERNIKOW, LOUISE. Review of <u>Such a Strange Lady</u>, by Janet
    Hitchman. <u>New York Times Book Review</u>, 9 November, sec. 7,
    p. 51.
        Says that this, in spite of the author's limited source
    material, is "awfully intelligent, compassionate, interest-
    ing, and . . . a very good read."

1975

13   BRADY, CHARLES A. "The Lady Proves Fascinating; But the Book
     is Inadequate." Buffalo Evening News, 4 October.
          Review of Such a Strange Lady, by Janet Hitchman. De-
     scribes this book as "fascinating" on account of its sub-
     ject, but otherwise "inadequate, undistinguished, pell-mell,
     curiously unsympathetic."

14   CARY, NORMAN REED. "The Creative Act in Theology and Art."
     In Christian Criticism in the Twentieth Century: Theologi-
     cal Approaches to Literature. Port Washington, N.Y.:
     National University, Kennikat Press, pp. 60-62, 120.
          In his discussion of the implications of the Trinitarian
     doctrine for creativity, includes discussion of Sayers's
     concept of creativity from her book The Mind of the Maker.

15   CATTOI, LOUISE. "That Strange Sayers Woman." Milwaukee Jour-
     nal, 26 October.
          Review of Such a Strange Lady, by Janet Hitchman. A
     synopsis with two critical comments, remarking that it is
     "sympathetically presented" and wishing for an index.

16   CHRISTOPHER, JOE R[ANDELL]. "Charles and Dorothy." Mythprint
     11 (March):3.
          Cited in Christopher, 1973.8.

17   COLE, MARGARET. "Frustration and Success." Books and Bookmen
     20 (May):35-36.
          In this review of Hitchman's Such a Strange Lady, com-
     pares Sayers's popularity with Agatha Christie's in the
     early years of Sayers's writing and later, after she quit
     writing detective fiction. Remarks about her wandering
     popularity as she turned to religious drama and broadcast-
     ing, and its revival with the Lord Peter television series
     and The Man Born To Be King television drama. Comments on
     the good and bad points of Hitchman's book remarking that
     it is "not quite just" and that Sayers deserved better.

18   COX, J. RANDOLPH. "Detection in the Guilt-Age." Armchair
     Detective 8, no. 2 (February):111-20.
          Very briefly discusses the history of Sayers's detective-
     fiction writing from Whose Body? through Busman's Honeymoon,
     commenting that her characters became more real as she went
     along. Sees her as a representative of the Golden Age of
     detective fiction throughout its course.

1975

19 CRADDOCK, JOHN. Review of Such a Strange Lady, by Janet
    Hitchman. Sunday News and Courier/Charleston (S.C.)
    Evening Post, 26 October.
        Calls this a "series of sketches" tritely written and
    having faulty chronology.

20 DUPREY, RICHARD A. "Plays or Penances." In Just Off the
    Aisle: The Ramblings of a Catholic Critic. Westminster,
    Md.: Newman Press, pp. 188, 191.
        Compares Sayers to Henri Ghéon, a French religious play-
    wright, commenting that they both received their ideas for
    their plays from many sources and wrote in much the same
    style. Gives as the major difference Sayers's "formality
    as opposed to Ghéon's almost childlike candor."

21 EAMES, JOHN DOUGLAS. The MGM Story: The Complete History of
    Over Fifty Roaring Years. New York: Crown, p. 165.
        Short movie reviews arranged by year include Busman's
    Honeymoon/Haunted Honeymoon, made in 1940. Lists author,
    stars, brief history, and includes one illustration.
    Assesses the movie as "lightweight" causing little
    excitement.

22 ESSEX, ROSAMUND. "In Bad Taste?" Church Times (28 February):
    7.
        Review of Such a Strange Lady, by Janet Hitchman.
    Recognizes that Hitchman lacked much information that would
    have made a better biography, but feels that she was unkind
    in her emphasis--failing to bring out Sayers's true worth
    as a person, yet making much of her faults.

23 FRANKENBURG, CHARIS URSULA. Not Old, Madam, Vintage; An
    Autobiography. Suffolk: Galaxy Press, 196 pp., passim.
        A long-time friend of Sayers mentions her several times.

24 GILBERT, MICHAEL. "Mistress of Murder." Sunday Telegraph,
    2 March, p. 13.
        Reviews Such a Strange Lady, by Janet Hitchman, consider-
    ing it a fitting introduction to the sort of person and
    writer Sayers was. Feels that a scholarly biography, com-
    plete with footnotes and bibliography, would not become her
    in spite of the fact that she added a great deal to the
    lives of those who knew her and read her works. Comments
    on the quality of her detective stories and their staying
    power, and says that the depiction of her characters shows
    some lack of imagination.

25 GREEN, PETER. "A Clergyman's Daughter." <u>Times Literary</u>
    <u>Supplement</u>, 28 February, pp. 223-24.
        A study of Sayers's life (from its Good Fairy/Bad Fairy
    beginning to its end) and her work from both his own knowl-
    edge and <u>Such a Strange Lady</u>, by Janet Hitchman. Wonders
    why Hitchman was chosen and if it was necessary for the
    book to be so "slapdash." Comments that "if her [Sayers's]
    life was, in several respects, a tragedy, her professional
    career verged on the epic."

26 HANSCOM, LESLIE. "Lord Peter's Peculiar Creator." <u>Newsday</u>,
    12 October.
        Review of <u>Such a Strange Lady</u>, by Janet Hitchman. A
    synopsis. Commends Hitchman for the apt title and for
    bringing "alive the personality of a very strange lady
    indeed."

27 HARRISON, JOSEPH G. "The Woman Behind Detective Peter
    Wimsey." <u>Christian Science Monitor</u>, 10 November, p. 18.
        Review of <u>Such a Strange Lady</u>, by Janet Hitchman.
    Praises both the biographer and the biographee. Feels that
    this interesting biography would have been finer for having
    had use of better resources, but that it gives the first
    glimpse of what a fascinating person Sayers was.

28 HART, HAROLD. "Accident, Suicide, or Murder? A Question of
    Stereochemistry." <u>Journal of Chemical Education</u> 52 (July):
    444.
        This review by a chemist of <u>The Documents in the Case</u>
    notes the scientific errors: the Sayers/Eustace formula
    for synthetic muscarine was inaccurate and should have been
    known to be so, and the sodium flame described as green
    should have been yellow. Even so, considers the book en-
    joyable, especially to organic chemists.

29 HITCHMAN, JANET. <u>Such a Strange Lady: An Introduction to</u>
    <u>Dorothy L. Sayers (1893-1957)</u>. London: New English
    Library, 203 pp.
        An entertaining, tantalizing introduction to the life of
    Sayers. Written without access to her personal papers,
    Hitchman admits that much is "supposition, a reading be-
    tween the lines of her published work."

30 _____. "'This Blasphemous Outrage': The Row Over <u>The Man</u>
    <u>Born To Be King</u>." <u>Listener</u> 93 (30 January):140-42.
        Combines discussion of the controversy with excerpts
    from interviews--with the producer, Val Gielgud; with the
    actors, John Laurie and Robert Speaight; with Sayers; with

1975

a spokesman for the loudest protestor, a member of the
Lord's Day Observance Society--and with letters from Dr.
James Welch, BBC's Director of Religious Broadcasting.

31 KEATING, H. R. F. Murder Must Appetize. London: Lemon Tree
    Press, 63 pp., passim.
        Includes Sayers's works in a discussion of the qualities
    that avid readers were looking for in the "golden" days of
    detective fiction. Calls her the "co-queen" of the age.

32 LOCHHEAD, MARION. Review of Such a Strange Lady, by Janet
    Hitchman. Library Review 25, no. 2 (Summer):89.
        Remarks that Hitchman finds Sayers a good writer but an
    unlovable person. Comments on Sayers's writings, briefly
    mentioning her story-telling ability, her scholarship, and
    her prefaces to the Dante translation.

33 MAIO, KATHLEEN L. Unnatural Woman: A Feminist Study of
    Dorothy L. Sayers. Women and Literature Ovular.
    Goddard/Cambridge Graduate Center, (October), 98 pp.,
    processed.
        A study of the feminist aspects of Sayers's writing.
    Discusses each novel from the point of view that Sayers was
    a feminist though not always recognized as such, even by
    herself. Has a chapter on Sayers's elitism.

34 MARSHALL, ARTHUR. Review of Such a Strange Lady, by Janet
    Hitchman. New Statesman 89 (21 March):386-87.
        Credits Hitchman with giving an endearing portrait of
    Sayers in spite of the lack of help from the Sayers family
    and executors. Comments on the increasing interest in
    Sayers.

35 MEISER, BARBARA F. Review of Such a Strange Lady, by Janet
    Hitchman. Library Journal 100 (1 November):2043-44.
        Recommends this biography of Sayers for Wimsey fans.
    Calls it readable but "unmeticulous."

36 MILES, CLARK. "Such a Strange Lady." Pasadena Star News,
    9 November.
        Senses, after reading this book by Janet Hitchman, that
    Sayers was a series of paradoxes.

37 MINER, VIRGINIA SCOTT. "There Could Be No Happiness for Bril-
    liant Dorothy L. Sayers." Kansas City Star, 23 November.
        Review of Such a Strange Lady, by Janet Hitchman. A
    synopsis without critical comment.

38 MORAN, MAUREEN; PAINTER, SUSAN; and REDMOND, JAMES. "The
    Twentieth Century." Year's Work in English Studies
    56:366-67.
        Includes comments on Such a Strange Lady, by Janet
    Hitchman. Complains of the lack of critical analysis, and
    the "ludicrous and embarrassing" use of asides and slang.
    Concludes that future biographers will thank her but "fu-
    ture work there must indeed be."

39 MYERS, DORIS T. "Lord Peter Wimsey's Answer to Pilate."
    Cimarron Review, no. 33 (October):26-34.
        Contends that Sayers replies to Pilate's question, "What
    is truth?" in her detective novels as well as in some of
    her other works. Discusses Sayers's ideas of truth as
    found in the novels, giving examples to substantiate her
    conclusions. Brief bibliography.

40 NEVIN, JOY LYNN. "Strange Life of Dorothy Sayers." San
    Rafael Independent Journal, 8 November.
        Review of Such a Strange Lady, by Janet Hitchman. Sees
    this as an "unimaginative, vaguely hostile account," whose
    author "does not appreciate the intelligence and humor of
    the Wimsey books." Nevertheless, gives Hitchman credit for
    holding the reader's interest.

41 P. H. S. "The Times Diary." Times (London), 10 January,
    p. 14.
        Reports an interview with John Laurie who played John
    the Baptist and Judas in the radio performances of The Man
    Born To Be King both in 1941 and 1975. Laurie briefly re-
    calls the disputes and difficulties accompanying the 1941
    broadcast.

42 ROBINSON, KENNETH. "'Cleverer Than What I Am'." Listener 93
    (10 April):472-73.
        Reviews the updated edition of The Man Born To Be King
    for rebroadcasting. Comments on favorable and unfavorable
    changes made and on his own reaction to the dialogue and
    the portrayal of Christ. Considers the cast, musicians,
    and producer excellent. For Sayers he borrows the line
    from her Matthew--'A lot cleverer than what I am'.

43 SATTERTHWAITE, ALFRED W. "To the Editor: Such a Strange
    Lady." Times Literary Supplement, 28 March, p. 338.
        This stepson of John Cournos objects to Peter Green's
    speculations (TLS 28 February 1975) concerning the rela-
    tionship between Sayers and Cournos.

1975

44   WADE, ROSALIND. "Dorothy Sayers: An Appreciation."
      Contemporary Review (London) 226 (June):332-33.
          Review of Such a Strange Lady, by Janet Hitchman. Along
      with a few points made about Hitchman's Sayers biography,
      reviewer briefly mentions some facts about Sayers's life
      and works.

45   WALSH, ANNE C. "Mysteries: Literary Chic for Autumn Read-
      ing." Phoenix Gazette Marquee Books, 11 October, p. 18.
          Includes some of the biographical notes from Such a
      Strange Lady, by Janet Hitchman, with no critical comment
      except that Americans are apt to devour it.

                            1976

1   ANON. "Do You Remember the Mustard Club?" Witham, Essex:
      Dorothy L. Sayers Historical and Literary Society.
      Archives, 6.16, processed, 2 pp.
          Handout produced by Colman's for their 1976 Mustard Club
      anniversary. Includes information that Sayers wrote most
      of the advertising copy for the Club and Club's recipe
      book. Recipes were concocted and tested by her husband,
      O. A. Fleming.

2   ANON. Review of Such a Strange Lady, by Janet Hitchman.
      Booklist 72 (15 January):662.
          Brief resumé.

3   ANON. Review of Such a Strange Lady, by Janet Hitchman.
      Choice 12 (February):1571.
          Considers it a "good depiction of Sayer's [sic] enthu-
      siastic, untidy life." Mentions differences between Ameri-
      can and English editions.

4   ANON. "Society Formed to Honour Dorothy Sayers." Times
      (London), 29 March, p. 16.
          Announces the formation of The Dorothy L. Sayers His-
      torical and Literary Society, its location, purposes, and
      director, Mr. R. L. Clarke. Calls Sayers the "creator of
      that most elegant of sleuths, Lord Peter Wimsey; translator
      of The Divine Comedy into terza rima; and popular
      theologian."

5   CASEY, ELLEN MILLER. Review of <u>Such a Strange Lady</u>, by Janet
    Hitchman. <u>Bestsellers</u> 35 (11 February):358-59.
        Recognizes that Sayers would have disliked this book be-
    cause she carefully guarded her privacy. Finds Hitchman an
    unsympathetic biographer, not liking mysteries, apologetics,
    or Dante. Also comments on the poor quality of the writing,
    although appreciating the fact that it whets the appetite
    for a better study.

6   CAWELTI, JOHN G. "The Art of the Classical Detective Story."
    In <u>Adventure, Mystery, and Romance: Formula Stories as Art</u>
    <u>and Popular Culture</u>. Chicago: University of Chicago Press,
    pp. 106-38.
        Discusses Sayers's detective fiction as among that at
    the top of the classical detective story and the reasons
    for his conclusions. Uses <u>The Nine Tailors</u> to illustrate.
    Compares her work primarily to that of Agatha Christie.

7   CHRISTOPHER, JOE R[ANDELL]. "Detective Fiction in the Wade
    Collection." <u>Armchair Detective</u> 9, no. 4 (October):274-75.
        Gives a brief history of the Wade Collection at Wheaton
    College in Illinois and discusses its scope.

*8 _____. "Dorothy L. Sayers and the Inklings." <u>Mythlore</u> 4
    (September):8-9.
        Cited in his "An Inkling Bibliography." <u>Mythlore</u> 4
    (March):34.

9   _____. "Dorothy Leigh Sayers: A Chronology." <u>Sayers Review</u>
    1, no. 1 (September):1-13.
        As each bibliographer builds on the work of another this
    chronology is built on information from Hitchman's <u>Such a</u>
    <u>Strange Lady</u> and Sandoe's "Contributions Toward a Bibliog-
    raphy of Dorothy L. Sayers," with additions from his own
    research. Includes entries from her birth in 1893 to 1975,
    giving biographical data, dates of her published works,
    speeches, and dramatic works.

10 _____. "Wimseycalities: The Doyle Syndrome." <u>Sayers Review</u>
    1, no. 1 (September):26-27.
        Reviewing in poetic form the incidents involving detec-
    tives who disappear or die, then reappear, suggests that
    Sayers was right to stop the Wimsey stories.

1976

11   CLARKE, RALPH L., and CLARKE, MOLLY. A Summary of the Life
      and Works of Dorothy L. Sayers, D. Litt. MA (Oxon).
      Witham, Essex: Dorothy L. Sayers Historical and Literary
      Society. Archives, 6.1, processed, 8 pp.
           A factual account of the life of Sayers and some com-
      mentary on her work. This will be updated and corrected as
      further information is available. Includes one addendum
      and data on the founding of the Society.

12   CURRAN, TERRIE. "The Word Made Flesh: The Christian Aesthetic
      in Dorothy L. Sayers' The Man Born To Be King." Sayers Re-
      view 1, no. 1 (September):14-25.
           Using quotations from several of Sayers's works, Curran
      discusses the development of characters, particularly Judas,
      in The Man Born To Be King to show whether or not it is in
      line with Sayers's philosophy of a Christian aesthetic as
      stated in "Towards a Christian Aesthetic" and in The Mind
      of the Maker. Compares her solutions to some of the prob-
      lems of the drama with solutions to similar problems in the
      Medieval Mystery Cycles. Reprinted in 1979.29.

13   DOROTHY L. SAYERS HISTORICAL AND LITERARY SOCIETY. Bulletin.
      Witham, Essex: Dorothy L. Sayers Historical and Literary
      Society.
           Includes news notes of various sorts, items of informa-
      tion related to Sayers and the Society, and notices of new
      books, sometimes with reviews.

14   _____. Proceedings of the Seminar, 1976-. Witham, Essex:
      Dorothy L. Sayers Historical and Literary Society.
      Archives, 6.18, processed.
           Papers presented at the annual seminar held at the home
      of the Society, Witham, Essex, England.

15   EPISCOPAL BOOK CLUB (Eureka Springs, Ark.) Embertidings
      (Spring):[1-6].
           Announces Sayers's Emperor Constantine as the club's
      book selection for its members. Discusses her idea of the
      excitement to be found in the divine drama (the Gospel) as
      seen in some of her works, including this play. Gives some
      biographical and bibliographical facts. Admits to her be-
      ing strange in some ways but calls her a "remarkable per-
      son," skillful in writing and translating, and "a superb
      and intelligible theologian and a fearless defender of
      sound doctrine."

1976

16 ETHERIDGE, ANNE. "Lord Peter Returns, Followed by Murder."
    New York Times, 19 December, sec. 2, pp. 33-34.
        Most of this is a discussion of Ian Carmichael's career,
    including the effort that went into persuading someone to
    produce the Sayers detective stories for television. Also
    includes some discussion of the extensive work done on all
    BBC productions. Compares Carmichael and Wimsey, but
    merely mentions Sayers as author of the then-running Five
    Red Herrings.

17 FULLER, EDMUND. "Hercule Poirot's Last Case." Wall Street
    Journal, 14 June, p. 12.
        Includes review of Such a Strange Lady, by Janet
    Hitchman, commenting that it is "written with balance, per-
    ception, compassion, and wit," and justifying its title.
    Praises the "extraordinary versatility" of Sayers's work.
    Ranks her with Christie as one of the two great ladies of
    detective fiction, viewing The Nine Tailors as "transcend-
    ing the category in many ways." Says she produced some of
    the "most closely reasoned Christian apologetical writing
    in the modern Anglican Church." Calls her translation of
    Dante "crackling, stimulating, controversial."

18 GRELLA, GEORGE. "Murder and Manners: The Formal Detective
    Novel." In Dimensions of Detective Fiction. Edited by
    L. N. Landrum, Pat Browne, and R. B. Browne. Bowling
    Green, Ohio: Popular Press, pp. 37-57.
        Discusses the characteristics of the detective novel,
    illustrating several of them from the works of Sayers.

19 HITCHMAN, JANET. "Champagne in the Well." Listener 95
    (4 March):264.
        In an article on a variety of subjects, discusses the
    quality of book-reviewing in America, as seen in reviews of
    Such a Strange Lady. Her objection is not to what was said
    but the poor quality of the writing--not professional but
    as if done by college students. Admits that other writers
    may not share her impressions.

20 _____. "Times Past." Listener 95 (8 January):23.
        In this article on radio programing, she quotes from a
    talk never given by Dorothy L. Sayers "(because the men did
    not like it)" but which was later published as "The Human-
    Not-Quite-Human."

1976

21   HOFFMAN, NANCY Y. "Mistresses of Malfeasance." In <u>Dimensions</u>
     <u>of Detective Fiction</u>. Edited by L. N. Landrum, Pat Browne,
     and R. B. Browne. Bowling Green, Ohio: Popular Press,
     pp. 99-101.
        Calls Sayers an "astute crime critic, creator of the
     Lord Peter Wimsey stories, fascinated by the potential in
     the union of crime and medical science." Says Sayers "im-
     plicitly predicted in her stories [that] the modern world
     would fear its scientists while seeking science's cure-
     alls," and "science fiction is replacing the detective
     story."

22   HOLLOW, JOHN. Review of <u>Such a Strange Lady</u>, by Janet
     Hitchman. <u>Ohio Review</u> 17, no. 2 (Winter):102-5.
        A critical review, characterizing the book as "short and
     forced." Complains of Hitchman's failure to properly as-
     sess Sayers's detective fiction and her Dante work. Also
     laments her failure to confront the problem of responsi-
     bility of Sayers toward her husband and child while ignor-
     ing how much she did for both. Concludes with an imagined
     Wimsey comment, "She is Miss Sayers, don't you know."

23   LACHMAN, MARVIN. Review of <u>Such a Strange Lady</u>, by Janet
     Hitchman. <u>Mystery Nook</u> (August).
        Feels that, even deprived of many Sayers resources,
     Hitchman could have discussed Sayers's work in the field
     of detective fiction. Nevertheless, finds it an interest-
     ing study of her life.

24   KING, DANIEL P. Review of <u>Such a Strange Lady</u>, by Janet
     Hitchman. <u>Books Abroad</u> 50 (Summer):664.
        Comments that Hitchman best describes her own book as
     an "introduction" to Sayers.

25   LARSON, JANET KARSTEN. "Jolly Strange Lady." <u>Christian</u>
     <u>Century</u> 93 (28 April):419-21.
        Review of <u>Such a Strange Lady</u>, by Janet Hitchman. Dis-
     cusses both the biography and Sayers's works. Criticizes
     Hitchman for using less-than-adequate resources, thus fail-
     ing to give glimpses of the true Sayers. Remarks that
     Sayers's works show an understanding of the oneness of the
     aesthetic upon which they are all based.

26   McMENOMY, CHRISTE [ANN]. "British Sayers Studies: The
     Dorothy L. Sayers Historical and Literary Society."
     <u>Sayers Review</u> 1, no. 1 (September):28.
        Announces the formation of the society in 1976 and in-
     cludes a report from the secretary, R. L. Clarke.

27 O'CONNOR, JOHN J. Review of Five Red Herrings (Masterpiece
    Theatre production). New York Times, 17 December, sec. 3,
    p. 26:1.
        Brief resumé with little critical comment other than
    that Ian Carmichael bears "scant physical but ample stylish
    resemblance" to Sayers's Lord Peter.

28 PATON-SMITH, SHEILA LAKE. "Memories of D. L. S." Dorothy L.
    Sayers Historical and Literary Society. Archives, 6.28,
    processed, 13 pp. in 6.
        Enlightening reminiscences about Sayers by those who
    knew her.

29 Sayers Review 1- (September 1976-).
        A journal of miscellany which furnishes a hearing for
    Sayers material of various sorts, primarily literary writ-
    ings about her and her works. Other information is in-
    cluded; that is, announcements of meetings, forthcoming
    works, reviews, bibliographies, etc. Edited by Christe
    McMenomy.

30 SCHREURS, ANN. "Letter." Dorothy L. Sayers Historical and
    Literary Society. Archives, 5.2, processed, 4 pp.
        The daughter of Sayers's husband discusses his marriages
    and her disagreement with Janet Hitchman's account of him
    in Such a Strange Lady.

31 SPEROW, CAROLE. "An Introduction to Dorothy Sayers."
    Chronicle of the Portland C. S. Lewis Society 5 (July-
    September):3-12.
        An analysis of Sayers's thought as revealed primarily in
    her essays and plays. Discusses four concepts in particu-
    lar: Christian doctrine, Creativity and Work, Education,
    and Women. Adds some comments on some of Sayers's other
    viewpoints.

32 SWEETING, EVE. "The Reluctant Lord Peter Wimsey."
    Colchester Evening Gazette, 9 June.
        An interview with Eric Whelpton, erstwhile friend of
    Sayers, in which he discusses that friendship.

33 TILLINGHAST, RICHARD. "Dorothy L. Sayers: Murder and
    Whimsy." New Republic 175 (31 July):30-31.
        Gives a brief biographical sketch, commenting on some of
    Sayers's works. Remarks that her verse translations of
    Dante "show that she had no ear for poetry." Feels that
    romance stood in the way of pure detective writing, but
    what she lacked in plot she often made up for in atmosphere
    and characterization. In his discussion of Lord Peter and
    Harriet he wonders who Lord Peter personifies.

1976

34   WOLFE, PETER. Review of <u>Such a Strange Lady</u>, by Janet
       Hitchman. <u>Journal of Popular Culture</u> 10 (Fall):454-55.
            A resumé interspersed with some critical remarks. Com-
       pliments Hitchman on telling the Sayers story "with wit and
       warmth."

<u>1977</u>

1   AIRD, CATHERINE. "The Devout: Benefit of Clergy." In <u>Murder
       Ink</u>. Edited by Dilys Winn. New York: Workman, p. 469.
            A single paragraph discussing Sayers's two "affectionate
       pen portraits of Anglican clergymen."

2   BAKER, RUSSELL. "A Gentleman's Gentleman." <u>New York Times</u>,
       30 January, sec. 6, p. 6.
            Mentally impersonating Lord Bellamy (?), Baker, in his
       Sunday spoof, is threatening to replace his butler, Hudson,
       and looks at Sayers's and Lord Peter's Bunter as a true
       gentleman's gentleman--a man superior to the gentleman he
       serves and who still maintains his impeccable behavior.

3   BANDER, ELAINE. "The Case for <u>Sir Charles Grandison</u>: A Note
       on Barbara Reynolds's 'The Origin of Lord Peter Wimsey'."
       <u>Sayers Review</u> 1, no. 4 (July):8-9.
            Argues that Sir Charles, of Samuel Richardson's <u>Sir
       Charles Grandison</u>, might have served Sayers as the model
       for Lord Peter Wimsey, although considering him a less
       likely one than Philip Trent as contended for by Barbara
       Reynolds. See 1978.34.

4   _____. "Dorothy L. Sayers and the Apotheosis of Detective
       Fiction." <u>Armchair Detective</u> 10 (October):362-65.
            Shows the transformation of Sayers's work from the early
       solution of puzzle-type problems by Lord Peter in her de-
       tective fiction, through the themes of her novels of man-
       ners and Lord Peter's changing from a "cardboard character"
       to a more human one, to her discussions of genuine problems
       of life in "The Wimsey Papers" in the <u>Spectator</u> during the
       early months of World War II, when she used Lord Peter as
       her spokesman.

5   BRENION, FREDERICK M. "Theology for Average People." <u>Sayers
       Review</u> 1, no. 4 (July):14-15.
            Quotes from two Sayers letters: one reprinted in <u>An
       Introduction to Religious Philosophy</u> by Geddes MacGregor,
       suggesting that people go to the primary source to learn
       about God instead of asking her; the other reprinted in

The Revolt Against Reason by Arnold Lunn, concerning scholastics and their arguments about angels.

6 CARMICHAEL, IAN. "The BBC Through a Monocle." In Murder Ink. Edited by Dilys Winn. New York: Workman, pp. 109-12.
Relates the difficulties encountered with the BBC after Carmichael's agent had suggested he prepare to do a Lord Peter television series. Comments on his enjoyment of the preparation and the role.

7 CASSIS, A. F. The Twentieth-Century English Novel: An Annotated Bibliography of General Criticism. New York: Garland, 436 pp., passim.
Lists critical "works on the English novel as a literary genre," arranged as follows: criticism in books, in periodical literature, and in dissertations.

8 CHRISTOPHER, JOE R[ANDELL]. "The Delightful Art of Bibliography." Sayers Review 1, no. 4 (July):1-7.
Reviews An Annotated Guide to the Works of Dorothy L. Sayers, by R. B. Harmon and M. A. Burger. Outlines the format and commends the numbering system. Follows with lengthy comments on omissions, errors, and what he sees as inconsistencies.

9 CLARK, S. L. "The Female Felon in Dorothy L. Sayers' Gaudy Night." Publication of the Arkansas Philological Association 3, no. 3:59-67.
An analysis of Sayers's ideas on intellectual integrity and feminism as brought together in the culprit, Annie Wilson, in Gaudy Night, and reflected in the thinking of the other characters.

10 CRAIG, BARBARA. "Letter." Witham, Essex: Dorothy L. Sayers Historical and Literary Society. Archives, 5.4, processed, 2 pp.
Remarks about Gaudy Night as a picture of Somerville College.

11 DALE, ALZINA STONE. "The Man Born To Be King: Dorothy Sayers' Best Plot." Sayers Review 1, no. 2 (January): 1-16.
Summarizes Sayers's talents that enabled her to write this play: "amused interpreter," "Christian artist," and "translator extraordinary," commenting that the translation in this case is from old to modern language. Analyzes the development of the plot, working from Sayers's introduction and earlier drafts of the play series in the Wade Collection (1976.7). Reprinted: 1979.29.

1977

12   EAGLE, DOROTHY, and CARNELL, HILARY, comps. The Oxford Lit-
     erary Guide. Oxford: Clarendon Press, 461 pp., passim.
        A dictionary of places associated with writers. In-
     cludes brief note concerning each place, its place in the
     life of the author or authors, with biographical material,
     index of authors, and map section. Reviewed by Joe
     Christopher in Sayers Review 1, no. 3 (April 1977):7.

13   EDWARDS, LEE. "Love and Work: Fantasies of Resolution."
     Frontiers: a Journal of Women Studies 2, no. 3 (Fall):
     31-38.
        Characterizes Gaudy Night as a combination of detective
     fiction, the novel of manners, and "psychological biog-
     raphy." Sees it as Sayers's expression of principles that
     determine the role of woman in society vis à vis single-
     ness, work, and marriage. Comments that she "writes better
     mysteries because she can grapple with complicated emo-
     tional and sexual realities in her own life."

14   FLANDERS, ALDEN B. "Dorothy L. Sayers: The Holy Mysteries."
     Anglican Theological Review 59 (October):366-86.
        Sees Sayers's writings as all "of a piece, growing from
     a single root, all aiming at the same goal." Considers her
     work a mythological means of confronting the basic issues
     of her life--her career, her motherhood, her marriage, and
     her religion. Discusses this idea in relation to her writ-
     ings. In the issue for July 1978, pp. 333-35, there is a
     reply by A. S. Dale, followed by a response by Flanders,
     pp. 335-37.

15   FORBES, CHERYL. "Dorothy L. Sayers--For Good Work, For God's
     Work." Christianity Today 22 (4 March):16-18.
        Discusses Sayers's work in the light of her personality
     and Christian beliefs. Feels that her attitude toward her
     work set her apart from other writers of detective fiction.
     Brings together from her writing Sayers's philosophy of
     work.

16   _____. "Introducing a 'Strange Lady'." Christianity Today
     22 (4 March):38.
        Review of Such a Strange Lady, by Janet Hitchman.
     Criticizes Hitchman's use of "psychological speculation,
     rumor, and biographical literary criticism" in this book,
     and of putting herself instead of Sayers to the fore dur-
     ing the first half of the book. Remarks that once she
     left herself out and put Sayers first, she is both "in-
     formative and entertaining."

17 GREGORY, E. R. "From Detective Stories to Dante: The Transitional Phase of Dorothy L. Sayers." <u>Christianity and Literature</u> 26, no. 2:9-17.
   Quotes from Sayers's works in tracing the growth of her writing from detective fiction to Dante. Sees her coming full circle from her concept of the mystery story as having the "rounded (though limited) perfection of a triolet" to her immersion in a "poem that had 'the rounded . . . perfection of a triolet' without its limitations."

18 _____, ed. Introduction to <u>Wilkie Collins: A Critical and Biographical Study</u>, by Dorothy L. Sayers. Toledo, Ohio: Friends of the University of Toledo Libraries, 121 pp.
   Pages 7-24 make up the introduction by Gregory, in which he discusses various facets of this Sayers work: her intentions to eventually complete the Collins biography, Collins's influence on her work, her "compositional habits," and his own editorial principles. See also 1979.28.

19 HALL, TREVOR H. "Dorothy L. Sayers and Sherlock Holmes." <u>Proceedings of the Seminar, 1977</u>. Witham, Essex: Dorothy L. Sayers Historical and Literary Society. Archives, 6.18, processed, pp. 12-29.
   Deals with the relationship between Sayers and Doyle as writers and Holmes and Wimsey as detectives, and with the dating of "Dr. Watson, Widower." Includes discussion which followed. Revised: 1980.5.

20 HARMON, ROBERT B., and BURGER, MARGARET A. <u>An Annotated Guide to the Works of Dorothy L. Sayers</u>. New York: Garland, 296 pp.
   A critical bibliography of works by and about Sayers, showing careful research. Since it is the first in book form and attempts to include several kinds of information, it is not comprehensive but provides a starting point for further research. Includes critical comment, editions and issues of books, and locations of shorter works. Lists: Novels; Short stories; Essays; Dramatic works; Poetry; Translations; Miscellaneous works; Criticism; Sources; Adaptations; Chronology; and a list of Sayers papers in the Wade Collection (1976.7). Indexed.

21 HITCHMAN, JANET. "On Writing <u>Such a Strange Lady</u>." <u>Sayers Review</u> 1, no. 4 (July):16-21
   Reprint of speech given at the Dorothy L. Sayers Historical and Literary Society seminar, November 1976. Comments on the difficulties encountered in getting source

material and on her impressions of Sayers from the material she could get.

22   HODGE, JONATHAN. "Chronology." Sayers Review 1, no. 4 (July):10.
     Brief comments on Sayers's rearrangement of natural phenomena to suit her stories.

23   HODGE, MARY ANN. "'The Dragon's Head,' Retold by L. A. Hill." Sayers Review 1, no. 3 (April):6.
     Reviews this retelling of Sayers's story, "The Learned Adventure of the Dragon's Head" for children. Considers the adaptation competent and a "fairly good introduction" to Sayers. Mentions several changes that seem unfortunate.

24   JAMES, P. D. "Ought Adam to Marry Cordelia?" In Murder Ink. Edited by Dilys Winn. New York: Workman, pp. 68-69.
     On the question of detectives and marriage, discusses Sayers's attitude as shown in her writing along with her own ideas.

25   _____. "The Wimsey Saga." Times (London), 2 July, p. 7.
     Begins a discussion of Sayers's first four novels with a compliment: "She brought to the detective novel originality, intelligence, energy and wit . . . new style and a new direction, and did more than almost any other writer of her age to make the genre intellectually respectable. Says these novels "give one as much of the feeling of the hectic, disillusioned doom-laden years between the wars as any fiction of the time."

26   KEATING, HENRY RAYMOND FITZWALTER, ed. Agatha Christie: First Lady of Crime. New York: Holt, Rinehart & Winston, 224 pp., passim.
     An anthology of essays in some of which Sayers is mentioned.

27   KROUSE, AGATE NESAULE, and PETERS, MARGOT. "Murder in Academe." Southwest Review 62 (Autumn):371-78.
     Discussion of detective fiction with a campus background. Includes several paragraphs on Sayers's Gaudy Night, partly resumé, partly criticizing her failure to achieve her intention of exalting academe and intellectual integrity.

28   LEE, G[EOFFRY] A. "The Birthplace of Dorothy L. Sayers."
      Witham, Essex: Dorothy L. Sayers Historical and Literary
      Society. Archives, 6.5, processed, 2 pp.
          Describes the home in which Sayers was born. Includes
      references.

29   _____. "Dorothy L. Sayers and a Personal Problem: Some Notes
      on Cocksparrow Hall, Westcott Barton, Oxfordshire." Witham,
      Essex: Dorothy L. Sayers Historical and Literary Society.
      Archives, 6.7, processed 2 pp.
          Summarizes information given to Dr. G. A. Lee concerning
      the house in which Sayers's son, Anthony Fleming, was
      raised. Includes paragraph about Ivy Shrimpton, Sayers's
      cousin, who raised him.

30   _____. ["The Wimsey Saga."] Proceedings of the Seminar,
      1977. Witham, Essex: Dorothy L. Sayers Historical and
      Literary Society. Archives, 6.18, processed, pp. 2-12.
          Shows the "consistency of imagination" in Sayers's fic-
      tion through a study of the chronology of the works which
      covered a period of twenty years of narrative. Says she
      thereby "retained control of her material," developing her
      main characters credibly as the series progressed. In-
      cludes ensuing discussion. See also 1977.31.

31   _____. "The Wimsey Saga: A Chronology." Proceedings of the
      Seminar, 1977. Witham, Essex: Dorothy L. Sayers Histori-
      cal and Literary Society. Archives, 6.18, processed,
      pp. 54-57.
          Enlarged and reprinted: 1978.30.

32   McCOLMAN, DONNA J. "Dorothy L. Sayers." American Reference
      Books Annual 9 (1978):603.
          Review of An Annotated Guide to the Works of Dorothy L.
      Sayers, by R. B. Harmon and M. A. Burger. Comments on the
      broad scope of the work, the good balance of works covered,
      the arrangement, the quality of the annotations, and the
      indexing. Remarks that it should set a standard for further
      Sayers research.

33   McMENOMY, CHRISTE [ANN]. "A Glossary of Foreign Terms and
      Quotations in the Wimsey Novels." Sayers Review 1, no. 3
      (April):8-20.
          Translations listed chronologically by novel, in the
      order in which they occur, by chapter rather than by page.
      This had been requested so that an understanding of the
      quotations and terms might add to the reader's enjoyment
      of Sayers's works.

1977

34   MARVIN-CARRELL, JOY K. "A Comparison Between Dorothy L.
     Sayers' Plays: <u>The Man Born To Be King</u> and <u>The Emperor
     Constantine</u>." Paper presented under the direction of
     Dr. Barbara Reynolds at Wheaton College, Illinois, pro-
     cessed.
         Compares the two plays, calling them "both portrayals of
     'theology in action'," exploring the "incarnational reality
     of Christ." Develops this theme.

35   MITCHELL, DONALD R. "Presentation to English Department
     Chapel Honoring Dorothy L. Sayers, 27 September 1977."
     Wheaton, Ill.: Wheaton College, processed, 2 pp.
         Concludes a statement of who Sayers was with the rea-
     sons for including her works in the Wade Collection.

36   _____. Review of <u>Such a Strange Lady</u>, by Janet Hitchman.
     <u>Christian Scholar's Review</u> 6, no. 4:338-39.
         Comments on Hitchman's failure to heed her recognized
     limitations for writing this biography. Credits her with
     a good description of Sayers's determination to maintain
     the integrity of her work when others desired changes.
     Considers Hitchman "out of her depth" in writing about
     Sayers as theologian or Dante scholar, but admits that she
     whets the appetite for a "truly discerning" biography.

37   MOODY, AUBREY. "In Memoriam." <u>Sayers Review</u> 1, no. 2
     (January):20-23.
         Address given at the Commemoration Service held as part
     of the Dorothy L. Sayers Historical and Literary Society
     convention, November 1976. Remarks on her kindness, then,
     using quotations from her writings, addresses the quality
     of her faith and her ability to make doctrine and its im-
     portance clear to other people. Comments, finally, on her
     attitude toward day-to-day Christian living.

38   MURDOCH, DERRICK. <u>The Agatha Christie Mystery</u>. Toronto:
     Pagurian Press, 14, 128-29, 131.
         In this book on Christie, Murdoch briefly compares her
     and Sayers as women and as writers.

39   P. H. S. "Touch of Wimsey With Style." <u>Times</u> (London),
     30 August, p. 10.
         A note concerning the coming book by Wilfred Scott-
     Giles: <u>The Wimsey Family</u>, saying that it was the result of
     a lengthy correspondence between Sayers and Scott-Giles
     concerning the "history" of the Wimsey family.

40 PARKER, ALYSON. "Lord Peter Today." Sayers Review 1, no. 4
    (July):11-12.
        Quotes from the foreword to The Adventure of the Peer-
    less Peer, by John H. Watson, M.D., edited by P. J. Farmer,
    concerning Lord Peter's inheritance of Holmes's villa and
    some Watson manuscripts which had been sold to the 17th
    Duke of Denver.

41 PATE, JANET. "Peter Wimsey." In The Book of Sleuths: An
    Illustrated Chronicle of the Detective Genre. London:
    New English Library, pp. 49-52.
        An illustrated biography of Wimsey, including a bio-
    graphical note about Sayers and a bibliography of detective
    works and performances.

42 PENZLER, OTTO; STEINBRUNNER, CHRIS; and LACHMAN, MARVIN, eds.
    Detectionary. Woodstock, N.Y.: Overlook Press, pp. 30,
    93-94, 100, 164, 186.
        Includes brief biographical notes on Sayers's Montague
    Egg, Lord Peter Wimsey, and Bunter. Also outlines plots
    of Murder Must Advertise and Whose Body?

43 PENZLER, OTTO. "Lord Peter Wimsey." In The Private Lives of
    Private Eyes, Spies, Crimefighters, & Other Good Guys. New
    York: Grosset & Dunlap, pp. 194-200.
        An illustrated biography of Wimsey, including a bibliog-
    raphy of films and detective fiction.

44 PEPPER, SHEILA. Review of An Annotated Guide to the Works of
    Dorothy L. Sayers, by R. B. Harmon and M. A. Burger.
    Library Journal 102 (15 May):1170.
        Tells the scope of this work, commenting on its expert
    quality, the value of the annotations, and the treatment
    given Sayers.

45 PHILLIPS, IVY. "Letter." Witham, Essex: Dorothy L. Sayers
    Historical and Literary Society. Archives, 5.3, processed,
    4 pp.
        Notes from a Sayers contemporary on her school life, with
    comments on the inaccuracy of some of Janet Hitchman's ac-
    counts in Such a Strange Lady.

46 REYNOLDS, BARBARA. "Dorothy L. Sayers, Interpreter of Dante."
    Proceedings of the Seminar, 1977. Witham, Essex: Dorothy
    L. Sayers Historical and Literary Society. Archives, 6.18,
    processed, pp. 31-53.
        Discusses Sayers's "interpretation of Dante under three
    headings: Dante the writer, Dante the allegorist, Dante

the Christian." Shows from her writings the special abilities and experiences that enabled her to interpret The Divine Comedy for the modern reader. Includes ensuing discussion. Partially revised and reprinted: 1979.29.

47 _____. "Dorothy Sayers Remembered." Address given at Wheaton College, Wheaton, Illinois, 27 September, processed, 2 pp.
   Gives a sense of the true warmth of Sayers's personality, and of the practical nature of her faith.

48 RICHARDS, KATHLEEN. "An Evening's Lecture and Discussion." Witham, Essex: Dorothy L. Sayers Historical and Literary Society. Archives, 6.14, processed, 16 pp.
   Having served at one time as Sayers's secretary, Richards discusses Sayers's life in Witham . . . her activities, manner of dress, community and personal relationships, and her temperament.

49 SCHAEFFER, SYLVIA. "Sayers and C. S. Lewis." Sayers Review 1, no. 4 (July):12-13.
   Comments on Sayers as a letter writer, quoting from some of hers to C. S. Lewis.

50 SCOTT-GILES, C. W[ILFRED]. "The Wimsey Pedigree." Sayers Review 1, no. 3 (April):1-5.
   Summarizes the material to be published later in his book The Wimsey Family (1977.51). Reprinted from Proceedings of the 1976 Seminar of The Dorothy L. Sayers Historical and Literary Society.

51 _____. The Wimsey Family: A Fragmentary History Compiled from Correspondence With Dorothy L. Sayers. New York: Harper & Row, 88 pp.
   Gathers into one record the bits and pieces of history of the imaginary Wimsey family as they had been compiled by the author, Dorothy L. Sayers, and other friends. Includes material from Sayers's An Account of Lord Mortimer Wimsey, the Hermit of the Wash and Papers Relating to the Family of Wimsey.

52 SOAMES, EMMA. "'Ascot and Biggin, My Lord?'" Esquire 88 (December):141-43.
   An illustrated review of Wimsey's wardrobe worn for the Masterpiece Theatre productions of Sayers's works.

53 STEWART, J. I. M. "The Mysterious Mystery-Writer." <u>Times</u>
    <u>Literary Supplement</u>, 2 December, p. 1398.
        Reviews Dorothy L. Sayers's <u>Wilkie Collins</u>, edited by
    E. R. Gregory. Commends Gregory on the "excellent edition"
    and discusses Sayers's thoughts and works on Collins. Also
    mentions <u>An Annotated Guide to the Works of Dorothy L.</u>
    <u>Sayers</u>, giving its scope.

54 WINKS, ROBIN. "Mysteries." <u>New Republic</u> 176 (11 June):35.
        Includes a mention of R. B. Harmon, and M. A. Burger's
    "nice" annotations in their <u>An Annotated Guide to the Works</u>
    <u>of Dorothy L. Sayers</u>.

55 WINN, DILYS, ed. <u>Murder Ink: The Mystery Reader's Companion</u>.
    New York: Workman, 551 pp., passim.
        A potpourri of articles on all manner of subjects that
    have to do with murder in books. Includes excellent index.
    The following articles treat Sayers more fully than others:
    "Ought Adam to Marry Cordelia?" (1977.23), "The BBC Through
    a Monocle" (1977.6), and briefly, "The Devout: Benefit of
    Clergy" (1977.1).

<u>1978</u>

1   ANON. "July Books." <u>Human Events</u> 38 (17 June):16.
        Announcement of <u>The Whimsical Christian</u>.

2   ANON. Review of <u>Wilkie Collins: A Critical and Biographical</u>
    <u>Study</u>. <u>Choice</u> 15 (March):73-74.
        Tells scope of work. Considers Gregory's work admira-
    ble, and Sayers's criticism of Collins's work better than
    her biography of him.

3   ANON. Review of <u>The Whimsical Christian</u>. <u>New Yorker</u> 54
    (2 October):149-50.
        Comments that while Sayers's apologetics "convince only
    the convinced" she's a winner where her Christianity and
    literary criticism are combined. Cites especially her es-
    say "Oedipus Simplex," calling it "a thrilling display of
    intellectual fireworks."

4   ANON. Review of <u>The Whimsical Christian</u>. <u>Publishers Weekly</u>
    213 (29 May):43.
        Considers these essays good reading for the adult mind.
    Calls Sayers a "lay theologian who is a master wordcrafter,"
    with wide-ranging interests. Comments on her relationship
    to "the Inklings."

1978

5   ANON. "Sayers, Dorothy L[eigh]." In <u>The New Encyclopaedia</u>
     <u>Britannica</u>. <u>Micropaedia</u>. 10 vols. Chicago: Encyclopaedia
     <u>Britannica</u>, 7:938.
          Consists chiefly of remarks about her writing, comment-
     ing that her fiction was characterized by "precise and
     learned vocabulary, well-researched facts, and tight plot
     construction." References lead to other articles. In one
     she is said to have used her later writings to atone for
     her detective-fiction writing. In another she is mentioned
     with praise for her radio play, <u>The Man Born To Be King</u>.

6   BEAUMONT, LORD BEAUMONT OF WHITLEY. "Dorothy L. Sayers as a
     Lay Theologian." Address delivered 3 June. Witham, Essex:
     Dorothy L. Sayers Historical and Literary Society.
     Archives, 6.37, processed, 5 pp.
          Examines Sayers's theology as seen in her works. Com-
     ments on her gifts as a Christian writer, her insistence on
     logical thinking and expression, her summary of what she
     considered her talents for the presentation of Christian
     truth, and something of what she accomplished in this line.

7   BROWN, CAROL ANN. "Notes for a Lost Eulogy." <u>Bulletin of</u>
     <u>the New York C. S. Lewis Society</u> 9, no. 12 (October):1-6.
          A running commentary on Sayers's life and works. Empha-
     sizes her Dante works but includes critical comment on her
     total output.

8   CHRISTOPHER, JOE R[ANDELL]. "Trying to Capture 'White
     Magic'." <u>Mythlore</u> 5, no. 1 (May):36-37.
          An analysis of Sayers's poem, "White Magic" from her
     <u>Catholic Tales and Christian Songs</u>. Comments on her use of
     puns to bring out the resemblance between the hunt of
     Rhiannon in <u>The Mabinogian</u> and the search for Christ by a
     society that fails to understand Him.

9   CLARK, S. L. "Harriet Vane Goes to Oxford: <u>Gaudy Night</u> and
     the Academic Woman." <u>Sayers Review</u> 2, no. 3 (August):
     22-43.
          A lengthy analysis of the feminist/anti-feminist ele-
     ments in <u>Gaudy Night</u>. Points out Sayers's craftsmanship in
     drawing on both experience and literature to make her argu-
     ments. Concludes by listing some of the ways in which the
     detective, the detective writer, and the scholar are faced
     with a similar challenge. Shows how Sayers uses this fact
     to demonstrate that intellectual integrity has no gender.

1978

10   COBB, LAWRENCE W. "A Gift from the Sky: The Creative Process
      in Lewis and Sayers." Paper written for the New York C. S.
      Lewis Society, mimeographed, pp. 1-5.
          Quoting from C. S. Lewis's works and from Sayers's The
      Mind of the Maker, shows the similarities in their thinking
      on creativity. Endorses Sayers's ideas from the standpoint
      of his work in the field of building construction. In-
      cludes bibliography.

11   DALE, ALZINA STONE. "Caveat Christian." Christianity Today
      22 (8 September):36, 38, 40.
          From her experience in writing a juvenile biography of
      Sayers, she relates her discoveries of the characteristics
      of good biography. Discusses Sayers's rules laid down for
      her work on Wilkie Collins. Recommends that Christians
      writing biographies be careful to honor the people about
      whom they write, even as they recognize their faults.

12   _____. "Fossils in Cloud-Cuckoo Land." Sayers Review 3,
      no. 2 (December):1-13.
          Sees the relationship between real and imagined time in
      Sayers's Vane-Wimsey novels as being an important factor in
      the impression of authenticity which they give. Develops
      the idea that in them there is progression from less to
      more social commentary, placing the characters too much on
      the "public stage of modern life." Considers Sayers's de-
      cision to replace fiction with non-fiction in her writing
      a result of this development.

13   _____. Maker and Craftsman: The Story of Dorothy L. Sayers.
      Grand Rapids, Mich.: William B. Eerdmans, 158 pp.
          A simple straightforward biography of Sayers, originally
      intended as a means of introducing Sayers to young people.
      Shows careful research and gives a coherent picture of an
      interesting writer. Discusses various phases of her
      career.

14   De VOIL, PAUL. ["Dorothy L. Sayers as a Lay Theologian."]
      Proceedings of the Seminar, 1977. Witham, Essex: Dorothy
      L. Sayers Historical and Literary Society. Archives, 6.18,
      processed, pp. 1-17.
          Finds Sayers's theology primarily in her "deliberate
      treatises" and in her religious dramas. Looks at the basic
      doctrines he sees in these works and her expression of
      them. Includes ensuing discussion.

1978

15 Del MASTRO, M. L. Review of <u>Maker and Craftsman</u>, by A. S.
    Dale. <u>Library Journal</u> 103 (1 November):2240.
        Uncomplimentary comments, calling the work "shallow,"
    "unperceptive" and elementary, adding nothing to the knowl-
    edge or enjoyment of Sayers, whom the reviewer praises most
    highly.

16 DOLEND, VIRGINIA. "A Passion for Explication: Dorothy L.
    Sayers' Art of the Footnote." <u>Sayers Review</u> 3, no. 1
    (October):1-11.
        Selects Sayers's footnote writing to illustrate the
    thesis that her craftsmanship pervades all of her writing,
    making even the footnote "an act of form." Gives examples
    of four types of Sayers footnotes and shows how they demon-
    strate Sayers's thoughts concerning creativity and workman-
    ship.

17 DOROTHY L. SAYERS HISTORICAL AND LITERARY SOCIETY. Archives,
    1-, 1978-. Witham, Essex: Society.
        Lists the holdings of the Society. Available to members
    only.

18 GILBERT, COLLEEN B. <u>A Bibliography of the Works of Dorothy L.
    Sayers</u>. Hamden, Conn.: Archon Books, 263 pp.
        "A comprehensive description" of Sayers's works. De-
    scribes all new editions and issues of each title. Ar-
    ranged first chronologically by date of the first edition
    of each title, then by ensuing editions and issues of the
    same title. Includes: books, pamphlets, cards, and
    ephemera; contributions to books, pamphlets, and miscel-
    lanea; contributions to newspapers and periodicals; book
    reviews; broadcasts, play productions, films, and records;
    lectures; and manuscript collections. Indexed.

19 GRIFFIN, WILLIAM. Foreword to <u>The Whimsical Christian: 18
    Essays by Dorothy L. Sayers</u>. New York: Macmillan,
    pp. vii-x.
        Gives a concise, sympathetic view of Sayers as a person
    and writer, showing something of the whimsy of her nature
    and of her works.

20 HABER, RUTH. "'Tant que je vive'"--"'Placetne?'" <u>Sayers
    Review</u> 3, no. 2 (December):21-28.
        Discusses the numerous parallels between Sayers's Lord
    Peter mysteries and Dorothy Dunnett's Lymond chronicles.

21 HANNAY, MARGARET PATTERSON. "Dorothy L. Sayers: What <u>Do</u>
    Women Want?" <u>Free Indeed</u> 1, no. 1 (March/April):13-14.
        Discusses the problem of "woman's role," quoting from
    Sayers's experience and from her works, particularly <u>Are</u>
    <u>Women Human?</u> and <u>Gaudy Night</u>.

22 HANNAY, MARGARET P[ATTERSON]. "Harriet's Influence on the
    Characterization of Lord Peter Wimsey." <u>Sayers Review</u> 2,
    no. 2 (June):1-16.
        Examines the manner in which Sayers used Harriet Vane to
    transform Lord Peter from the "pasteboard paragon" he was
    in <u>Whose Body?</u> to the human being he ultimately became.
    Reprinted: 1979.29.

23 HARP, RICHARD L. "<u>The Mind of the Maker</u>: The Theological
    Aesthetic of Dorothy Sayers and Its Application to Poetry."
    <u>Sayers Review</u> 3, no. 1 (October):12-31.
        Summarizes the argument of the book, then discusses its
    debt to various ideas in the Old and New Testaments and to
    Augustine's <u>De Trinitate</u>. In a second section, quotes from
    Ben Jonson and Robert Frost, applying Sayers's principles
    of creativity to selected poems. Concludes that "Sayers
    provides us a starting point for any work of criticism" of
    all types of literature. Reprinted: 1979.29.

24 HARRISON, BARBARA GRIZZUTI. "Lord Peter Wimsey as Lord."
    <u>Commonweal</u> 105 (27 October):698-700.
        Review of <u>The Whimsical Christian</u>. Using many quota-
    tions from Sayers's works, attempts to show the strength,
    excellence, and oneness of Sayers's writings. Pays her a
    compliment Sayers would perhaps have appreciated: "She
    cannot be categorized. She is exhilarating and subtle."

25 HODGES, SHEILA. <u>Gollancz: The Story of a Publishing House,</u>
    <u>1928-1978</u>. London: Victor Gollancz, pp. 26, 33, 39-46,
    145-146, 150.
        Discusses Sayers's relationship with Victor Gollancz as
    friend and publisher. Speaks of the letters they exchanged
    concerning her books and the advertising of some of the
    books. Comments on Gollancz's reaction to <u>The Man Born To</u>
    <u>Be King</u> and her reactions to his Left Book Club.

26 HUGHES, R. Review of <u>The Whimsical Christian</u>. <u>Columbia</u>
    (Knights of Columbus) 58 (December):32.
        Calls these essays "delightful" and, among other things,
    says "she defends the faith with earnestness, satire,
    learning, and deadly serious humor."

1978

27   KELLER, JOSEPH. "Grey-walled Paradise: The University as
      Symbol in Dorothy L. Sayers's Gaudy Night." Sayers Review
      3, no. 2 (December):29-33.
          Discusses the idea that the setting of Sayers's Gaudy
      Night in Oxford is essential to the theme of the novel,
      since to her Oxford stands as a symbol of "uncompromising
      truth" and here Harriet is forced to face the truth about
      herself.

28   KELLER, KATHERINE, and AVENICK, KAREN. "Wimsey, William, and
      Work." Sayers Review 2, no. 3 (August):1-15.
          An in-depth study of Sayers's attitude toward work "as
      almost sacramental." See in the development of Sayers's
      fictional characters the relationship between their work
      and their ultimate moral worth.

29   LEE, G[EOFFRY] A., and DALE, ALZINA STONE. "The Wimsey Saga:
      A Chronology." Sayers Review 3, no. 2 (December):14-20.
          A biographical and literary record of the events of
      Sayers's life, 1890-1942. Includes important historical
      events. A reprint, with additions by A. S. Dale, of the
      chronology worked out by G. A. Lee and attached to the
      Proceedings of the Seminar, 1977 of The Dorothy L. Sayers
      Historical and Literary Society (1977.30).

30   McMENOMY, CHRISTE [ANN]. "Review: Wilkie Collins." Sayers
      Review 2, no. 3 (August):18-21.
          Reviews Gregory's edition of Sayers's Wilkie Collins:
      A Critical and Biographical Study, along with his comments
      about her craftsmanship. Discusses Sayers's view that
      Collins received his inspiration from experience rather
      than from literature and suggests that the assumption may
      be made that Sayers did the same. Comments on Sayers's
      narrow interest in Collins as artist more than as person.

31   PARKER, ALYSON. "Overheard." Sayers Review 2, no. 1 (May):
      33.
          Report of a brief conversation in the UCLA Graduate
      History Students' Lounge concerning Lord Peter's choice of
      a bride.

32   PATTERSON, NANCY-LOU. "Images of Judaism and Anti-Semitism in
      the Novels of Dorothy L. Sayers." Sayers Review 2, no. 2
      (June):17-24.
          Cites incidents in Sayers's writings that show her
      handling of contemporary attitudes towards Jews and blacks
      which would be unacceptable in a writer of her calibre
      today.

33 REYNOLDS, BARBARA. ["Epic and Romance in the Detective Fic-
        tion of Dorothy L. Sayers."] <u>Proceedings of the Seminar,</u>
        <u>1977</u>. Witham, Essex: Dorothy L. Sayers Historical and
        Literary Society. Archives, 6.18, processed, pp. 33-34.
            Discusses Sayers's detective fiction, showing that "epic
        and romance are two essential ingredients." Follows a
        study of her theoretical writings on the genre with illus-
        trations from her work. Includes ensuing discussion.

34 _____. "The Origin of Lord Peter Wimsey." <u>Sayers Review</u> 2,
        no. 1 (May):1-16, 21.
            Reviews at length the relationship between E. C.
        Bentley's Philip Trent in <u>Trent's Last Case</u>, and Lord Peter
        in the Wimsey novels. Identifies similarities and comments
        on the differences. Defends Sayers's development of char-
        acters, as a product of her broad literary background,
        against the narrow view of those critics who saw no further
        than Sayers herself, and her contemporaries as models.
        Discussion reported, pp. 17-20. Reprinted from <u>Proceedings</u>
        <u>of the Seminar, 1976</u>, Dorothy L. Sayers Historical and Lit-
        erary Society. Condensed version printed in <u>Times Literary</u>
        <u>Supplement</u>, (22 April 1977), p. 492.

35 _____. "Panegyric on Dorothy L. Sayers." Witham, Essex:
        Dorothy L. Sayers Historical and Literary Society.
        Archives, 6.36, processed, 2 pp.
            Pays tribute to Sayers's achievements in the fields of
        literature, aesthetics, and religion.

36 REYNOLDS, WILLIAM. "Dorothy Sayers and the Drama of Ortho-
        doxy." <u>Sayers Review</u> 3, no. 1 (October):32-[45].
            Discusses five Sayers plays: <u>He That Should Come</u>, <u>The</u>
        <u>Zeal of Thy House</u>, <u>The Devil to Pay</u>, <u>The Just Vengeance</u>,
        and <u>The Emperor Constantine</u>. For each one gives date of
        first performance, resumé of the play, and a discussion of
        the themes. For some he also notes the problems involved
        in the writing, concluding with some general critical com-
        ments. Reprinted: 1979.29.

37 SULLIVAN, MARY. "Delicious Dorothy." <u>Sign</u> 58 (October):
        42-45.
            Review of <u>The Whimsical Christian</u>. Calls this a "Chris-
        tian smorgasbord--nourishing, delicious, and filling."
        Quotes the editor and Sayers at length.

1978

38 TAMBLING, JEREMY. ["Dorothy L. Sayers's Place Among the
      Translators of Dante."] Proceedings of the Seminar, 1977.
      Witham, Essex: Dorothy L. Sayers Historical and Literary
      Society. Archives, 6.18, processed, pp. 17-32.
          Follows a brief discussion of the theory of translation
      with a discussion of Sayers's critical approach and of her
      translation of The Divine Comedy. Illustrates from her
      works. Includes ensuing discussion.

1979

1 ANON. Review of As Her Whimsey Took Her, edited by M. P.
      Hannay. Choice 16 (November):1166.
          Comments on Sayers's versatility, and the increase in
      critical interest in her work. Gives the scope of this
      book, highly praising its scholarly "apparatus." Considers
      the essays a reflection of the persons writing them but
      finds them "unfailingly scholarly, solid, and delightful."
      Comments on the harsh attitude displayed toward Janet
      Hitchman's biography.

2 ANON. Review of As Her Whimsey Took Her, edited by M. P.
      Hannay. Publishers Weekly 215 (7 May):76.
          Remarks that these essays should appeal to discriminat-
      ing readers as well as students of literature. Gives brief
      description and comments that the authors agree that
      "Sayers was a logical constructionist, a master of her
      craft, and that her Christian convictions dominate her
      writing."

3 ANON. Review of Dorothy L. Sayers: A Literary Biography, by
      R. E. Hone. Publishers Weekly 215 (7 May):76.
          Describes the book as objective yet warmly sympathetic,
      well-researched, a "plodding" but interesting portrayal of
      a woman "as compelling as any of the characters she
      created."

4 ATKISSON, LOVELLE VERN. "An Exploration of Dorothy Sayers'
      Theory of Creative Process As It Applies to Humanities
      Education." Ed.D. dissertation, George Peabody College
      for Teachers, 1976. Ann Arbor, University Microfilms
      International, 85 pp.
          A single chapter is devoted to Sayers's philosophy of
      creativity as found in her writings. A case is then built
      for development of the "expressive arts" of man--otherwise
      spoken of as "humanities"--through the creative process in
      education, using Sayers's concept of creativity as a basis.

Practical examples are given, making "creativity the general framework subject which serves as a unifying factor
for individual units."

5   BAILEY, CARL. "Sleuthing Bibliophile: The Popular Art of
     Dorothy L. Sayers." Antiquarian Bookman (19 March).
          Discusses Sayers as a person, Lord Peter as "scholar-
     detective," her Wilkie Collins work, her detective writing,
     her religious plays, and her Dante translation, plus the
     C. B. Gilbert work, A Bibliography of the Works of Dorothy
     L. Sayers.

6   BASNEY, LIONEL. "The Nine Tailors and the Complexity of Inno-
     cence." In As Her Whimsey Took Her. Edited by M. P.
     Hannay. Kent, Ohio: Kent State University Press,
     pp. 23-35.
          Discusses Sayers's ability to integrate "detective-
     interest and a seriously intended 'criticism of life'."
     Looks at her use of the normal conventions of detective
     literature, while developing a novel in which the complex-
     ity of assigning guilt and innocence fall partly outside
     the boundaries of these conventions.

7   BELL, JOSEPHINE. "A Face-to-Face Encounter With Sayers." In
     Murderess Ink. Edited by Dilys Winn. New York: Workman,
     pp. 55-57.
          Very briefly states her impression of Sayers, both at
     Godolphin School and as a member of the Detection Club.

8   BILL, RISE. Review of Maker and Craftsman, by A. S. Dale.
     Best Sellers 39 (June):92.
          Calls this "an earnest tribute" to Sayers, gives a
     brief resumé and follows with two sentences of critical
     comment commending its conciseness and remarking on its
     tantalizing quality.

9   BRAND, CHRISTIANNA. Introduction to The Floating Admiral, by
     Certain Members of the Detection Club. Boston: Gregg
     Press, pp. v-xiv.
          Discusses the Detection Club and its members, giving
     several biographical details about Sayers.

10   BREEN, JON. "Murder in Print." Wilson Library Bulletin 54
     (November):176.
          Includes reviews of Dorothy L. Sayers: A Literary Biog-
     raphy by R. E. Hone, and As Her Whimsey Took Her, edited by
     M. P. Hannay. Characterizes Hone's work as a "summary"
     presenting Sayers as a fine and noble woman. Feels that it

is better than Maker and Craftsman by A. S. Dale but not as
good as recent biographical-critical works on other mystery
writers. Finds the desired critical material in the collection edited by Hannay.

11 BUNGE, CHARLES A. "Current Reference Books." Wilson Library
Bulletin 53 (May):650.
Includes review of A Bibliography of the Works of
Dorothy L. Sayers, by C. B. Gilbert, and describes the
scope of this "scholarly" bibliography.

12 CARPENTER, HUMPHREY. The Inklings: C. S. Lewis, J. R. R.
Tolkien, Charles Williams, and Their Friends. Boston:
Houghton Mifflin, pp. 189, 224.
Brief references to Sayers, and to Lewis's, Williams's,
and Tolkien's reactions to her and some of her works.

13 CHRISTOPHER, J[OE] R[ANDELL]; GREGORY, E. R.; HANNAY,
M[ARGARET] P[ATTERSON]; and MAYLONE, R. R. "Dorothy L.
Sayers's Manuscripts and Letters in Public Collections in
the United States." In As Her Whimsey Took Her. Edited by
M. P. Hannay. Kent, Ohio: Kent State University Press,
pp. 215-77.
Gives full bibliographic descriptions and annotates the
works in the following collections: The Marion E. Wade
Collection (1976.7); Manuscripts and Letters at the Humani-
ties Research Center, University of Texas at Austin; Let-
ters at the University of Michigan, Ann Arbor; Letters in
the Houghton Library, Harvard University; Letters in the
Special Collections Department, Northwestern University
Library.

14 CHRISTOPHER, JOE R[ANDELL]. "Lord Peter Views the Telly."
Armchair Detective 12 (January):20-27.
A study of the dramatization of four of Sayers's novels:
Clouds of Witness, The Unpleasantness at the Bellona Club,
Murder Must Advertise, and The Nine Tailors--in which the
television versions are compared with the novels. Points
out the advantages and disadvantages of the changes made.
Concludes that the "adaptations retain in their visual way
much of the artistry" of Sayers.

15 _____. Review of A Bibliography of the Works of Dorothy L.
Sayers, by C. B. Gilbert. Choice 16 (October):992.
Describes the contents, comments on its "scholarship and
completeness," and remarks that it "will be the standard
primary bibliography of Sayers for years to come."

16   _____. Review of <u>Dorothy L. Sayers: A Literary Biography</u>, by
      R. E. Hone. <u>Choice</u> 16 (November):1172.
          Considers this biography an important addition to Sayers
      scholarship. Compares it to those of Hitchman and Dale.
      Gives brief resumé, commenting on the biography's lack of
      serious error.

17   _____. Review of <u>Maker and Craftsman</u>, by A. S. Dale. <u>Arm-
      chair Detective</u> 12, no. 2 (Spring):180.
          Speaks of the "use of social background" as the "major
      feature of this book" which he calls a biographical step
      ahead of <u>Such a Strange Lady</u>, by Janet Hitchman. Writes on
      Dale's treatment of the Sayers mysteries. Points out and
      corrects some errors.

18   _____. Review of <u>Maker and Craftsman</u>, by A. S. Dale. <u>Choice</u>
      16 (May):387.
          Properly assesses this factual biography as written for
      young people and of interest also to Christian writers and
      women writers. Summarizes the basic facts given, mention-
      ing only one factual error.

19   Del MASTRO, M. L. Review of <u>As Her Whimsey Took Her</u>, edited
      by M. P. Hannay. <u>Library Journal</u> 104 (September):1698.
          A derogatory review commenting that the essays "draw what
      strength they have from the lucid prose of Sayers herself."
      Makes an exception of the one by R. L. Harp (1978.23).

20   _____. Review of <u>Dorothy L. Sayers: A Literary Biography</u>, by
      R. E. Hone. <u>Library Journal</u> 104 (September):1698.
          Compliments Hone on his presentation of Sayers as "a
      living picture of a complex woman" and on the "integrity
      and good craftsmanship" of the work.

21   DIXON, JAMES GEORGE. "The Canterbury Festival Plays in Pro-
      duction." Ph.D. dissertation, Northwestern University,
      1977. Ann Arbor: University Microfilms International,
      pp. 218-48, 260-79.
          A history of the Canterbury Festival from 1928-1958.
      Covers four subject areas for each production: background,
      rehearsal process, the performance, and the response. Also
      considers the playwrights themselves as they relate to the
      four main emphases. In discussing <u>The Zeal of Thy House</u>
      quotes from Sayers's introduction to <u>The Man Born To Be
      King</u> which shows her theory of play writing and produc-
      tion. While not a work of "detailed critical examination"
      the author's critical thinking does come through in this
      scholarly work and includes quotations from critical
      reviews.

1979

22   DUNLAP, BARBARA J. "Through a Dark Wood of Criticism: The
     Rationale and Reception of Dorothy L. Sayers's Translation
     of Dante." In As Her Whimsey Took Her. Edited by M. P.
     Hannay. Kent, Ohio: Kent State University Press,
     pp. 133-49.
          Discusses Sayers's consuming need to make as good a
     translation of The Divine Comedy as possible and the effort
     she put into it. Comments on various critical reviews.

23   DUNN, ROBERT PAUL. "'The Laughter of the Universe': Dorothy
     L. Sayers and the Whimsical Vision." In As Her Whimsey
     Took Her. Edited by M. P. Hannay. Kent, Ohio: Kent State
     University Press, pp. 200-12.
          Sees in Sayers's life and work an acceptance of the
     reality of human limitations along with the recognition of
     a redeeming spiritual reality that transforms "all of one's
     endeavors." Calls this her "comprehensive comic view of
     the universe" or "whimsical vision." Illustrates from her
     works, both detective and theological.

24   DURKIN, MARY BRIAN. "Dorothy L. Sayers: A Christian Humanist
     for Today." Christian Century 96 (14 November):1114-19.
          Traces the concepts of "integrity in communication" and
     pride--here called "the root of every sin against integ-
     rity"--in Sayers's fiction and non-fiction. Considers
     briefly the renewed interest in her works, commenting that
     they merit careful attention "for they speak to the
     troubled times of today."

25   ESSEX, ROSAMUND. "'Strange Lady'?" Church Times (2 March).
          Review of Maker and Craftsman, by A. S. Dale. Gives a
     resumé with quotations. Says the style cannot be compared
     to the sparkle of Janet Hitchman's in Such a Strange Lady,
     but that, unlike that book, it "gives the jam, but the
     bread-and-butter as well." Comments that some of Dale's
     explanations would irritate English readers.

26   FULLER, EDMUND. "The Versatile Creator of Lord Peter
     Wimsey." Wall Street Journal, 20 August, p. 12.
          Review of Dorothy L. Sayers: A Literary Biography, by
     R. E. Hone, and of As Her Whimsey Took Her, by M. P.
     Hannay. Compares Hone's book to Such a Strange Lady, by
     Janet Hitchman. Says it "gives a better integrated account
     of her life in depth, making some of the more unusual as-
     pects of Sayers's character appear less eccentric." Fol-
     lows some biographical material with the comment that
     Sayers died "full of honors from her extraordinarily varied
     career." Commends Hannay's book to all Sayers devotees

after outlining its scope. Discusses The Mind of the Maker, which she views as Sayers's greatest work.

27   GAVIN, FRANCIS. Review of As Her Whimsey Took Her, edited by
      M. P. Hannay. Best Sellers 39 (October):263-64.
         Remarks that this begins the critical work on Sayers for
      which her fans have waited. Gives the scope and comments
      on omissions. Says that the writing is almost too enthu-
      siastic in some of the essays but more realistic in others.
      Mentions those especially enjoyed.

28   GREGORY, E. R. "Wilkie Collins and Dorothy L. Sayers." In
      As Her Whimsey Took Her. Edited by M. P. Hannay. Kent,
      Ohio: Kent State University Press, pp. 51-64.
         Expresses the many ways in which Sayers was influenced
      by her extensive knowledge of Wilkie Collins's work. Re-
      views some of the documents available that show her inter-
      est in him and his works. See also 1977.18.

29   HANNAY, MARGARET [PATTERSON], ed. As Her Whimsey Took Her:
      Critical Essays on the Work of Dorothy L. Sayers. Kent,
      Ohio: Kent State University Press, 301 pp.
         A major collection of essays arranged in five sections:
      Detection, Drama, Translations, Aesthetics, and Bibliog-
      raphy. Most are "revised from scholarly papers" read at
      various seminars listed in the preface. While none of the
      essays is primarily biographical, much about Sayers's life
      is revealed in them. See 1976.12; 1977.11, 46; 1978.22,
      23, 36; 1979.6, 13, 22, 23, 28, 36, 42, 46, 48, 49.
      Indexed.

30   HARRISON, BARBARA GRIZZUTI. "Above All, Laughter and
      Delight." New York Times Book Review, 15 July, pp. 9, 24.
         Taking Hone's Dorothy L. Sayers: A Literary Biography
      and Hannay's As Her Whimsey Took Her together, deplores
      their absence of humor in dealing with Sayers, who "never
      fails to inspire laughter and delight," commenting that the
      essays "confuse seriousness with earnestness." Further
      criticizes Hone for failing to synthesize Sayers's life and
      work, for his "theorizing in the absence of evidence," and
      for failing to match the quality of Sayers's writing.
      Criticizes Hannay's arrangement for compartmentalizing
      Sayers, but finds the bibliography of great value, com-
      menting that parts "deserve to be read as text."

1979

31 HONE, RALPH E. <u>Dorothy L. Sayers: A Literary Biography</u>.
    Kent, Ohio: Kent State University Press, 234 pp.
       A detailed, chronological, critical commentary on
    Sayers's life and works, including letters, addresses, and
    essays. Includes commentary on her writings from other
    sources. Indexed.

32 MILLER, PATRICIA. "Theme in the Novels of Dorothy L. Sayers."
    Wheeler Essay Award. Wheaton, Ill.: Wheaton College,
    processed, 10 pp.
       Sees in all of Sayers's novels the concept of a struggle
    between "responsibility to truth versus responsibility to
    people," in line with Sayers's view that the detective
    story is a "constructional element in a work of universal
    scope."

33 MOORE, ARTHUR J. Review of <u>The Mind of the Maker</u>. <u>Commonweal</u>
    106 (2 March):124.
       Brief comments on the reissue of Sayers's analogy of the
    creativity of God and of man. Remarks that Lord Peter has
    almost overwhelmed her other works and welcomes this one
    with joy.

34 NICKEL, GORDON. "Dorothy, Dante and Detectives." <u>Mennonite</u>
    <u>Brethren Herald</u>, 16 February, pp. 31-32.
       Review of <u>Maker and Craftsman</u>, by A. S. Dale. Commends
    the author for "making sense" of a difficult writer, and
    doing so in a pleasant and provocative way. Remarks on the
    references to the "Inklings." Finds the strongest quality
    Dale's portrayal of Sayers's Christianity.

35 PANEK, LeROY. <u>Watteau's Shepherds: The Detective Novel in</u>
    <u>Great Britain, 1914-1940</u>. Bowling Green, Ohio: Bowling
    Green University Popular Press, 232 pp., passim.
       In his chapter on Dorothy Sayers (pp. 72-110) discusses
    the characters and themes of Sayers's novels and her devel-
    opment of them. Analyzes the quality of her writing from
    <u>Whose Body?</u> to <u>Busman's Honeymoon</u>, showing the changes in
    her thinking, and how she revealed them in her work. Com-
    ments that "her novels confront problems and do not give
    easy answers [and] may be her best pieces of theology."

36 REAVES, R. B. "Crime and Punishment in the Detective Fiction
    of Dorothy L. Sayers." In <u>As Her Whimsey Took Her</u>. Edited
    by M. P. Hannay. Kent, Ohio: Kent State University Press,
    pp. 1-13.
       Examines the moral issues with which Sayers was con-
    cerned and the manner in which she wove them into her de-
    tective fiction.

37 REDFERN, JOHN. "The Dorothy Sayers Story." <u>Methodist</u>
    <u>Recorder</u> (London), 15 March.
        Review of <u>Maker and Craftsman</u>, by A. S. Dale. Gives
    some biographical facts from the book. Comments that Dale
    approached Sayers in a spirit of reverence, and whispered
    where she might have shouted. Credits Dale with having
    worked hard on this book but also mentions a few factual
    errors.

38 REYNOLDS, BARBARA. "Dorothy L. Sayers, Interpreter of Dante."
    In <u>As Her Whimsey Took Her</u>. Edited by M. P. Hannay. Kent,
    Ohio: Kent State University Press, pp. 123-32.
        Refutes Sayers's self-deprecating statement that her
    mind was unprepared for the impact of Dante's <u>Divine</u>
    <u>Comedy</u>. Illustrates from her writings that she well
    understood at her first reading the message Dante brought,
    "the vigour of the story-telling," and the technical abil-
    ity required to combine these in an artistic manner. Re-
    prints a revised section of 1977.46.

39 RYKEN, LELAND. <u>Triumphs of the Imagination: Literature in</u>
    <u>Christian Perspective</u>. Downers Grove, Ill.: Inter-Varsity
    Press, 262 pp., passim.
        Quotes from some of Sayers's writings in this work on
    the relationship of literature to the Christian faith. Re-
    views <u>The Mind of the Maker</u> and "Towards a Christian Aes-
    thetic." Sees the former as "the classic work on the
    contribution of Christian doctrine to an understanding of
    artistic creativity."

40 SPRAGUE, ROSAMOND KENT. "The Energy of Dorothy L. Sayers."
    <u>New Oxford Review</u> 46 (January/February):7-9.
        With the remark "that her reflections on work constitute
    her major contribution to Christian thought," brings to-
    gether and discusses some of these reflections from
    Sayers's writings.

41 STERN, PETER L. Review of <u>A Bibliography of the Works of</u>
    <u>Dorothy L. Sayers</u>, by C. B. Gilbert. <u>Book Collector's</u>
    <u>Market</u> 4 (September/October):39-40.
        Praises Gilbert's work highly, commenting that "There
    is not another bibliography in the mystery field of suffi-
    cient quality to be placed next to it on the shelf." Gives
    brief description. Regrets lack of information on dust
    jackets and the poor quality of the photographs.

1979

42   STOCK, R. D., and STOCK, BARBARA. "The Agents of Evil and
     Justice in the Novels of Dorothy L. Sayers." In As Her
     Whimsey Took Her. Edited by M. P. Hannay. Kent, Ohio:
     Kent State University Press, pp. 14-22.
          Investigates the manner in which Sayers developed her
     ideas of good, evil, and justice through the characteriza-
     tion and milieu in her detective novels. Comments on the
     growth in her artistic ability to accomplish her goals from
     the early novels to her later plays.

43   SWAN, ANNALYN. "Inspired Wimsey." Time 114 (13 August):
     72-73.
          Reviews of Dorothy L. Sayers, by R. E. Hone and As Her
     Whimsey Took Her, edited by M. P. Hannay. Follows some
     thoughts about Sayers as revealed in Hone's book with the
     comment that he failed to analyze Sayers's books or career
     and therefore should not have called this a "literary biog-
     raphy." Because Hannay's book "addresses the most fasci-
     nating aspect of Sayers's career: how the same sensibility
     could embrace low crime and high church" says it comes off
     as a better book. Nevertheless, implies that these books
     illustrate the "'unmitigated Grimth' that Sayers deplored."
     Wishes that Sayers's biography could have been researched
     and written by Lord Peter.

44   SYMONS, JULIAN. "The Detection Club." New York Times Book
     Review, 30 September, p. 14-26.
          Tells the history of this club to which Sayers also be-
     longed, and comments on her contributions and the zest with
     which she made them.

45   TETLOW, JOSEPH A. Review of The Mind of the Maker. New
     Catholic World 222 (September/October):234.
          A highly complimentary discussion of the value of this
     work for today. Says it is "about several things simul-
     taneously" and calls it "graceful, erudite, witty." Gives
     a paragraph to her analogy of divine and human creativity
     and considers its impact on artists, theologians, and the
     "me" generation.

46   THORPE, LEWIS. "Dorothy L. Sayers as a Translator of Le Roman
     de Tristan and La Chanson de Roland." In As Her Whimsey
     Took Her. Edited by M. P. Hannay. Kent, Ohio: Kent State
     University Press, pp. 109-22.
          Remarks on the competent teacher under whom Sayers had
     studied at Oxford, at which time her interest in these
     works had begun. Discusses also the quality of her work and
     something of her feeling for these great poems. Demonstrates

that her interest came full circle, illustrating from her poems in OP. I, published in 1916, through her Tristan in Brittany, published in 1929, to her Song of Roland, published shortly before her death in 1957.

47   TINDER, DONALD. "The Great State of Lewisiana." Christianity Today 22 (5 October):48.
      Discusses the explosion of works about C. S. Lewis and mentions Lewis's friendship with Sayers, saying that she is beginning to be studied more. Lists several new works about Sayers and her writings.

48   TISCHLER, NANCY [M.] "Artist, Artifact, and Audience: The Aesthetics and Practice of Dorothy L. Sayers." In As Her Whimsey Took Her. Edited by M. P. Hannay. Kent, Ohio: Kent State University Press, pp. 153-64.
      Analyzes, then synthesizes Sayers's ideas concerning aesthetics and creativity as seen in her works, especially "Creative Mind," "Toward a Christian Aesthetic," The Mind of the Maker, The Zeal of Thy House, and Gaudy Night.

49   WEBSTER, RICHARD T. "The Mind of the Maker: Logical Construction, Creative Choice and the Trinity." In As Her Whimsey Took Her. Edited by M. P. Hannay. Kent, Ohio: Kent State University Press, pp. 165-75.
      A philosophical discussion of Sayers's The Mind of the Maker. Sees her idea of Trinity as narrow but still able to break down the barrier between today's religion as "stained-glass-window syndrome" and religion that permeates the life of an individual.

50   WINN, DILYS, ed. Murderess Ink. New York: Workman, 304 pp., passim.
      Includes many references to Sayers and her work.

1980

1   ANON. "Notes on Current Books: Literary Studies." Virginia Quarterly Review 56 (Winter):22.
      Review of As Her Whimsey Took Her, edited by M. P. Hannay. In brief remarks on this collection of essays, finds those essays most interesting that are on Sayers's detective fiction and on her translations. Enjoyed seeing Lord Peter stories criticized by academics. Considers her translations her "finest scholarly achievement."

1980

2   ANON. Review of <u>Dorothy L. Sayers: A Pilgrim Soul</u>, by Nancy
    M. Tischler. <u>Publishers Weekly</u> 217 (8 February):78.
        Considers this an "eloquent" and "admiring but not un-
    critical" biography that will "help readers to understand
    and perhaps sympathize with" Sayers.

3   CHRISTOPHER, JOE R[ANDELL]. "Dorothy Sayers at Fifty."
    <u>Mythlore</u> 7 (March):40.
        A sonnet in terza rima to a friend on the subject of
    Sayers's discovery of and love for Dante's <u>Divine Comedy</u>.

4   DURKIN, MARY BRIAN. <u>Dorothy L. Sayers</u>. Twayne's English
    Author Series, no. 281. Boston: G. K. Hall, Twayne
    Publishers, 204 pp.
        A scholarly, tightly written critical commentary on
    Sayers, primarily on her work. Within each chapter the
    works are discussed individually and at the same time
    within the context of the entire Sayers output in the genre
    under discussion. Traces the development of her ideas and
    techniques and comments on the public reception of her
    works. Indexed.

5   HALL, TREVOR H. <u>Dorothy L. Sayers: Nine Literary Studies</u>.
    London: Duckworth, 143 pp.
        These scholarly essays present the fruit of Hall's
    painstaking research on various aspects of Sayers's life
    and writing. The first three, dealing with the relation-
    ship between the Doyle/Holmes and Sayers/Wimsey sagas, and
    with the dating of "Dr. Watson, Widower," are revised from
    his paper (1977.18). Other essays are: "<u>The Nebuly Coat</u>"
    (compared to <u>The Nine Tailors</u>), "Atherton Fleming: A Lit-
    erary Puzzle," "<u>The Documents in the Case</u>," "Dorothy L.
    Sayers and Robert Eustace," "The Dates in <u>Busman's Honey-</u>
    <u>moon</u>," and "Dorothy L. Sayers and Psychical Research."
    Indexed.

6   OHANIAN, SETA. "Dinner with Dorothy L. Sayers; or, 'As My
    Whimsey Feeds Me'." <u>Journal of Popular Culture</u> 13, no. 3
    (Winter):434-46.
        A menu (pictured) of tales and novels, each representing
    something edible. Discusses Sayers's talents for detective-
    fiction writing, her use of themes other than detective,
    and her success or lack of it in achieving her goals.

7   PATTERSON, NANCY-LOU. "Eve's Sharp Apple: Five Transgressing
     Women in the Novels of Dorothy L. Sayers." Sayers Review
     3, no. 3 (April):1-24.
          A discussion of the "unsympathetic" women characters in
     Sayers's Unnatural Death, The Documents in the Case, Five
     Red Herrings, Gaudy Night and Busman's Honeymoon. Attempts
     to show how Sayers depicted "human weakness and sin" in the
     women considered, and the way they failed in their rela-
     tionships with others.

8   REYNOLDS, BARBARA, and SAYERS, DOROTHY L. "Like Aesop's Bat."
     VII: An Anglo-American Literary Review 1 (March):81-93.
          Reynolds presents Sayers's final essay intended for pub-
     lication in Nottingham Mediaeval Studies, found among the
     papers of Lewis Thorpe, Reynolds's late husband. Reynolds
     tells the story of how Dr. Thorpe had requested the article
     following a spirited correspondence between him and Sayers
     over the translation of the controversial "Hoese" in The
     Song of Roland.

9   REYNOLDS, WILLIAM. "Two Books About a Strange Lady."
     Reformed Journal 30 (January):25-26.
          Reviews of Maker and Craftsman, by A. S. Dale and of
     Dorothy L. Sayers: A Literary Biography, by R. E. Hone.
     Considers the strongest feature of Dale's book to be a
     plausible explanation for Sayers's change from writer of
     detective fiction to Christian dramatist and translator.
     Finds the book uneven in its approach to its audience,
     speaking sometimes to the young and at other times to
     adults. Remarks that Hone's book may be seen as a founda-
     tion for the work of future Sayers students. Finds his
     greatest strength is in the way he deals with Sayers as a
     writer, especially in his analyses of her plays and novels.
     Thinks that both books fall short in the area of compara-
     tive criticism--where Sayers's work stands in relation to
     other writers. Criticizes Hone for putting substantive
     material in his notes.

10   SCOTT, NAN C. L. "Dorothy L. Sayers and the Sacrament of
     Work." Living Church 180 (17 February):10, 11, 18.
          Gives four reasons for a widened interest in Sayers's
     work. Reviews As Her Whimsey Took Her, edited by M. P.
     Hannay, discussing her introduction and the essays, some
     individually. Also reviews Such a Strange Lady, by Janet
     Hitchman and Dorothy L. Sayers: A Literary Biography, by
     R. E. Hone, comparing and contrasting them and concluding
     that "Reading both provides a corrective of sorts for the
     deficiencies of each."

1980

11   SCOWCROFT, P. L. "Music and Dorothy L. Sayers' Detective Fic-
      tion." Witham, Essex: Dorothy L. Sayers Historical and
      Literary Society. Archives, 2.28, processed, 5 pp.
          Shows, through various conversations and incidents, that
      Lord Peter's creator had considerable musical knowledge,
      not just a passing interest. Comments also on the various
      forms of musical entertainment available in the 1920s and
      1930s, and Sayers's use of them in her fiction.

12   _____. "Railways and the Detective Fiction of Dorothy L.
      Sayers." Witham, Essex: Dorothy L. Sayers Historical and
      Literary Society. Archives, 2.29, processed, 4 pp.
          Summarizes the use of railway transport in Sayers's
      novels. Concludes that she had the ability to compete with
      men like Freeman Wills Crofts--a retired railway engineer.
      Comments on the social background she gives through her de-
      piction of "half-forgotten railways and railway practices."

13   TISCHLER, NANCY M. Dorothy L. Sayers: A Pilgrim Soul.
      Atlanta: John Knox Press, 167 pp.
          A thoughtful study of Sayers, fitting her life and her
      writings into what Tischler sees as a pilgrimage similar
      to that of Christian in Bunyan's Pilgrim's Progress.
      Largely derived from a careful study of the themes in
      Sayers's work, gives an image of a brilliant scholar,
      strong Christian character, sometimes eccentric but loving
      and lovable, whose works exhibit the "consistency of her
      imagination." Indexed.

14   _____. "Dorothy and Beatrice." Sayers Review 3, no. 3
      (April):25-34.
          After giving a short resumé of Sayers's life and works,
      comments on her preparation for her translation of The
      Divine Comedy, then discusses Sayers's perception of
      Beatrice as shown in her writings about Dante and his work.
      Concludes with a statement of the meaning of the Beatrician
      vision for Sayers's life and work.

15   WINKS, ROBIN. "Robin Winks on Mysteries." New Republic 182
      (16 February):37.
          Includes reviews of Hone's Dorothy L. Sayers: A Liter-
      ary Biography and Hannay's As Her Whimsey Took Her.
      Characterizes Hone's book as "affectionate, careful, and
      entertaining." Compares it favorably to Hitchman's Such a
      Strange Lady. Praises his thoughts on Sayers's religious
      essays, and comments that Sayers ends up seeming less
      strange than some would make her. Remarks that Hannay's
      book, being composite, is predictably uneven--some good,

some foolish, some solid. Commends the bibliography of
manuscripts and letters in United States collections.

1981

1   BRABAZON, JAMES. <u>Dorothy L. Sayers: A Biography</u>. New York:
      Charles Scribner's Sons, 352 pp.
      The first biography of Sayers authorized by her son,
      Anthony Fleming, who made available to Brabazon all the
      letters and documents in his possession. Fleming also co-
      operated with John Cournos's stepson to secure Brabazon's
      access to all available Cournos-Sayers correspondence.
      Factual evidence has taken the place of guesswork, some-
      times corroborating, sometimes denying the latter.
      Ranges from harsh realism to warm sympathy and under-
      standing. Shows clearly that her childhood and early ado-
      lescent experience was not of the best sort for helping so
      gifted a child respond to life situations. Gives insight
      into her relationships with people. Discusses her works
      as part of her life experience without giving long critical
      analyses.

2   GAILLARD, DAWSON. <u>Dorothy L. Sayers</u>. New York: Frederick
      Ungar, 136 pp.
      Looks at Sayers's detective fiction from the point of
      view of her development as a writer, from the short story
      form, through the detective novel primarily as puzzle, to
      the detective novel that combined the puzzle with a view of
      contemporary society and the people of which it was com-
      posed. Carefully illustrates this thesis from Sayers's
      detective fiction. Gaillard's introduction gives a bio-
      graphical sketch.
      In a final chapter, "Values and Aesthetics: A Touch of
      the Eternal in Sayers's Detective Fiction," Gaillard dis-
      cusses some of the philosophical concepts that inform
      Sayers's work. These include her attitude toward war,
      work, woman's place in society, integrity, and the divine
      pattern of life as manifested in man's behavior.

3   JAMES, P. D. Foreword to <u>Dorothy L. Sayers: A Biography</u>, by
      James Brabazon. New York: Charles Scribner's Sons,
      pp. xiii-xvi.
      A critical analysis of Sayers's detective fiction, de-
      scribing the talents she brought to it and showing why
      "Forty years after publication of the last novel, readers
      in airport departure lounges all over the world reach for
      a Dorothy L. Sayers story. . . ."

Index

Abbott, Bromley, 1957.1
"Above All, Laughter and Delight," 1979.30
"Accident, Suicide, or Murder?" 1975.28
"According to Miss Sayers," 1943.12
Acocella, Joan Ross, 1974.1
"Action on the Map," 1972.8
Adams, J. Donald, 1954.1
Adams, Phoebe-Lou, 1975.1
Adventure, Mystery, and Romance, 1976.6
"Aesthetic Theology," 1942.9
Agate, James, 1939.1
The Agatha Christie Mystery, 1977.38
"The Agents of Evil and Justice in the Novels of Dorothy L. Sayers," 1979.42
Aird, Catherine, 1977.1
Alpert, Hollis, 1973.1
The Anatomy of Murder, 1937.40
Anderson, Isaac, 1929.1; 1932.1-3; 1933.2-3; 1934.1-2; 1935.1; 1936.1-2; 1937.1; 1938.1; 1940.1
"An Anglican Prophetess," 1947.12
Annan, Gabriele, 1975.2
An Annotated Guide to the Works of Dorothy L. Sayers, 1977.8, 20, 32, 44, 53-54
"Anthology, Scholar Covers Field," 1929.9
"Aristotle's 'Poetics'," 1954.2
Armstrong, Anne, 1933.11
"Art of Bell-Ringing," 1934.3

"The Art of the Classical Detective Story," 1976.6
"Art With and Without Dogma," 1949.11
"Artist, Artifact, and Audience," 1979.48
"As for Detectives," 1929.8
As Her Whimsey Took Her, 1979.1-2, 9, 19, 26, 27, 29-30; 1980.4, 10, 15
"'Ascot and Biggin, My Lord?'" 1977.52
"At the Bellona Club," 1928.7
Atkins, Steward, 1930.9
Atkisson, Lovelle Vern, 1979.4
"Author Defends Dogma in Religious Volume," 1949.19
Avenick, Karen, 1978.28

Babington, Margaret, 1958.8
Backhouse, Janet, 1975.10
Bailey, Carl, 1979.5
Baird, J. W., 1956.2
Baker, Russell, 1977.2
"Baker Street Notes," 1934.4
Bander, Elaine, 1977.3-4
Barnes, Melvyn, 1975.11
Barton, John M. T., 1943.5
Basney, Lionel, 1973.5; 1974.3; 1979.6
Barzun, Jacques, 1941.16; 1942.9; 1971.4
"B.B.C. Life of Christ," 1942.2
"The BBC Through a Monocle," 1977.6
Beaujohn, Paul, 1937.21